CHILDHOOD AND OLD AGE – EQUALS OR OPPOSITES?

CHILDHOOD AND OLD AGE – EQUALS OR OPPOSITES?

Edited by
Jørgen Povlsen
Signe Mellemgaard
Ning de Coninck-Smith

ODENSE UNIVERSITY PRESS 1999

Childhood and Old Age
© The authors and Odense University Press 1999
ISBN 87-7838-490-7
Cover design by UniSats ApS
Cover Illustration: "Modern" by Lena Cronqvist (1975)
Printed by Special-Trykkeriet Viborg a-s

Published with support from
The Aging Research Centre and
LEGO A/S

Odense University Press
Campusvej 55
DK 5230 Odense M
Phone: +45 6615 7999
Fax: +45 6615 8126
E-mail: Press@forlag.sdu.dk
Internet: www.oup.dk

Distribution in the United States and Canada:
International Specialized Book Services
5804 NE Hassalo Street
Portland, OR 97213-3644
USA
Phone: +1-800-944-6190

Contents

Introduction ... 7

I: Age as Discourse

Allison James: Bodies of Knowledge: Growing Up and Growing Old ... 17

Ning de Coninck-Smith: "He Wished Nothing But Good for the Children; But Knew that Many Had Been Harmed by It". Film Censorship in Denmark 1896-1922 ... 31

Anne Løkke: Infancy and Old Age as Causes of Death ... 55

Stephen Katz: Fashioning Agehood: Lifestyle Imagery and the Commercial Spirit of Seniors Culture ... 75

Lene Otto: Memories, Age and Biographical Discourse ... 93

II: Age in Practice

John R. Gillis: A World of Their Own Making: Families and the Modern Culture of Aging ... 109

Maxine Rhodes: Complete Motherhood: The Mother-Infant Relationship in the First Few Days of Life, 1920 to 1950 ... 125

Jørgen Povlsen: When Men Are Made into Boys. Old Boys in the Danish Sports Movement – The Sporting Fellowship of Elderly Men in the Beginning of the 20th Century ... 137

Patricia Stamp: Power to the Elders: The Politics of Aging Amongst the Kikuyu Women of Kenya ... 161

Erhard Chvojka: Wise or Childish? Ambivalent Images of Grandparents in the Course of the 19th Century ... 185

III: Age in the Future

Lene Koch: Age in the Future. Some Implications of New Reproductive and Genetic Technologies ... 205

Introduction

As distinct areas, the two stages of life which we call Childhood and Old Age have recently been the subject of intense research throughout the world. It has been both interesting and challenging for us, as editors of this book, to allow a meeting of minds involved in these two areas of research. Our aim has been to throw light on the mutual relationship that exists between these two ages of life and to this end we have asked experts with different scientific backgrounds to analyse the constitution of these ages of life and the ways in which they manifest themselves.

This book takes as its point of departure the idea that indiviual stages of life should not be viewed in isolation. The cultural, social and medico-biological constitution of old age can, for example, best be understood with reference to the historical emergence and development of other stages of life such as childhood, – and vice versa. Different ages and phases of life do not exist autonomously but are intimately related by the fact of their common origins in an interplay between discourse and praxis forms, their relatedness is not linear and simple, but rooted in mutual opposition, in paradoxality and complexity.

Though seemingly mutual opposites, old age and childhood share a number of characteristics. Both young and old are institutionalised and transformed into objects of age-related pedagogical practices. The two ages of life are marginalised in relation to the labour market since both children and old people in Western societies are considered non-productive individuals. Children and old people are not only each positioned on the fringes of life but they also share the same conditions of dependency, although the quality of this dependency is quite dissimilar.

Childhood and old age have yet other similarities, in that they both appear to have become the objects of increasing commercialisation. Almost identical developing patterns of aestheticisation and stylisation have modelled children and old people as consumers of products for self-staging.

Childhood and old age are apparently represented by common notions in language, literature and myth. Certain myths concerning old age receive sustenance in apparently irresistible comparisons to childhood; on the one hand positive interpretations are attached to the resemblances of the two life ages as when grandparents and grandchildren are assumed to have an instinctive close relationship – they understand each other in a special way without jeopardising the mutual relationship of legitimate authority. On the other hand old age is still, to a certain extent, associated with the occurent low status of childhood manifested in negative use of language and imagery. Expressions such as "being in one's second childhood" convert old people metaphorically into children. Infantilization of old people, therefore, exerts an influence on the construction of old age itself.

Even though the two life phases exhibit similarities, and even though, historically, their constitution appears to have developed in tandem, childhood and old age are structurally and semantically different – simply because children look towards the future, while the elderly represent the past.

The study of life ages has received renewed attention as a result of changing intergenerational relations. Age and ages of life are central concerns when the western industrial society of the future is the subject of debate. Many emphasize the threatening socio-economic consequences of a global increase in the number of people who become older and older, as well as pointing to the possibility of radicalized generational conflicts. Others express concern about the consequences of new reproductive technologies on the concept of age, and for our perceptions of generational relations. Or they envisage to changes to old age caused by medical technology and its potential for extending life, – by means of organ transplantation, for example, – or for actively reducing life, – by euthanasia.

In research into life ages and aging it has become more and more customary, in recent years, to regard aging not as a biological phenomenon, but rather as a social and cultural construct. This construct is manifested in the way people, at different times and in different cultures, have treated aging. This applies both at the everyday level and at the symbolic level.

Several interpretations of this development are possible. Some researchers (e.g. Bauman 1992, Meyrowitz 1985; Gillis 1996) have observed a marked blurring of the demarcation lines of different age groups in late modern society – a merging of age groups which is demonstrated by symbolic behaviour of the elderly inappropriate to their real age. Old people want to stay young and children want to become adults before their time – youth seems to extend into all other age groups. This development seems to point towards a future society where age itself is not important, in the sense that age is not associated with rights, privileges or responsibilities, and where young and old can meet on equal terms. Other researchers see the development of new phases of life as 'young olds' or 'old olds' not as a sign of a merging of life phases, homogenization or de-differentiation, but rather as a further differentiation and hierarchical ranking of the various life phases (Laslett 1991).

This book should be regarded as a manifestation of the movement within age and life phase research which, in recent years, can be observed from a medico-biological, universalising and standardising paradigm – hinging primarily on the question of normality v. abnormality – towards a critical humanistic research concentrating on discrepancy, paradox and diversity. In this book, the intention has been to focus on contradictions and diversity as they are seen in the interplay between the cultural and social construction of ages or life phases and the concreteness and materiality of lived life.

Studies of the structural and institutional history of childhood and old age, like discourse about and representation of these times of life, should be viewed in relation to studies of the lived life and to children's and old people's every-day experiences. The structure of this book reflects these intentions. The first part of the book concentrates on the discursive level. The contributors discuss how discursive practices have defined aging and age groups and ascribed specific meanings to them. The articles illustrate this problem area partly in general terms and partly by concrete examples and, in addition, show how the concepts of age develop in a universe of gender differences and social and cultural divisions.

The first section of the book *Age as Discourse* is introduced by Allison James in the article *Bodies of Knowledge: Growing Up and Growing Old*, and strikes up the main theme: Are old age and childhood similar or dissimilar? Children and old people, as a group, are generally characterised by what they have in common, – a lack of attributes perceived as qualifications for the real world. They lack what makes adulthood normal, they are dependent and they are without gender. But where old age is seen as negative, a deficiency, a loss, a decline, youth is the age of growth and possibilities. Where youth represents the future, old age represents the end of the future. Even though all societies have some form of age-grading, the western world has a special version which is the product of a long history of discourse.

By reviewing central works in recent research in the sociology of the body, Allison James concludes that neither a naturalism which stresses the body as a natural entity and as a biological base for the social or cultural structures of the society nor a constructionism which focuses on the body as a result of particular discourses and power relations are sufficient as perspectives on the relation between body and age. Instead, she advocates a view that allows us to see the body as something active and experiencing. We are our bodies at the same time as having them. Hence the import of the notion of embodiment: age is fundamentally an embodied knowledge, she argues. The experience of growing older takes place in an interplay between physiological circumstances and social manifestations, and is situated both in the course of life and at a particular historical time.

Ning de Coninck-Smith in her article *He Wished Nothing But Good for the Children* looks at a concrete area where childhood is formed as a specific age category, where the borderline between the child, as the innocent and often vulnerable, and the adult or young adult is established. The discussion concentrates on the introduction of film censorship at the beginning of this century. If certain films, because of their erotic or violent scenes, should not be seen by children, this required a definition of what children were. Ning de Coninck-Smith looks closely at the discussion of age limits and the moral panic of which the film censor is an example. Age limits are in this way connected to conceptions of gender and to class distinctions, and the discussion of these therefore highlights social and cultural images of times of life.

In the definition of age and age categories with their respective characteristica, certain professions have played a decisive role as enforcers of discourse. Ning de Coninck-Smith draws attention to among others the teaching profession which played the role of childhood expert, whilst Anne Løkke in her article *Infancy and Old Age as Causes of Death* examines the role of medicine and statistics in the definition of age. To previous generations it was common knowledge that just as people could die of old age, so could they die of infancy. In the 19th century this understanding was replaced by the notion of infant death as unnatural. Medical doctors exercised their authority and medical expertise in the fight against this unnatural phenomenon – a medicalization of infant welfare took place. Løkke views this re-categorisation which took place in the last half of the 19th century as the result of a movement towards regarding infant mortality as a problem that could be prevented and avoided – and she sees a parallel to this in the re-categorisation of the sicknesses of old age. For both these categories, death must have a specific cause.

In *Fashioning Agehood: Lifestyle Imagery and the Commercial Spirit of Seniors' Culture*, Stephen Katz concerns himself with the opposite end of the life phase and examines a completely different discourse production of an age category. He examines how age is created in contemporary advertising and its imagery. As a point of departure in the discussion of positive imaging of aging in contrast to the ageist perception of old age, Katz reflects on the commercialisation of seniors' culture which seems to lead to a one-sided fixation of discourses and representations of old age that mirror one way of growing old and mask the material realities of the aging process.

As a conclusion to the first part of the book Lene Otto in her article

Memories, Age and the Biographical Discourse argues against regarding life stages as general phenomena. Instead she argues for focusing on cultural diversity. Images of age and the life cycle cannot be assumed to have a general history, but are inscribed in spheres of cultural diversity. Even if people employ the same concepts, the content of these will vary for different cultural groups. Her point of departure is that life ages should be regarded as part of a biographical discourse, a compulsion to relate a life history. She therefore refuses to regard the individual's identity and experience as phenomena that exist before, or independent of, a more official state or scientific discourse. On the contrary, the two levels are preconditions of each other and can only exist in, and with, each other. In this way Lene Otto very explicitly problematises the relationship between discourse and praxis.

From the many articles in this book it is evident that discourses do not live independent of other forms of praxis. But it is obvious, too, that there is no substantial agreement as to how exactly to describe the relation between discourse and non-discursive practices. Thus, while Allison James describes ageing as an embodiment of knowledge and sees this as a way of bridging the gap between the social constructionist account stressing discourse and accounts of the aging experience stressing the lived experience of people, Lene Otto argues that we should not regard discourse as a factual empirically existing entity, but rather as tool for the researcher. Notwithstanding the differences, it is clear that it is untenable to see discourse as a simple and unequivocal contrast to the lived life; the two must be seen in relation to each other. Age as discourse is therefore linked to age as praxis.

The second section *Age in Practice* presents articles that concentrate on age as lived experience. In his article *A World of Their Own Making* John Gillis claims that in modern society the family has assumed the role that religious communities, for example, previously played, by giving age a meaningful content. Since Victorian times the family has become an institution which concerns itself with manifesting the transition between age categories and has become the most important manager of the cultural practices, images and myths which surround age and aging. For more than a hundred years we have lived with a linear, objective externalised time which replaced the pre-modern conception of a life course and the non-separation of time from place which characterised this world view. With industrialism and the era of the nation state a flooding time – a uniform, standardised time – emerged. But this time was not merely transferred to people's lived life. It was carved up and divided by new rituals, the domicile of which was the family. Linear time has always existed simultaneously with a cyclic, subjective time where points of time recur, a time that human beings take possession of. 'The time we live with' is combined with 'the time we live by'. In this way age has become for us something both external and reified and something subjectively experienced.

Gillis observes a de-chronologisation in recent years; age has received a less precise definition and aging has become less standardised, the life cycle has become more undefined. This de-chronologisation has been accompanied by a proliferation of age-related rites – we are re-inventing our life ages. Gillis thus emphasizes people's appropriation and adaptation of general social conditions.

In her article on infant welfare *Complete Motherhood: The Mother-Infant Relationship in the First Few Days of Life, 1920 to 1950,* Maxine Rhodes moves in the same direction as Gillis. By focusing on the "maternity service" and its role in controlling and modelling maternal and infant behaviour, she demonstrates how this knowledge – disseminated from above, via text books on midwifery and popular childcare manuals with advice on infant welfare – was not just uncritically forced upon midwives and mothers. The knowledge was imparted in diffuse manner in the network surrounding the new mother. The notion of infancy was constructed not only by dissemination knowledge from medical text books and teaching manuals – from experts to lay people – but by interpreting and employing this knowledge in a flexible manner dependent on the place and the circumstances.

In his contribution *When Men Are Made into Boys* Jørgen Povlsen investigates the existence of various bodies and embodiments in old age. From around the turn of the century a specific cultural understanding of age, age grading and aging became visible in connection with the burgeoning sports movement. The paradox phenomenon "Old Boys" (Sports veterans) on a micro level contains the story of the plasticity of the age-concept, on a macro level it points further at the relativity and diversity of ways of growing old. Povlsen reveals the playing with age and embodiments of age in a framework of masculinity, aging and sport. Povlsen focuses on the interaction between the physical construction (old body) and the experienced physicality (boy's body), thereby questioning if the aging body of sport can point the way to other interpretations of the relationship between old age and childhood.

As early as in the first chapter of the book Allison James states that all cultures undoubtedly have some form of age-grading, and that the western world has constructed its own version. Patricia Stamp gives an example of the construction of age and age categories in a different culture in her article on Kikuyu women's age categories in Kenya, *Power to the Elders: the Politics of Aging amongst the Kikuyu Women of Kenya*. It is obvious that age is not merely a biological phenomenon among Kikuyu women. As in other East African countries both men and women go through several socially defined life phases separated by certain rites. In Kikuyu society women's youth and old age have distinct similarities which separate them from adulthood and differences that separate them from each other. Women's status is first and foremost determined by motherhood; this is what gives them prestige, but young women as well as old have quite a large degree of freedom and self-determination. In contrast to the young, older Kikuyu women can exploit their position to obtain a fairly substantial degree of power, and especially in pre-colonial times age-grading was the basis of women's power and political strategy.

As noted, age categories and life phases can be said first to receive significance when contrasted to other ages. Age groups become the basis for interchange – as Stamp has shown with the Kikuyus – and it is in relation to other life ages that the elderly are granted rights and duties. Erhard Chvojka in his article *Wise or Childish? Ambivalent Images of Grandparents in the Course of the 19th Century* approaches the problem complex of age and the inter-generational from a historical viewpoint. From the late 1700's the modern role of grandparents was associated with the new middle class conception of the family. Old people were assumed to have a special pedagogic effect on children, even though this image of grandparents also met its opposite: grandfathers were often portrayed as wise and experienced authorities, yet they were still an easy target for ridicule in their second childhood. Grandmothers who had not the same aura as grandfathers in their role of serious teachers, were often described as inadequate as child rearers, as ignorant, inattentive and irrational. Chvojka discusses the relationship between the normative rules for the interplay between grandparents and grandchildren – as they appear in pictures – and the social practices and personal experiences as expressed, for example, in autobiographies. As in other articles in the book, it is stressed that these two levels – cultural stereotypes and social reality – should not be sharply segregated because the division between them is artificial, and Chvojka reviews his material in a constant interaction between individual reflections and the visual dimension. The difficult division between discourse and praxis is thus thematised.

The point of departure of this book has been that age may be viewed as a social and cultural construction created in a historical setting. Therefore, it is relevant to ask in what way will the future be shaped differently from the situation we know at present. Recent demographic research clearly points to a scenario of increased life expectancy. This has given rise to a growing interest in longevity as it is manifested in centenarians and super-centenarians research.[1] These demographic changes may completely reform our attitude to age. In the future more generations will be alive at the same time, and thus a drastic change may take place in the relationship between young and old. Not only may old age change its appearance but the whole distribution of life ages may also be given a new character.

At the other end of the life span the question of age is extended into the uterus. In the closing chapter of this book *Age in the Future: Social Implications of New Reproductive and Genetic Technologies*, Lene Koch looks more closely at the importance of new reproductive and genetic technologies. In her opinion these new techniques will decisively alter our perception of age, generation, family and kinship – when, for example, twins can be born with an intervening period of years, or when grandmothers can be mothers of their own grandchildren. In this way our perception of what is natural will be challenged, and we will have to ask ourselves where the line is between life and death, between not-yet-life and life, or life and no-longer-life. Technology will in this way fundamentally change our perception of life ages, aging and identity.

Most of the articles contained in this book were presented at a conference Childhood and Old Age – Equals or Opposites? which took place at Odense University from 7th – 9th April 1997. We thank the Danish Research Council for the Humanities, the Danish Social Science Research Council, LEGO A/S, and The Aging Research Centre at Odense University for economically supporting the arrangement of the seminar. The Aging Research Centre and LEGO A/S have given economic support to the publication of this book.

---

1. B. Jeune and J. Vaupel 1995; A.R. Thatcher, V. Kannisto. and J. Vaupel 1998.

References

Gillis, J.: *A World of Their Own Making. A History of Myth and Ritual in Family Life.* Oxford University Press, 1996.

Jeune, B. and Vaupel, J. (eds.): *Exceptional longevity. From prehistory to the present*. Odense University Press, 1995.

Laslett, P: *A Fresh Map of Life: The Emergence of the Third Age.* Harvard University Press, 1991.

Meyrowitz, J.: *No Sense of Place. The Impact of Electronic Media on Social Behavior.* Oxford University Press, 1985.

Thatcher, A.R., Kannisto, V. and Vaupel J.: *The Force of mortality at ages 80 to 120.* Odense University Press, 1998.

I
Age as Discourse

Bodies of Knowledge:
Growing Up and Growing Old

Allison James

Family photograph albums provide us with a splendid iconography of the ways in which bodies mark out the passage of time between growing up and growing old. Placed side by side these photographs register, year upon year the subtle changes which bodies undergo: children's bodies become at first fatter, then thinner and taller and their faces mature from the round face of the toddler to the more angular adolescent. It is a photographic sequence which marks out and is held to celebrate their literal coming of age, their growing into adulthood. Photographs of adult bodies also mark out the passage of time but our enchantment with these changes seems less – firm flesh becomes slack, faces crisscross with lines, backs stoop. Thus, in the advertising copy of modern western societies, as noted elsewhere,[1] 'growing up' is positioned positively and visual images of 'the child' are used to promote the future, progress, health and vitality. 'Growing old', on the other hand, is signalled as a period of decline, accompanied by the onset of physical and social dependency with, as Haraven notes, the aged being characterised as 'useless', 'inefficient', 'unattractive', 'temperamental', and 'senile'.[2]

Taking these starkly contrasting images of childhood and old age as a starting point, this article explores images and experiences of ageing across the life course. First, it considers the ways in which images of childhood and old age are, within western industrial societies, counter-poised in the popular imagination and everyday social practice to provide radically different evaluations of different periods in the life course. Second, and following on from this, it asks why is it that images of childhood provide potent metaphors for dealing with what is considered to be the pressing 'problem' of old age within modernity when it is clear that the infantilising practices which follow from such a perspective may be experienced, by those who become subject to them, as deeply humiliating?[3] Exploring the idea that bodily change is used as a marker of social identity this paper argues that considerable insight into these practices can be gained by an analysis which conceptualises age as a form of embodied knowledge, something which Featherstone and Wernick argue is all too often lost sight of in studies of the ageing process.[4]

Central to the argument presented here are two key assumptions. First, if the passing of time is literally mapped onto and into bodies – from the loss of puppy fat through to the greying and loss of hair – then the ageing process must necessarily be understood as a constantly reflexive intersection between the physical and social experience of having and being a body, an experience which is constantly changing in and through the life course. An adequate sociological understanding of the ageing process cannot therefore simply be a matter of assessing the social consequences of natural, physiological change. Rather it must address the agency of the ageing body and how people experience the complex interplay between the physical and social manifestations of the ageing process. It must account for the actual practical, experience of being young and being old through a "focus on embodied persons relating to each other through the visible body, the body which sees and can be seen".[5] A second, and related assumption, is that central to our understanding of ageing must be therefore the recognition that that reflexive interaction is, itself, temporally situated both within the life course of the individual and within historical time: the body "is irreducibly historical… structured through human values and the exigencies of the historical world".[6] Thus, this paper argues, to take seriously a theory of ageing as embodied knowledge we must see the body as temporally located within particular cultural settings at particular historical moments.

THE BODY AND SOCIOLOGY

According to Shilling the body, until recently, has been an 'absent presence' within mainstream sociological theory. Theories of agency and social action have simply assumed the existence of 'the body' (through postulating but not engaging with the actor) and have offered little critical appreciation of the body as both the medium of and for social action.[7] More recently, however, this omission has begun to be addressed within social theory and, as Shilling and Csordas have observed, two opposing traditions have emerged.[8] The first approach begins from the view that the body is a natural entity and it is argued that it is the body which provides the 'biological base' for the social, moral, economic and political structures of society. Thus, the naturalistic perspective holds that:

"the capabilities and constraints of human bodies define individuals, and generate the social, political and economic relations which characterise national and international patterns of living. Inequalities in material wealth, legal rights and political power… are given, or at the very least legitimised, by the determining power of the biological body".[9]

Within this view, for example, sexual difference is taken to be a given feature of bodies and held to account for the 'natural' propensity of women for mothering and of men for dominance, bodily differences which are taken to provide justifications for gendered social and political inequalities. This naturalistic approach is clearly the main stay of sociobiology and medical models of the body but it can also be found within contemporary sociological theorising. Some branches of feminism use the 'naturalistic' model to muster a powerful set of arguments for celebrating women's identities and, in feminist research on, for example, eating disorders and reproduction a naturalistic perception of the body is the starting point for exploring the ways in which social differences and gender inequalities are mapped onto or exploit the particularities of women's biology.[10] Within social anthropology, naturalistic views of the body are used for the more descriptive task of demonstrating cultural variation through analysis of "the cultural meaning [to] be distilled from the treatment of body products such as blood, semen, sweat, tears, faeces, urine and saliva".[11]

The second perspective which embraces a largely social constructionist view, sees the body as, instead, "the outcome of social forces and relations", the product of particular discourses.[12] In such accounts of the body, materialist explanations are rejected and attention is given instead to the ways in which the body is constrained and shaped by society. For example, for Foucault, the body is primarily a product of discourses of power, its material form becoming almost immaterial to his analysis: what is of interest is the way in which the body is imprinted by society.[13] Less radical formulations see the body as a receptor of cultural meanings, which are then displayed upon the body, or the body as reflecting or representing sets of social relations which can be 'read off' its surfaces. Thus Featherstone's body is visualised as a product of consumer culture, Turner's the outcome of complex historical and social processes and Mauss's a clear indication of the varied workings of culture, a visible and immediately apparent demonstration of cultural difference.[14]

What neither of these perspectives does, however, is provide an adequate account of the agency of the body. In their focused concentration on the study of the body both approaches simply take the fact of embodiment for granted. They do not give explicit attention to the notion of an active, experiencing body.[15] In Csordas's view, this lacuna is regrettable for, in agreement with Shilling[16], he maintains that a number of theoretically productive links can be forged between these different theoretical perspectives by explicitly addressing the social experience of the physical body which people have.

Shilling begins to open up such an approach to embodiment through his suggestion that the body is 'unfinished' at birth. What he terms the 'finishing' of the body by and in society is the process whereby the material object (the body) takes on particular forms and characteristics through its engagement with social structures and institutions – be this the havoc reaped upon the body by starvation and war or the anorexic models which are fast becoming the unwelcome by-product of the western fashion industry. But to understand how it is that such a reshaping of the material body actually takes place requires a more incisive exploration, one which centres on the experiencing body itself – here is the importance, then, of the notion of 'embodiment' or what Turner calls 'bodiliness'.[17] As Lyon and Barbalet note, such an approach has a lot to offer for, although

> "the body is a subject of (and subject to) social power... it is not merely a passive recipient of society's mold, and therefore external to it. The human capacity for social agency, to collectively and individually contribute to the making of the social world comes precisely from the person's lived experience of embodiment. Persons do not simply experience their bodies as external objects of their possessions or even as an intermediary environment which surrounds their being. Persons experience themselves simultaneously in and as their bodies".[18]

For an understanding of ageing across the life course such an approach, which attempts to bridge naturalistic and constructionist accounts of the body, takes on a particular poignancy for, if Shilling is correct in arguing that the body is only completed through action in society, then it is surely during both childhood and old age that this process of 'finishing' (embodiment) becomes particularly stark. Both these periods of the life course are marked by rapid physiological change. When compared to the bodily experiences of adults, therefore, young and old people are both likely to have a greatly enhanced subjective awareness of bodily change, albeit that these changes, as discussed below, are open to strongly contrasting social and moral evaluations. Focusing on either ends of the life course provides potentially seminal instances of ageing as embodied knowledge.

Hitherto, however, accounts of ageing, whether in relation to the very young or old, have more usually been interpreted from within either largely naturalistic or constructionist frames, with notions of age as an embodied experience rather rare. The bio-medical gaze of gerontology has worked, for example, to shape both sociological and social policy accounts of ageing into what Featherstone and Wernick term, the 'social bookkeeping tradition' whereby a great deal of statistics are collected about particular aspects of the ageing body "in order to assess, and argue about, the distribution of resource to the frail, the sick and the infirm".[19] Similarly, accounts of childhood have, until fairly recently, been dominated by models adapted from developmental psychology, leading to a view of children's social behaviour as being largely the outcome of the particularities of their incompetent and as yet underdeveloped bodies.[20] From within a naturalistic perspective, therefore, the bodies of old and young people are held to account for particular age-based experiences of social marginality or dependency. More recently, however, the pendulum has swung in the opposite direction with a great deal of attention being paid to the social construction of ageing at either end of the life course. At their most extreme, as paralleled in the work of the body previously described, accounts of childhood and old age are represented as simply the product of discourses, as cultural constructions of ageing which are inscribed upon or read off the surfaces of the body.[21]

And from these kinds accounts there is, of course, much insight to be gleaned into how the social process of ageing takes place in society in terms of age-based ideologies or the patterning of inequalities in relation to health and welfare. However, exactly how ageing is actually experienced by people and the ways in which this experience might be made sense of as a form of embodied knowledge is perhaps an even more intriguing question and one which, as Featherstone and Wernick observe, is less commonly asked.[22] This omission is particularly significant when, as noted elsewhere, infantilising and stigmatising practices are played out upon the bodies of elderly people.[23] Such practices cannot be regarded as somehow the 'natural' or inevitable outcome of the ageing process. How then are they experienced? Why do they occur?

Growing up through the life course over time

Common to all societies are systems of social classification which conceptually order and control the changes which time brings to the material body. Systems of status and age-grading, though often varying according to gender, nonetheless work to render orderly the physical changes in the body that the march of time produces. Registered in language, particular sets of terms are used to separate out one age status group from another; child is distinguished from toddler, adolescent from adult, adults from 'the elderly'. In making such distinctions these terms allocate social identities and responsibilities and in this way mark out the differences between categories of person across the life course, often ascribing to them particular sets of social qualities or attributes. Thus, in modern western societies it has been suggested that an elliptical path of ageing can be traced which depicts,

> "different qualitative experiences during the life course as an individual moves from childhood, through the adult years to old age. It emphasises the centrality of adult life, in contrast to the relatively weaker and more marginal positions of child and an elderly person".[24]

Across the life course, therefore, "whilst the movement towards person hood by the child is celebrated and anticipated, ageing is seen as an unwelcome movement out of person hood, as something to be hidden and or disguised".[25] That this is, however, not the 'natural' or inevitable outcome of biological change can be seen through cross-cultural comparisons of the ageing process. Sankar's study of Buddhist nuns, for example, reveals that old age is welcomed as a sign of the growth of maturity while MacCormack's research among the Sherbo people of Sierra Leone shows how the incoherent ramblings of an infirm mind, which in western industrial societies is associated with the onset of dementia, is more positively interpreted as a sign of the elderly person's contact with the ancestors. And in Japan a moral cosmology centred on the image of 'okina' (literally old man) works to provide a positive, rather than negative image of old age.[26]

However, whilst evaluations of old age (and also of childhood[27]) can be shown through such examples to vary across time and space and thus they help persuade us of the value of social constructionist accounts of ageing, it is also the case that the materiality of ageing – the ageing experience which people have in and as their bodies – has also to be accounted for. And it is by seeing age as embodied knowledge that this bridge can be built for, although the physical changes which the body undergoes over time can in many ways be regarded as universal, and as largely (though not wholly) undifferentiated by time and space, the ways in which these changes are experienced do in fact change. And they do so precisely because of the intersection between 'the body' and 'society'. Thus growing up through the life course, though clearly embracing the physiological process of ageing from childhood to old age, has to be also accounted for as a generational specific phenomena: to grow up or to grow old is to acquire a particular embodied knowledge at a particular moment in time.

This can be illustrated through an historical account of the ways in which views about the child's body and physiology changed during the nineteenth century and the social, moral, economic and practical consequences for children which this changed view of their bodies had. Taken together, these changes can be said to contextualise children's own experience of ageing, to quite literally constitute a particular embodiment of children. Steedman, for example, argues that it was the nineteenth century that,

> "fixed childhood, not just as a category of experience, but also as a time span… [through] the development of mass schooling, and its

grouping of children together by age cohort. In the same period the practices of child psychology, developmental linguistics and anthropometry provided clearer pictures of what children were like, and how they should be expected to look at certain ages."[28]

During this period ideas of child growth and development became a trope around which a whole variety of social, political and educational ideologies and reforms were woven, with the peculiarity of the child's changing physiology becoming seen as the very embodiment of time passing, giving visible material form to the notion of the biological clock:

"The building up of scientific evidence about physical growth in childhood described an actual progress in individual lives, which increased in symbolic importance during the nineteenth century, whereby that which is traversed is, in the end, left behind and abandoned, as the child grows up and goes away. In this way childhood as it has been culturally described is always about that which is temporary and impermanent, always describes a loss in adult life, a state that is recognised too late. Children are quite precisely a physiological chronology, a history, as they make their way through the stages of growth".[29]

This changed view of the ageing process was accompanied, during the nineteenth century, by the opening up of the conceptual and social space of childhood. The special and distinctive features of childhood, often held to stem from the needs of children which the particularity of their bodies impart, were shored up by a variety of philanthropic, educational, welfare and political reforms, designed to improve the lives – the embodied experience – of children.[30]

Central to this endeavour, therefore, was a gradual firming up of what the child's body was. Progressed and popularised through the nineteenth and twentieth centuries, contemporary ideas of the child's body coalesced around the idea of the significance of change and growth: to grow up as an adult was to out grow (or, more precisely, to grow out of) the body of a child. And it became clear that this process of biological development needed to be measured and monitored. In Britain, as Armstrong has shown, the charting and surveying of the child population which began to take place at this time gradually defined and firmed up limits of normality for that childlike body. Different kinds of children, who differed from this norm, were thereby identified and their particular needs classified and attended to:

"nervous children, delicate children, neuropathic children, maladjusted children, difficult children, oversensitive children and unstable children were all essentially inventions of a new way of seeing childhood". [31]

Thus, in her account of the work of labour party activist McMillan, Steedman shows how, measured against such visions of normalcy, the retarded growth apparent amongst the population of working class children took on great political and social significance:[32]

> "[Child physiology] structured around the idea of growth and development... allowed for comparisons to be made between children, and, most important of all as a basis for a social policy on childhood, it rooted mental life in the material body and the material conditions of life. In this way, working-class children could be seen as having been robbed of natural development, their potential for health and growth lying dormant in their half-starved bodies".[33]

McMillan believed, that is was through a purposive and healthy education based on open air schools that the children of the poor could be rescued from deprivation and restored "to become agents of a new social future".[34]

But this kind of account provides only part of the story. It fails to explore how children themselves live with their changing biology, a biology which both shapes what they are and what they can do and one which, at the same time, invites particular perceptions of what, as children, they should be and should do. If ageing – be it for children or older people – is to be seen as the acquisition of embodied knowledge in and over time then account must be taken of the materiality and experiential subjectivity of the body in the same moment as the body is objectified within the social world. Such an approach, as noted earlier, sees the body as neither simply the product of social relations nor a determinant of them:

> "The shapes, sizes and meanings of the body are not given at birth and neither is the body's future experience of well being: the body is an entity which can be 'completed' only through human labour".[35]

Thus, for example, it is certain that the historical shaping of perceptions of children's bodies described above had a number of consequences for children which were very material indeed. There was, for example, a decline in infant mortality, from 148 per 1000 live births in 1841-5 to 50 in 1941-5[36]; the incidence of tuberculosis declined from the 1930s onwards, following the discovery of the importance of vitamins and fresh air,[37] children's bodies increased in weight and size according to age, a direct result of state interventions to improve food provision, housing and sanitation for the children of the poor and, through education policy, to encourage physical exercise within the curriculum.[38]

Thus it could be argued that it was children's (and their parents') active engagement with these changing health practices, combined with a more general improvement in the social and economic conditions of their everyday lives, that contributed to the changing physiology of children's bodies. Increases in children's height and weight and a decline in chronic sickness did not occur as a somehow 'natural' follow on from increased knowledge about nutrition or better housing. Nor was this simply a matter of seeing children differently. It was through children's literal embodiment of social policies and welfare reforms centred on improving their health and welfare that the image of 'the child' gradually came to encompass more universal images of hope for the future, and of bodily change and development providing a safe passage into the adult world.

And as Haraven notes such a change in both the conceptualisation and practical living conditions for those at one stage of life has, necessarily, an effect upon others:

> "The emergence of 'old age' as social, cultural and biological phenomenon can best be understood in the context of other stages of life. The social conditions of children and adolescents in a given society are related to the way in which adulthood is perceived in that society. Conversely, the role and position of adults and the aged are related to the treatment of children and youths."[39]

Thus, that by the beginning of the twentieth century a negative, rather than positive, view of old age had emerged as predominant has to be understood as a response to the increasing valorisation of childhood and youth as categories in the life course which had preceded it.

INFANTILISATION AND EMBODIED KNOWLEDGE

The above extended historical discussion of the development of concepts of childhood in relation to changing ideas about children's bodies illustrates how, through focusing upon ageing as an embodied concept, it is possible to capture more incisively the complex interplay of the many social and material factors which come to centre upon the body and thus to explore how these also work to shape people's own everyday experience of that body. In this final section I turn, therefore, to a particular experience of embodiment which, during the latter part of the twentieth century has been identified as a problem which warrants attention. This is the infantilisation of elderly people, that is the treating of elderly people as if they were children. Explored in greater detail elsewhere[40] in this final section I tease out some further ramifications by an explicit focus on ageing as embodied knowledge.

Previously it was argued that infantilisation practices arise as response to the onset of dependency in old age as a way to soften the degradations which time can wreak upon the ageing body:

> "a selective and culturally specific reading of the body and mind of the child forms the basis for the western conception of childhood as a period of culturally legitimated dependency which, in turn, provides the grounding for parallels perceived between their bodies and those of elderly people. Through metaphoric recourse to the positively perceived 'limitations' of the child's body adults shield themselves from the approaching vision of illegitimate social dependency in old age. In doing so, however, the basis for the denial of elderly personhood is formed. At its most extreme this can lead to the social death of those who are merely growing old".[41]

Thus, signs of bodily decay – such as loss of speech or of continence – are interpreted as childlike because they contravene the usual signs of independent adulthood and, perhaps more significantly, foretell of death itself.

But, this represents a partial and selective reading of older bodies. Infantilising parallels choose to ignore the wrinkles which enfold the elderly woman's face, the loss of her mobility or her bent arthritic frame . These are visibly not features of the body of a child. Infantilising parallels also choose to ignore the personal qualities and characters of those who are elderly and infirm so that, for example, entry into residential homes for the elderly is assessed in terms of physical capabilities. This means, as Hazan notes, that very elderly people risk becoming defined primarily by their bodies through the effective obliteration of "their life history and social identity, and reducing them to their physical and mental disabilities".[42]

If, as has been argued here, ageing is to be understood as an embodied knowledge then clearly those who are in deep old age and at the receiving end of practices of infantilisation will provide one of the richest source for exploring the ways in which this knowledge is gained and made use of. If their social identities are constructed by others largely and as time passes increasingly through the medium of the body – via particular practices of bodily care and other forms of social exclusion – then a person's experience of and as their body must surely take on a greater significance in relation to the self. Indeed, the body must become increasingly self-conscious as the elderly person becomes more self-conscious about their bodies. It is perhaps not surprising therefore that the forms of resistance to infantilising practices which elderly people adopt are promulgated through the body, rather than through language. From her fieldwork in a residential home for elderly people Hockey describes such acts of defiance:

> "a new and very overweight resident demanded without success to be given a wheel chair. When staff made her stand up in the corridor she slid down the wall, two or more care assistants being required to return her to her feet. When they put her commode on the other side

of the room to make her walk across to it she infuriate them by urinating in her coffee mug. Another scarcely mobile woman invariably set off on her long journey to the toilets whenever the lunch bell was rung... Endeavouring to circumvent her late arrival in the dining-room, a care aide asked her some 15 minutes before lunch if she needed the toilet. Managing not to hear the question until it had been shouted repeatedly the resident held up her hand and replied: "Please teacher. I don't. Not yet"".[43]

Like small children who have limited forms of linguistic expression the body provides a significant medium of expression. And through such example the body is demonstrated to be, indeed, a body of knowledge.

Conclusion

This article has argued for a perspective on ageing which engages with notions of embodiment across the life course so that the processes of both growing up and growing old can be viewed in their spatial and temporal specificities and understood as a subjective and reflexive experience. It has suggested that the body be regarded as both a sign of time passing for an individual and as a representation of the temporal location of that individual within the life course, embodied experiences which are themselves subject to historical change.

That ageing is an embodied knowledge there is therefore no doubt. Indeed it is something which finds explicit recognition in Britain in the commonly voiced wisdom that 'you are as old as you feel'. However, until recently the private consolation which this aphorism provides has not spilled over into more public arenas – as we have seen, the visibility of the changes marked upon the ageing body has taken a predominant role in marking out social identity. However, it may be that such attitudes are beginning to change. A recent advert promoting Age concern, the British charity for elderly people, is designed to combat negative views of ageing and age discrimination at work. It features a strikingly attractive 50 year old woman, ample breasted, wearing a plunging black bra and is captioned by the phrase: the first thing some people notice is her age. But, in truth, this is the last thing that one notices. Age is, ironically, rendered immaterial through the medium of the body.

---

1. J. Hockey and A. James 1993.
2. T. Haraven 1995.
3. J. Hockey and A. James 1993.

4. M. Featherstone and A. Wernick 1995.
5. M. Featherstone and A. Wernick 1995, p.2.
6. N. Crossley 1996.
7. C. Shilling 1993.
8. Ibid. and T.J. Csordas 1994.
9. C. Shilling 1993.
10. K. Chernin 1983 and M. O'Brien 1989.
11. T.J. Csordas 1994, p. 5.
12. C. Shilling 1993, p. 16.
13. Michel Foucault 1979 cf. N. Crossley 1996.
14. M. Featherstone1982; B.S. Turner 1984, and M. Mauss 1950.
15. T.J. Csordas 1994, p. 6.
16. C. Shilling 1993.
17. B.S. Turner 1984.
18. M.L. Lyon and J.M. Barbalet 1994, p. 54.
19. M. Featherstone and A. Wernick,A. (eds) 1995, p. 1.
20. A. James and A. Prout (eds.) 1990.
21. In relation to childhood as a social construction see discussion in James, Jenks and Prout 1998.
22. M. Featherstone and A. Wernick (eds) 1995.
23. J. Hockey and A. James 1993.
24. Ibid., p. 28.
25. Ibid., p. 87.
26. A. Sankar 1984, C. MacCormack 1985, and S. Wada 1995.
27. J. Hockey and A. James 1993 and H. Hendrick 1990.
28. C. Steedman1995, p. 7.
29. C. Steedman 1992, p. 37.
30. H. Hendrick 1997.
31. D. Armstrong 1983, p. 15.
32. A fuller account of the work of Margaret McMillan can be found in Steedman.
33. C. Steedman 1992, p. 25.
34. Ibid., p. 35.
35. C. Shilling 1993, p. 124-25.
36. C. Woodroffe et al. 1993.
37. L. Bryder 1992.
38. B. Mayall 1996, p. 25-26.
39. T. Haraven 1995, p. 121.
40. J. Hockey and A. James 1993.
41. J. Hockey and A. James1995, p. 143.
42. H. Hazan 1980, p. 30.
43. J. Hockey and A. James 1993, p. 173.

Bibliography

Armstrong, D. *The Political Anatomy of the Body.* Cambridge: Cambridge University Press, 1983.

Bryder, L. "Wonderlands of buttercup, clove and daisies: tuberculosis and the open-air school movement" in R. Cooter (ed.) *In the Name of the Child: health and welfare 1880-1940.* London: Routledge, 1992.

Chernin, K. Womansize. *The Tyranny of Slenderness*. London: The Women's Press, 1983.

Crossley, N. "Body-subject/Body-power: Agency, inscription and control in Foucault and Merleau-Ponty". *Body and Society* 2.2 (1996): 99-116.

Csordas, T.J. *Embodiment and Experience: the existential ground of culture and self*. Cambridge: Cambridge University Press, 1994.

Featherstone, M. "The body in consumer culture". Theory, Culture and Society 1 (1982) 18-33.
Featherstone, M. and Wernick, A. (eds.) *Images of Aging*. London: Routledge, 1995.

Foucault, M. *Discipline and Punish: the birth of the prison*. Harmondsworth: Penguin, 1979.

Haraven, T. "Changing images of aging and the social construction of the life course". In M. Featherstone and A. Wernick (eds.) *Images of Aging*. London: Routledge, 1995.

Hazan, H. *The Limbo People*. London: Routledge and Kegan Paul, 1980.

Hendrick, H. "Constructions and reconstructons of British childhood: an interpretative survey, 1800 to the present". in A. James and A. Prout (eds.) *Constructing and Reconstructing Childhood*. Lewes: Falmer Press, 1990.

Hendrick, H. *Children, Childhood and English Society 1880-1990*. Cambridge: Cambridge University Press, 1997.

Hockey, J. and James, A. *Growing Up and Growing Old*. London: Sage, 1993.

Hockey, J. and James, A. "Back to our futures: imaging second childhood". In M. Featherstone and A.Wernick (eds.) *Images of Aging*. London: Routledge, 1995.

James, A. and Prout, A. (eds.) *Constructing and Reconstructing Childhood*. Lewes: Falmer Press, 1990.

James, A., Jenks, C., Prout, A. *Theorising Childhood*. Cambridge: Polity Press, 1998.

Lyon, M.L. and Barbalet, J.M. "Society's body: emotion and the "somatization" of social theory" in T.J. Csordas *Embodiment and Experience: the existential ground of culture and self*. Cambridge; Cambridge University Press, 1994.

Mauss, M. "*Les techniques du corps*". Sociologie et Anthropologie. Paris: Presses Unversitaires de France, 1950.

MacCormack, C. "Dying as transformation to ancestorhood: the Sherbo coast of Sierra Leone" *Curare, Sonderband* 4 (1985): 117-26.

Mayall, B. *Children, Health and the Social Order*. Buckingham: Open University Press, 1996.

O'Brien, M. *Reproducing the World*. Boulder, CO: Westview Press, 1989.

Sankar, A. "'It's just old age'. Old age as a diagnosis in American and Chinese medicine". In D. Il. Kertzer and J. Keith (eds.) *Age and Anthropological Theory*. Ithaca, NY: Cornell University Press, 1984.

Shilling, C. *The body and Social Theory*. London: Sage, 1993.

Steedman, C. *Childhood, Culture and Class in Britain: Margaret McMillan 1860-1931*. London: Virago,1990.

Steedman, C. "Bodies, figures and physiology: Margaret McMillan and the late nineteenth-century remarking of working-class childhood", in R. Cooter (ed.) *In the Name of the Child: health and welfare 1880-1940*. London: Routledge, 1992.

Steedman, C. *Strange Dislocations: Childhood and the idea of human interiority 1780-1930*. London : Virago, 1995.

Turner, B.S. *The Body and Society*. Oxford: Basil Blackwell, 1984.

Wada, S. "The status and image of the elderly in Japan: understanding the paternalistic ideology". in M. Featherstone and A.Wernick (eds.) *Images of Aging*. London: Routledge, 1995.

Woodroffe, C. et al. *Children, Teenagers and Health: the Key Data*. Buckingham: Open University Press, 1993.

"He Wished Nothing But Good for the Children; But Knew that Many Had Been Harmed by It"[1]

Film Censorship in Denmark 1896-1922

Ning de Coninck-Smith

The movies came to Denmark in 1896. The first movies were shown in a wooden pavilion on the City Hall Square and the new medium quickly found a wide popular audience. It was cheap entertainment: 25 *øre* for adults, 10-15 *øre* for children. Saturday evening was the big evening, while in the course of the week it was children and the young who were the regular guests. If the cinema wasn't quite simply closed. The show lasted at most half an hour and consisted of 4-5 short films ranging from scenes from nature and popular life, through current affairs to farces and dramatic scenes.

Cinemas mushroomed in closed-down shops and even more casual venues. Such a cinema lay in the street Mysundegade in the Vesterbro district of Copenhagen, and was called *Loppen*, 'the Flea'. The name, like the English 'fleapit', came from the fact that the audience were packed so close that they could not avoid getting fleas. But the atmosphere wanted nothing, if we are to believe an old Copenhagener:

> "We children could get in there before seven for 5 *øre*, in the three front rows – the normal price was 15 *øre* anywhere in the hall. "You get in right away!", proclaimed a barker at the door, and so you did, even if it was in the middle of the film. You could sit down wherever you liked in the hall, and you just sat on through the next show. A pianist hammered away at the old untuned piano, but it was still a great treat for us when the film appeared on the screen".[2]

Around 1911 proper cinema-building began, as film began to be an acceptable medium for more refined social circles and this was reflected in the palatial architecture of the cinemas. The films became longer and increasingly developed into melodramas and comedies – sometimes erotic – with the middle or upper classes as the preferred social setting. In the early years the popular and carnivalesque had been typical modes for short films. But they were still silent, accompanied by piano music, supplemented by a *contentum* – an instrument for playing background sounds. Working this was an attractive job for boys aged 12-14. It was only from the beginning of the 1930s that the talking film became widespread in Danish cinemas.[3]

Gunnar Sandfeld's major monograph *Den stumme Scene* (The Silent Stage), which appeared in 1966, based on the ministerial preliminaries to the 1913 Government Order,[4] as well as large numbers of contemporary newspaper articles and later memoirs, gives a thorough review of the public debate that led to the establishment of *Statens Filmcensur* (The National Board of Film Censorship) in 1913. After Sandfeld, several media and film historians have dealt with the subject in overview form. As regards the historical aspect, though, Sandfeld is still the authority.[5]

However, one question which has so far escaped the attention of the researchers is why the minimum age was set in 1913 at 16 – not for example at 14. At the time 14 was in fact the age of criminal responsibility and the age at which children normally left school, were confirmed and took their place at the back of the queue among the grown-ups.

It is this question I have set myself the task of answering. In the article I interpret the history of film censorship in the light of other contemporary efforts to make biological age a social and cultural parameter and a boundary marker between child and young person, young person and adult – in contrast to the socially determined age concept of earlier times.[6]

For the debate on the harmful influence of film on young minds was only one of many concerns that exercised adult discourse about the childhood and youth of the future in the decades around the turn of the century. With an analytical concept one can speak of moral panic – and insofar as it both had the media as its object and was played out in the media, the concept can be narrowed down to 'media panic'.[7] What these panics have in common is that they concern children and the young, that their course is by and large identical, and that the reaction to them is violent and emotional. Moral panics are reinforced by other forms of panics and cannot be rationally argued. On the other hand they function as norm-creating fora, and the media researcher Kirsten Drotner, for example, has claimed that the dissolution of norms in modern society can explain the intensity of the panic. That it is precisely children and the young who are in focus she explains by the fact that their behaviour is perceived as a threat to the bourgeois project of cultivation and education.[8]

Copenhagen Cinema before the 1st. World War. (Filmmuseet)

FREDERIKSBERG 1909

At its meeting in April 1909 the Frederiksberg District Council (Frederiksberg is now an independent council within the Copenhagen area) discussed a proposal to introduce 'pedagogical' film censorship at the fifteen cinemas found at that time in Frederiksberg.

The spokesman for the idea was Dr. Nandrup of the Right Party, and he argued for it by saying that the competition among the cinemas had now become so fierce that the cinema owners had found it necessary to lure the customers in by "means which were not beneficial to the young, since on the one hand the images shown, and on the other the advertising posters displayed, were often very unfortunate." Behind his formulation of the problem lay a more or less hidden criticism of the theatre censor in Copenhagen and Frederiksberg, P.A. Rosenberg, who was also responsible for the picture-houses. He was generally regarded by educationalists and right-wingers as far too liberal.

In his efforts to improve the 'conditions in picture-theatres', Dr. Nandrup could draw on the support of the Social Democrat councillor Friis-Skotte.

Yet there were strongly diverging opinions on how they were to proceed in the matter.

In the course of the summer Nandrup, working with the top officials of the educational system, ensured that the District Judge – the Chief Constable, who according to the Licensing Act was the licensing authority – could accept that Frederiksberg would in the future introduce a kind of adult accompaniment scheme where "children under 14-15 years of age can only be admitted when accompanied by adults unless the production in question has been recommended by the Director of Education …". Friis-Skotte, on the other hand, wanted local authority operation of the picture-houses and thus a guarantee of the soundness and entertainment quality of the programmes. But the District Judge was not prepared to give up his authority.

During the debate of the Council, Friis-Skotte tried to convince the councillors of the profitability of his proposal, as well as the pointlessness of introducing a special Frederiksberg system that, could not even be fully controlled. Children could simply cross the council boundary to the city or the Nørrebro district and see films there that were forbidden or cut in Frederiksberg. And anyway how could one be sure that they had been allowed to go to the cinema simply because they were in the company of someone over the age of 15?

Other councillors, too, raised sceptical voices; some even feared that a censorship system would have the opposite effect – and was more likely to lure more children in. Others thought that this 'craze' among the children and the young must be allowed to 'fizzle out'. But there seemed to be widespread agreement that film was a dubious medium, – and not only because of the nature of the films. It was just as much of a problem that children either sneaked in or "procured the money for the shows in dishonest ways".[9]

After these exchanges of opinions the case was submitted to the Education Committee. In December 1909 the Director of Education, Joakim Larsen, recommended, on behalf of the majority of the Education Committee, that the proposal for a guidance system should be tightened up so that children would in future only be allowed into picture shows which had been approved in advance by a censor. Such a proposal would help "to protect children from the unfortunate effects of picture-theatre productions with brutalizing or prurient content." On the other hand the majority of the Education Committee did not think that it was either practically or economically possible at that time to organize proper school showings that could "supplement and vitalize [the schoolchildren's] knowledge of nature and human life".[10]

The proposal of the Education Committee was given a rather lukewarm reception by the Council.[11] Yet despite its scruples the new scheme was adopted and from August 1910 "children under the age of 15" were not allowed into cinemas unless the programme had been approved by a censor.[12] The new local authority censorship was placed in the hands of the schoolteacher and English translator, A. Nicolaisen. In 1912 he was also given the power to censor the cinema advertisements in the street.[13]

The authorities in Frederiksberg did not act in a vacuum. The preceding years had seen some attention being paid to cinemas, and in 1907 the Ministry of Justice had enjoined chief constables to tighten up their supervision of the cinemas.[14] In teaching circles too concern had been aroused, and the Director of Education Joakim Larsen had sent for information from abroad – for example from his Swedish contact, the teacher Marie Louise Gagner, who had informed him about conditions in Germany. In several German cities, since 1908, teachers had formed committees which, in collaboration with the police, tried to control the situation in cinemas – and in some cases they had tried to start instructional school showings. Only in Berlin had a censorship system been practised earlier. Sweden had been inspired by the German systems; in Stockholm a teachers' committee worked on German principles; in Malmö and Helsingborg censorship had been left to an individual teacher in collaboration with the police.[15]

In Frederiksberg the Director of Education, Joakim Larsen, also tried to interest headmasters in the problem. In May 1909, for example, he asked them to visit selected cinemas, and paid visits to some himself.[16] In the long run, however, it was decided to copy the system from Malmö and leave the censorship to a specially selected teacher. So even before his formal appointment the schoolteacher Nicolaisen went on a study trip to Malmö.

Trial schemes, 1910-1930

Every month Mr. Nicolaisen sent in a report to the Director of Education in Frederiksberg. Here one could read, for example, that during the year from November 1911 he had paid 477 visits to Frederiksberg's 14-15 cinemas. Of the total of 2594 films that had been shown in the course of the year, he had prohibited 109 and ordered cuts in 94.[17] By his own account he spent at least two hours a day reviewing programmes and going from cinema to cinema, mostly by bicycle, otherwise by tram, or if in a hurry by cab. The paperwork had to be left to his wife, so he could do his work for the Frederiksberg educational authority.[18] In May 1913 Nicolaisen resigned as censor in Frederiksberg to take up an appointment as one of the first three state film censors. The other two were quickly replaced, while Nicolaisen functioned until his death in 1939 as a pedagogical film censor.[19]

While Nicolaisen was censor in Frederiksberg 'risqué nocturnal scenes', 'strangling scenes', 'kissing scenes', 'duels' and 'knife fights' were cut out.

And films that were 'strongly erotic', contained 'villainy', 'drunkenness and wildness', 'crudity' or an 'Apache dance' were prohibited for children and young people under the age of 15.

It was sex, violence and crime scenes that caught the eye of the censor. In an interview with *Biografteaterbladet* in December 1911, however, Mr. Nicolaisen did admit that it was difficult to lay down clear rules for what was harmful and what was not. In his own view he was trying to be as liberal as possible. "The main thing is that the children must be kept away from films which are swarming with crime and salaciousness." The main aim for Nicolaisen was to 'scotch unhealthy speculation.'

The intensity of both the prohibitions and the orders to make cuts abated somewhat in the course of the period covered by the reports. In Mr. Nicolaisen's view this was because the films were moving away "from explicit depiction of the many gruesome murders and titillating situations". From other sources, too, we know that film producers exercised a certain amount of self-discipline in their attempts to give the new medium a 'cultural' image.[20]

In the view of the censor the system had a beneficial effect – and it encountered very little opposition. But in a letter to the Director of Education in November 1911, he made no bones about the fact that it was difficult to monitor what happened when he was not present in the cinema. The police had no wish to get involved, so Nicolaisen sometimes had to get his wife to follow up on the cases.[21]

Frederiksberg was not alone in having a new censorship system. In Århus and Esbjerg there were similar initiatives.[22] In both cities it was Social Democrat politicians who led the way; but only in Århus did they succeed in setting up a system. In Esbjerg, the Police Commissioner did not wish to give up his own censorship rights. A few other cities were also fired by the idea, but this did not result in concrete schemes.[23]

Interestingly enough, it never came up for serious discussion in Copenhagen. In connection with a revision of the police regulations, the Evangelical city-councillor and schoolmistress, Johanne Blom, proposed in September 1909 that the new regulations should include a stipulation that "children under the age of 14 must not go to the picture-theatres, unless accompanied by parents or guardians." She also wanted "a prohibition of complete darkness in the picture-theatres during the intervals" and of showing moving pictures in the street, because it attracted children of all ages. "And it is an unfortunate circumstance that children are out so late on the streets." Finally she proposed that children should be forbidden to smoke in the street. The Police Commissioner thought that these stipulations fell outside the remit of the police, and anyway there were few supporters of Miss Blom's proposal among the City Councillors, although one or two thought that some limits should be imposed on "the hedonistic generation".[24]

The National Board of Film Censorship

Cinema and film circles were not entirely happy with the involvement of the teachers. Miss Blom's proposal to ban darkness in the cinemas aroused general amusement,[25] and the situation in Sweden was held up as an extreme example, especially by the theatre and film censor, P.A. Rosenberg. In an interview just after the Swedish Miss Gagner had given a lecture in Copenhagen at the annual meeting of the Danish Girls' Schools, he said:

> "Personally I will have no part whatsoever in far-reaching measures against the picture-theatres. Let them do what they like over in Sweden. What comes from the spirit must have freedom to develop, even if, like all things human, it does so through errors. I would remind the pedagogues of Grundtvig's demand for freedom for Loki as well as Thor, and the Evangelicals of the parable of the tares among the wheat …"[26]

The various local schemes, too, gave rise to disputes, and in April 1911 the Danish Association of Theatres for Moving Pictures submitted a request for uniform national film censorship to the Rigsdag or Parliament. Shortly before this, a delegation of representatives of a number of school and teachers' associations had been in audience with the Minister of Justice to get him to propose a bill for "effective, pedagogical central control of the images in the picture-houses". The initiative came from the association The Danish Girls' Schools and was co-signed by among others the National Association of Teachers, the teachers' associations of the lower and upper secondary schools, as well as a Christian teachers' and parents' association.[27] With this the central players – the teachers and the cinema owners – had shown their hands. The politicians were not involved until 1922, when the Cinemas Act was negotiated. Censorship was solely a matter for the Ministry of Justice.

The affair rolled on, and in the autumn of 1911 the theatre censor, Rosenberg was sent recommendations for a future film censorship system for his comments. In various interviews in the press he made it clear that his own plans tended towards a two-member committee consisting of himself and Mr. Nicolaisen, 'a sensible man' with whom he had an excellent working relationship. Rosenberg predicted that censorship would become stricter with the new scheme, since its decisions were to apply all over the country, and people in the countryside could not always 'bear' to see the same things as those in the city. Furthermore, the minimum age in his opinion should be set at 14.[28] It is evident from other sources that the deliberations of the Ministry tended towards setting the age limit at 15.[29]

In the summer of 1912, rumours were rife about who was to administrate the new film censorship. At the thought that it could be Mr. Nicolaisen the editor of the magazine *Filmen* wrote that such an appointment would "be met with the strongest of protests. In Frederiksberg, where Mr. Nicolaisen works as a pedagogical censor, he has created worse havoc than the most simple-minded constable in Rødovre. On the most foolish and prudish principles he has time and again interfered and has often gone to the most ridiculous extremes ..." Instead, the magazine wanted a representative of the film industry.[30]

The assessment of Mr. Nicolaisen was influenced by the cinema owners' scepticism about teachers, and did not do the censor's involvement full justice. For scattered interviews and small articles by Nicolaisen suggest that he was inspired by early ideas for educational reform and by dreams of placing the child and its needs at the centre of school activities. More specifically this meant that teaching was to be illustrative and practically oriented; and at a meeting of the Educationalists' Society in January 1911, Mr. Nicolaisen talked about his English teaching in the intermediate school. In his view oral language skills should be given a far higher priority than grammatical skills.[31]

When Nicolaisen described children as observers – "This [the children's] love of pictures is very different from the pleasure that adults can experience in pictorial art. Beauty is in the eye of the beholder. Children see with children's eyes. That is, the picture arouses a single idea in them and then their marvellous imagination can make up all the rest.."[32] – his view seems to be coloured by those of the British-American Child Study movement which regarded children and the young as social and cultural beings in their own right, of whose life the adult world on the whole knows nothing. In this country, the head teacher Olsen from Varde tried to assemble a Child Study circle at the end of the 1890's, but without success. However, what the people he was in contact with had in common was that they all had links with the English language. It is hardly inconceivable that Nicolaisen, who was an English translator and who was on a study trip in England in 1903 with ministerial support, came into contact with the Child Study movement in this way.[33]

Since, as mentioned above, the case file has disappeared, there is no documentation of whether the Ministry, in selecting Nicolaisen, took these qualities into consideration. Gunnar Sandfeld claims that Nicolaisen had proposed himself, while there had been an outside demand for a 'pedagogical' censor. But where the demand originated does not transpire from his account.[34] Whatever the situation was, Nicolaisen was one of the first teachers who had bothered to go to the cinema, even before it had become fashionable in better circles and he had had an eye not only for the educational possibilities, but also for children's fascination with the new medium.

Why two years had to pass before the order was signed, is another unanswered question. The case was prepared under a Venstre (i.e. old

Liberal) government, but it was a Social Liberal government that put it into practice. This was perhaps because the Social Liberal Party included among its members a particularly large number of teachers, who were extremely active in this issue.

Rhetoric and panic

Wherever children and the cinema were debated in the country, the rhetoric was by and large identical. The speaker had "learned from this city and elsewhere that the productions of these theatres by their very nature often have a harmful influence on the young" (Esbjerg City Council): "It was not rare for her to hear such parents speak of the 'cursed' picture-theatres that swallowed up the children's time and money. The situation was unfortunately such that the children often procured money for the shows in dishonest ways", (Miss Ankersted, District Councillor, Frederiksberg) and, "He wished nothing but good for the children; but he knew that many had been harmed by it", (Mr. Munck, Chairman, Child Welfare Committee, Frederiksberg) and "The lady knew many children who were such passionate devotees of these theatres that they tried to obtain tickets at any price ..." (Dagmar Petersen, City Councillor, Århus).

Statements at council meetings echoed those about children, the young and films found in the newspapers and periodicals, where, however the film debate took on a wider perspective, since it was linked with the struggle against Nick Carter and pulp magazines. This was expressed for example, in the journal *Forældre og Børn*, the organ of the Christian Society for Education in the Home and at School, which said of cinemas:

> " ...and then we were given the "Nick Carter" literature again in the form of moving pictures in the Cosmorama. And the harmful influence is so much greater than that derived from the reading of the books. As the sight of the pictures has a far stronger effect, more immediate and illustrative than reading the books, it also leaves a far deeper and more ineradicable impression on the minds of the young. It is not uncommon for the police, in arresting young offenders, to hear the confession that they had got the idea for the crime from a show at the picture-theatre." [35]

The youth magazine of the Social Democrats, *Fremad*, chose more or less to smother the cinemas with silence and focus instead on Nick Carter. At one point, however, cinemas along with music-hall shows, are described as "vapid", unlike the classic social realistic literature of J.P. Jacobsen, Johannes V. Jensen, Jeppe Aakjær and Johan Skjoldborg, whom working youth could benefit from studying.[36]

These statements were not only strongly agitatory and emotional, they were also wholly undocumented. In two articles in 1908 and 1910 in the periodical *Vor Ungdom*, the editor, Georg Bruun, tried to document that films had a harmful effect on unformed minds. He referred first to a German and then to an American survey. He, too, made a direct connection between Nick Carter and films: "It is in reality the same content as the pulp literature and shockers used to serve up – only dramatized." In his view there could,

> "on the whole [be] no doubt whatever that children's *intellectual* development suffers from the effect of their weekly mishmash of motley, flimmering, hectic ephemera, quite apart from the moral harm that is quite certainly the result."

And then, two years later,

> "But there is no doubt whatsoever that the moral dangers are far more threatening … Power over children is an indisputable fact, and there can hardly be any doubt that children's urge to imitate is strongly stimulated by the moving images of the picture-houses."[37]

In the opinion of Mr. Bruun, a headmaster, films and pictures were excellent pedagogical aids. The problem was simply that "private commercial initiative had pre-empted the schools and had exploited them [the children] in a way that involves imminent peril to the children's moral growth." An alternative had to be created, either in the form of school showings or travelling school cinemas, – and after chewing the matter over Bruun proposed in 1910 that once a pedagogical alternative had been found, one could proceed to denying 'children of school age' access to the public 'Cosmoramas'.

'No doubt', 'quite certainly', 'presumably' were common phrases in the debate on children and films, both oral and written. But it was all quite literally empty talk, for most of the debaters openly admitted that their knowledge was second-hand, although they compensated in full measure for their ignorance by stamping the new medium as both dangerous and alien.[38]

THE CINEMA AND THE CULTURE OF CHILDREN AND THE YOUNG

As mentioned above, teachers both in Germany and Sweden went in groups to the cinema to form their own impression of the new medium; and in Frederiksberg, too, the head teachers were ordered off to the picture palace. What they saw we do not know, but many older citizens of Copenhagen and Frederiksberg remembered far into their old age what had happened:

"We spent a lot of time at the good old Alleenberg, which was where the French School on Frederiksberg Allé was. It was an amusement establishment on a smaller scale, divided into three gardens … there were swings and roundabouts, shows, performances in the middle garden and at Sommerlyst, a skittle alley in Alleenberg, and a non-stop cinema, ticket price 10 øre – this was during the First World War, when you only saw fragments of scrapped films; in the middle of a raging shoot-out in a cowboy film – whoops! – suddenly there was a kissing scene with Asta Nielsen and Valdermar Zilander. Oh, we were careful then. We young people used the picture-house to have a bit of a squeeze. You could spend a whole Sunday killing time and forming cliques – the boys of the different parts of town kept well apart, and took care of their own girls; still, there could be big clashes between them …" [39]

"There were quite a few small picture-houses, and each show had five films on the programme. The first was a nature film, from a running train; number two would be something like that too – but number three would be the big film, usually one helluva guys like Chaplin, Nick Carter or Buffalo Bill, who could put a whole army of Indians in their place easy as pie. Then there were a couple of films that made up a whole one-hour show, and it cost 10 øre, where I'd got five øre as a discount on the Saturday shopping and begged the rest …"[40]

The memories[41] are evidence that the cinema was part of the culture of children and young people, like a number of other options – whether they were pulp fiction, music hall or the carnival. In the cinema you could get a glimpse of hitherto unknown – and perhaps even forbidden – adult worlds, while the darkness created an intimacy that you would otherwise only find in basements, attics, stairwells or more or less derelict houses and sheds. But the difference was that it was warm in the cinema. You could even have your dog with you if you wanted.

"Every now and then I was allowed to go the cinema. There was one on the corner of Linnésgade and Frederiksborggade. Every show consisted of four or five small films and lasted about one hour. Admission for children was 10-15 øre, and Basse [the dog] could get in free. The seats weren't numbered, so you just had to get there in good time to score the front row. One day Basse and I had a day out like that. I'd scored the front row and Basse sat on my lap. If there was anything that bored him he'd lie down and sleep like a log. He was good enough at following what was going on. That day they showed a film where a St. Bernard's saved a little girl. And Basse started in barking. There was a huge fuss, children and adults clapped and enjoyed themselves, and Basse was almost carried out of the hall. Outside, the doorkeeper said we could come every day that film was on and get in completely free, but I wasn't allowed. Mother wouldn't have it."[42]

Sneaking in was a sport that everyone knew about – but not everyone was as good at it. Staying in your seat and seeing the show at least one more time was a favourite trick that could be used in most cinemas. You could also sneak in during the breaks between films when the doors were opened for air, – or you could try to get in with old tickets found in a dustbin and hope you wouldn't be discovered. Not to mention those who bought a seat in the gallery and then sat in the first row.

Children and young people made use of the media. It was the pedagogue's gaze that turned the space of the cinema into a dark continent populated by aliens who had to be colonized at all costs.[43]

OTHER FORMS OF PANIC

Returning to the areas that were particularly active in the debate on children, young people and film, it emerges that in two of the three the soil had been prepared – by other campaigns and measures directed towards the life of children and the young. This had been most clearly manifested in Frederiksberg, where between 1903 and 1911 the Council had tried in various ways to abolish child labour. Particularly conspicuous were the milk boys from the older classes, who delivered milk every morning before they went to school. Child labour was to be weeded out of childhood, school was to be pushed into the foreground, and this council with its high concentration of milk boys intended to do its by, among other things restructuring school hours.[44]

During the council debate the Social Democrat Friis-Skotte, for example, thought he could see a connection between child labour and the large audiences of children and young people in the cinemas:

> "If one delved deeper into the question, then the root of the now so unfortunate circumstances would lie in child labour. He had spoken to so many people about this matter, and had received different answers according to whether he had asked day schools or half-day schools. It was the children from the latter schools who filled the theatres. These small 'breadwinners', who worked for half the day, narturally took home the wage that was their due, but not the extras. That was what they spent in the picture-theatres, and who could begrudge them that? Often there was no great happiness in these, the poorest homes. What was necessary was to abolish child labour, but

Holte Cinema, north of Copenhagen around the 1st. World War. (Filmmuseet)

that was a matter the legislature had to deal with. However, there was much to be gained from changing the present rules for school hours …"[45].

With urbanization and industrialization children – like adults – became wage earners, whereas they had previously mainly been paid in kind – food, clothes and clogs. Around the First World War this was still true of child labourers in the countryside, while children from the cities were paid in money. And here it was the tips that particularly aroused the attention of the adults, for with them the children were able to become consumers – without the adult world always being able to monitor what they spent their money on.

> "As a milk boy I earned 11 kroner a fortnight … I handed over the wages back home – that was quite natural. My father had praised me because I earned money for the rent then. – The tips were my own. I might have between 50 and 80 øre – so I was a well-off lad then. Not many other boys had as much pocket money a week as I did. 2 øre

was the regular amount we brothers and sisters got from Father on Sunday ... ...Oh yes, I was quite well off as a 12-year-old milk boy and a great spender with the girls. Chocolate and the then famous 'Fælledvej Grenades' [sweets] were enough to win the favour of the girls – that is, to be allowed to hold hands in the passage or take them into the giant picture-house on Åboulevarden by the old Ladegård ..."[46]

Since 1906 the authorities in Esbjerg had experienced several demonstrations and disturbances led by the boys in the oldest classes. This had prompted a teacher-initiated campaign against tobaccosmoking on the streets – and had in particular resulted in a regulation of 1911 stating that children must not be on the streets after 8 pm in winter and after 9 pm in summer.[47] The desire for a preventive type of film censorship was completely in line with this.

So it was not only that the campaign for film censorship echoed earlier campaigns; it was also carried on out of a concern for the children's use of the urban space. The same was true in Århus. From 1912, for example, we have a circular sent out to all teachers in the council, telling them to monitor "the children's behaviour outside school". The teachers were to ensure that the pupils' behaviour "is quiet and orderly on the streets, that they do not throw litter away in the woods or in the street, that they play without too much shouting and noise, and that they show consideration and respect for adults, especially the elderly."[48]

AGE AS A SOCIAL AND CULTURAL PARAMETER

With the rules for a national film censorship established in 1913, film censorship was not only age-determined, it was also made uniform. Until then it had been common practice to consider social conditions too. Cinemas that were visited by a more respectable audience could show films that socially second-rank or third-rank cinemas in the suburbs and workers' districts were not allowed to. It was also a widespread assumption that children in the city could 'bear' more than children in the countryside; or in the censor Nicolaisen's words of 1911, the effect of erotic images was not "as strong on the 16-year-old Copenhagener who was used to the cinema, as on the lad of the same age in the countryside."

The reputation of cinemas as entertainment for the whole family resulted in many very small children being taken along, not only in Denmark, but whereever the cinema gained ground. In Vienna, for example, a special ticket was issued for infants. The censor Nicolaisen took exception to this practice when he discovered that "infants quickly became strapping lads, [so] we of course also had to stop infants seeing forbidden films. For "Infants" 8-10 years old moreorless retain what they have seen."[49]

In the course of the debate on whether there should be film censorship or not, social considerations disappeared from the picture. Cinema owners thought the many local systems were inappropriate – and were prepared to accept age-determined censorship, rather than risk a total ban on showing films for children, who made up a large part of their audience. But the idea of a ban had no widespread support in educational circles either. It was considered impracticable and pedagogically inappropriate. They had to concede that children derived true pleasure from going to the cinema – again in Nicolaisen's words: "Listen to the sound of such a child's voice when the marvel man jumps up on the moon, falls down on the roof, topples houses, stops automobiles and all such things! The pleasure is genuine."[50]

The question, however, was where to set the age limit. In Sweden, which had passed the world's first film censorship act in 1911, films could be forbidden for children and young people under the age of 15, and they could only go to the cinema after 8 pm if they were accompanied by an adult – even if the film was intended for the youngest audience. In German cities, 14 had been set as the age limit. In addition, several places followed Sweden and prohibited children from going to the cinemas in the evening, and in Dresden children were totally forbidden to go to the cinema unless it was a so-called children's cinema.[51]

In Denmark the authorities chose a higher age limit – 16 – while none of the other regulations passed abroad found their way into Danish legislation. In the existing studies of the history of film censorship the age issue plays hardly any role[52] – and since the case files for the government order did not contain any relevant information regarding this question, it is not possible for us to look in more detail at what prompted the ministerial civil servants to draw the line at the age of 16.

But the story does not come to a dead end. Looking around at other aspects of everyday life we see that 16 was an age category that had earlier attracted legislative interest. For the interest, not only in children but also in young people, that materialized in the 1913 order was not as new as one might think. The age limit at 16 had first been introduced in Danish legislation with the Machinery Protection Act of 1889, where children and young people below the age of 16 were forbidden to work with dangerous machines. The stipulation was carried into the amended versions of the Factory Act of 1901 and 1913.[53]

Furthermore, around the turn of the century a teacher-driven campaign arose against child labour in general. The campaign gave rise to many local regulations, and, as mentioned above, the Frederiksberg Council was particularly active in the struggle against 'the milk boy abuse". As happened later in connection with the emergence of film censorship, there was some uncertainty about where the line should be drawn. New factory acts in 1901 and 1913 raised the age limits for children working in factories from 10 to 12 to 14. At the same time, a number of towns applied to the Ministry of Social Affairs for their own child labour regulations, which would regulate child labour in general, and not just in factories. On these occasions local authorities used a functional and cultural age concept. What was crucial was not how old they were, but whether the children were at school. Another factor was the extent to which child labor was used in the individual town. As a result some provincial towns got an age limit of 10, others 11, and others again of 12.[54]

In parallel with this, we see that the film censorship debate fluctuated between a socially and a biologically determined age concept. It was clear that an older view of when children were (small) adults and when they were children was being revised;[55] just as there was some doubt as to whether such an intervention in parents' rights was legal.[56] The first initiatives were thus an extension of the old tradition. The first gambit of the District Judge in Frederiksberg was a scheme for accompanging children up to the age of 14-15, roughly corresponding to the age when children were confirmed and left school. More or less at the same time, on the Copenhagen City Council, the schoolmistress Johanne Blom advocated a minimum age of 14, and the theatre and cinema censor shared this opinion. It is thought-provoking that 16 – as far as I have been able to ascertain – was not mentioned as a proposed minimum age. The only person who specifically talked about 16-year-olds was the teacher Nicolaisen, when he said in 1911 that young Copenhageners would be less affected by seeing certain things than young people in the countryside (cf. above). The uncertainty about the age limit reflected the fact that youth had not yet been made into a concept and become 'youth' with its own social and cultural characteristics. The debaters typically talked about children under a certain age limit and in the 1913 order establishing the Board of Censorship the wording was " …children under the age of 16 …" The same wording was used in the Swedish act of 1911.

The proposal of the Frederiksberg Education Committee – an age limit of 15 – was, compared with the rest of the debate, innovative, and it reflected the fact that the schools were expanding their area of responsibility beyond the seven first school years (Danish children started school at the age of seven). This interest in the young and their schooling can be traced back to the educational reforms of the turn of the century. The reform of the *gymnasium* or upper secondary school and especially the introduction of the intermediate school in 1903, as a halfway house between primary school and the *gymnasium* gave the State and local authorities far greater responsibility for the schooling of the young than before, when this had on the whole been a matter for private schools. The intermediate and lower secondary school pupils only left the school system when they were 15-16.[57]

The science of child and youth psychology also helped to ensure that the debate on youth took on anxiety-ridden undertones at an early stage. For the researchers placed particular emphasis on puberty as one of the most dangerous periods of life, when the erotic urges were awakened, while the young were still subject to their drives and spontaneous desires.[58] Puberty and youth were no longer no concern of the school; as one could read in the educationalists' periodical *Vor Ungdom* in 1913: "If that age [puberty] is the most dangerous in all of human life, it is quite absurd that society now says "stop" at the fourteenth year." [59]

SCHOLARIZATION, DOMESTICATION AND INFANTILIZATION

The scholarization of youth, although still on a relatively small scale – in 1921 only 2% of the average class passed the university entrance exam and 13% left school with an intermediate or lower secondary exam[60] – was an extension of the changes that had taken place in childhood in the preceding decades, when school had been incorporated into children's life, at the same time taking up more and more time at the expense of work.

However, childhood had not only been scholarized; it had also been domesticated and infantilized. This had resulted in a number of efforts to create a childlike universe in harmony with the special nature of the child, separate from the adult world. School played a central role in this process of change, which involved not only the children's time, but also their bodies and the space they moved in. For school took on the task of being a second home for the children. Teachers became experts in good childhood, and they worked determinedly in the service of childhood; in child welfare councils, as supervisors of holiday camps and school gardens. They were the driving forces behind the first youth recreation centres – or, as in the present context, the campaign for national film censorship.[61]

In the years around the First World War, it was the turn of the young to be scholarized, domesticated and infantilized. The new science of youth psychology was full of laments about youth growing into adulthood earlier and earlier. The explanation lay in urbanization and the city's many moral and consumption-related temptations. 'Hedonism' had spread like an epidemic among the young at the expense of an active, healthy outdoor life in easily controllable settings. Degeneration was just around the corner.[62]

In *Barnet* (The Child), a handbook published by the Danish Association of Teachers in 1911, one can read in the section on "the age of transition" that the solution to these problems was that the "homes must seek by all possible and appropriate voluntary means to keep the young in at the evenings, which must be made so comfortable and pleasant that the young feel no desire whatsoever to spend their evenings on roads and streets, exposed to all sorts of evils." The author of the article suggested that parents should find the time to talk to and listen to young people, read aloud for them, listen to music and play games. It was especially the boys who had to be kept occupied; young girls "are rarely bored, they are almost always happy to occupy themselves with needlework for a free hour in the evening ..."

The opposite of this idyll was "bad company ... Permission to be out late in the evening, idleness, the lack of good interests, too much pocket money, too many forms of bad entertainment, scandalous magazines, pulp literature etc."[63]

Statements like these heralded a battle for the time, bodies and space of the young, similar to those on behalf of the children. In the new upper secondary schools, sport, outdoor and scouting life were given a prominent place, and when the building of the new schools really picked up speed after the end of the First World War it was done with due consideration for all demands of hygiene and with plenty of light and air.[64] The film censorship order and the fixing of a minimum age of 16 can then be read as an element in the struggle for the time and space of both children and young people. For as we saw above, the cinema had become a new sanctuary, a supplement to the street for both children and the young.

The young were no longer just a labour market concern; both their schooling and their leisure time had become a social responsibility.

Moral panic and the naturalization of age

In Denmark, public debate on children, the young and films hardly never grew to such proportions as it did in Germany or Sweden. But this did not prevent a moral panic spreading as an echo of other ongoing moral campaigns related to the life and activities of children and the young people, primarily their working life, schooling and leisure time. And as we have seen such panic spread not only across national and district boundaries; it also spread from one area of concern to another. Moreover, it was not only at the rhetorical level that there was a knock-on effect. Expression of panic gave rise to a number of measures which, regardless of local differences, very quickly came to resemble one another.

The Danish debate was influenced by a certain amount of antagonism between the cinema owners and the teaching profession. The clear financial and artistic interests of the former did not always harmonize with the teachers' wish to protect the growing generations and to separate the worlds of children, the young people and adults. In the end, though, they met halfway – for the cinema owners were not interested in losing an important part of their regular audiences. In that case they would rather have censorship than a total ban on visits to the cinema, of the kind they knew about, for example from abroad.

The establishment of the National Board of Film Censorship in 1913 was only one of several initiatives aimed at the schooling, work and leisure life of children and the young people which contributed to an institutionalization of biological age and the setting aside of an older, social concept of age. Age was embedded in legislation and gradually developed into a parameter that could be used to draw an indisputable boundary between childhood and adolescence, adolescence and adulthood, a boundary which could also legitimize the right of society – personified at this time by the teaching profession – to affect the life not only of children but of the young people.

The result was that age was naturalized and its social and cultural origin lapsed from memory.

In the years around the First World War, youth, like childhood, became a collective, classless affair. The question is, however, whether it was also a genderless project. Several researchers have pointed out that in the infancy of film there was particular concern about girls' and women's fascination with the eroticized world of the cinema.[65] In Denmark it is noteworthy that it was precisely the teachers from girls' schools who took the lead in the struggle for a film censorship law; and the proposal to ban total darkness in the cinema was probably also born of concern about what could happen to the girls' morality under cover of darkness. But this interest in girls' moral constitution should in my view be related to the more general concern of the age with what in modern terminology we might call the new child and youth culture; for a consumption and leisure culture encompassing films, sweets, tobacco and pulp magazines saw the light of day as younger children were released from the labour market and the young began to make money.[66]

Finally, one could add that moral panic was also clearly more oriented towards the children of the working class than those of the bourgeoisie, if we are to believe the censor Nicolaisen's statements. All these worries merged together in the moral panic of the media that followed in the wake of the popularization of film.

Regardless of the efforts to give a moral panics a rationale in terms of mentality or cultural history, there remains an inexplicable element of irrationality in the statements and emotional outbursts one encounters in the debate – especially when they are set alongside with the children and young people's own memories. Perhaps we are dealing here with the essence of moral panic – that it creates a legitimate space where adult concern about the growing generations can be given free rein.

Acknowledgements

I would like to thank the following people for contributing useful information and comments: Ulrich Breuning; Henning Spurre Nielsen; Gitte Møller; Lene Koch; and Henning Pryds.

1. Child Welfare Committee Chairman Munck, Frederiksberg District Council 1909-10, meeting 11.10.1909, quoted from p. 143.
2. Pensioner Memoir No. 137, Københavns Stadsarkiv (Copenhagen City Archives), woman b. 1896. See also Memoirs No. 197, 885 and 1115, ibid.
3. For the early history of film, see Betænkning 1967; G. Sandfeld 1966, Engberg 1977 and Rasmussen 1961.
4. This possibility was not available when research for this article was undertaken. The central case file, Ministry of Justice Department 1, No. 1744, 1911 had disappeared from the National Archives in the autumn of 1995. Attempts have been made to 'clear up' the matter with the aid of the Letter Book, but with no substantial results. This article is, therefore based on other relevant files from the Ministry of Justice, but especially on the local history archive material from the three local authorities Frederiksberg, Århus and Esbjerg, which initiated trial schemes before the order establishing the National Board of Film Censorship was issued on 5.7.1913. In addition, I have used articles from newspapers or specialist educational journals in Denmark and abroad. During the winter 1998/99 the case-file showed up again. But it did not contain any further information that could be used to answer the questions of this article.
5. See for example J. Schytte 1996, K. Bruhn Jensen 1997, pp. 126-148 and N.J. Dinnesen and E. Kau 1983.
6. On the social and cultural history of age, see H. Chudacoff 1989 pp. 9f.
7. See for example U. Boëthius 1989 and 1995, and K. Drotner 1990.
8. K. Drotner 1990, pp. 135 and 143. A good discussion of the concept of moral panic can be found in E. Goode and N. Benh-Yehuda 1994.
9. Frederiksberg Kommune 1909-10, Vol. II, cit. p. 140.
10. Frederiksberg Kommune 1909-10, Vol. II, cit. p. 247.
11. Frederiksberg Kommune 1909-10, Vol. II, pp. 249ff.
12. Frederiksberg Kommune 1910-11, Vol. I, cit. p. 18.
13. For information on the censorship case, Frederiksberg, see also G. Sandfeld 1966, p. 244.
14. Ministry of Justice Circular No. 164, 29.6.1907.
15. Miss Gagner's travel report and various items of information in the folder Biografteatersagen, Frederiksberg skolekommission journalsager 1909 in Frederiksberg Town Hall archives (in the following referred to as Censorship case, Frederiksberg) and in Frederiksberg Skolekommissions forhandlingsprotokol 1909-1910. On the situation in Scania, Sweden, see Bergengren pp. 87-92. The German teachers' action was aimed at pulp and other cheap literature, and display windows. Cf. Maase 1994 and 1996. The same links were made in Sweden, where Marie Louise Gagner was one of the leading figures. See U. Boëthius 1989 and Svensk biografisk leksikon, Vol. 76, Stockholm. 1964.
16. Letter to headmasters from Joakim Larsen dated 17th May 1909 in Censorship case, Frederiksberg.
17. Reports in Censorship case, Frederiksberg.
18. Letter from Nicolaisen to Headmaster Joakim Larsen, 18th November 1911 and various letters in Censorship case, Frederiksberg. See also the newspaper Politiken, 1st May 1913.
19. Kraks Blå Bog 1938, Hof og Stat Kalenderen 1940.
20. K. Bruun Jensen 1997, pp. 136-147.
21. Letter from Nicolaisen to Headmaster Joakim Larsen, 18th November 1911 in Censorship case, Frederiksberg.
22. Århus Education Committee, Case Nos. 133:1910 and 390:1910 (Erhvervsarkivet) Esbjerg City Council, Case No. 236-1910 (City History Archives, Esbjerg).
23. See G. Sandfeld 1966, p. 248 and a request from the Education Authority in Fredericia for information on the film censorship scheme, letter of 27.5.1911 in Censorship case, Frederiksberg.

24. Printed debates of City Council, Vol. 70. 1909-1910, Meeting 13th September 1909, cit. p. 817-818. See also p. 827, p. 884, pp. 1036-1037 and p. 1041.
25. Nordisk Biografteater Tidende, No. 2, 1909, p. 21.
26. Biografteaterbladet, October 1911, cit. p. 72.
27. See Bog og Naal, November 1911, p. 169, December 1911, pp. 184-185, Folkeskolen No. 3, 1912, pp. 43-44. On the further course of events, see G. Sandfeld 1966 pp. 269ff.
28. Biografteaterbladet, No. 3, 1911, p. 39 and Politiken 3rd December 1911.
29. JM., 1. kt., File Q 7865, 1913, including draft circular dated 1911 (National Archives).
30. Filmen No. 12, 1913, cit. p. 170.
31. Det pædagogiske Selskabs Aarsberetning 1910-11, meeting 11th January 1911, pp. 24-28.
32. Cit. Biografteaterbladet, No. 6, December 1911, p. 83.
33. For the Child Study movement, see de Coninck-Smith 1997a.
34. G. Sandfeld 1966, pp. 274-75.
35. Forældre og Børn, No. 15, 1912, cit. p. 124.
36. Fremad No. 24, 1914.
37. Vor Ungdom, 1908, cit. p. 125 and Vor Ungdom, 1910, cit. p. 311, emphases in original.
38. K. Maase 1996, p. 121.
39. Pensioner Memoir No. 490, man b. 1898 (Copenhagen City Archives).
40. Pensioner Memoir No. 1985, man b. 1900 (Copenhagen City Archives).
41. Pensioner Memoir No. 123, No. 137, No. 197, No. 215, No. 296, No. 435, No. 487, No. 490, No. 723, No. 759, No. 790, No. 885, No. 894, No. 966, No. 988, No. 1031, No. 1085, No 1087, No. 1115 and No.1530 (Copenhagen City Archives).
42. Pensioner Memoir No. 1530, woman b. 1898 (Copenhagen City Archives).
43. K. Maase 1996, p. 115.
44. de Coninck-Smith 1997b.
45. Frederiksberg Kommune 1909-1910, cit. p. 138.
46. Pensioner Memoir No. 1115, man b. 1902 (Copenhagen City Archives).
47. de Coninck-Smith 1991.
48. Århus Education Committee, Case File 82:1912 (The Danish National Business Archives).
49. Biografteaterbladet No. 6, 1911, pp. 84-85, cit. p. 89. On the situation in Vienna see Bernold, p. 155.
50. Biografteaterbladet No. 6, 1911, p. 84. Cf. also Marie Louise Gagner, Tionde Nordiska Skolmötet ... 1910, p. 67 and Johanne Blom, Bog og Naal, p. 166.
51. Betänkande med Förslag till Förordning innefattanda vissa bestämmelser angående Förevisning af Biografbilder ... Bihang til Riksdagens Protokol, 1911, Andra Samlingen, Andra Avdelingen, Fjärda Bandet, Sthlm. 1911, pp. 3ff.
52. G. Sandfeld, p. 256 for example says that the age limit from 1911 was 16 in Sweden – it was 15.
53. L. Albæk Nielsen 1988.
54. de Coninck-Smith 1997b.
55. See, for example, the teacher Natalie Henke's paper in Tionde Nordiska Skolmötet, Stockholm. 1910 ... pp. 79-80. On the other hand I have seen no references to arguments linking the age limit of 14 with the age of criminal responsibility, which at this time was 14.
56. Cinema owners, among others, pointed out this problem in a letter to the Director of Education in Frederiksberg. Letter of 20.6.1910 in Censorship case, Frederiksberg.
57. de Coninck-Smith 1999.
58. See, for example, R. P. Neuman 1974-75.
59. C. Tybjærg Hansen: Pubertet og Skole i Vor Ungdom 1913, cit. p. 42.
60. H.C. Johansen 1991, p. 51.
61. de Coninck-Smith 1999. See also Marie Louise Gagner in Tionde Nordisk Skolmötet, Stockholm. 1910 ... pp. 75-76.

62. Hall 1904 Vol. I, pp. XVI- XVII.
63. P.C. Bjerregaard & F. Sadolin 1909 cit. p. 605 and p. 606. The author of the specific chapter was the doctor P. C. Bjerregaard.
64. de Coninck-Smith 1996.
65. K. Drotner 1990 and 1991, M. Bernold 1990 and interview with the censor Nicolaisen in Biografteaterbladet No. 6, 1911 p. 85.
66. See de Coninck-Smith 1997b.

Bibliography

Albæk Nielsen, Lizette. "Det industrielle børnearbejde og årsagerne til dets ophør". *Arbejderhistorie* 31 (1988): 49-63.

Bergengren, Johan: "När filmen kom til Malmö och andra skånska städer". Jan Aghed et al. *Skånske Kinematografen. En bok om film i Skåne och skånska filmare.* Sydsvenska Dagbladets årsbok, 1977, s. 57-92.

Bernold, Monika. "Kino(T)raum. Öber den Zusammenhang von Familie, Freizeit und Konsum". *Familie: Arbeitsplatz order Ort des Glücks? Historische Schnitte ins Private.* Ed. Bernold Monika et al. Vienna: Picus Verlag, 1990. 135-163.

Betænkning om filmcensur. Betænkning nr. 468. Copenhagen 1967.

Bjerregaard, P.C., & Frode Sadolin, eds. *Barnet. Haandbog for Hjem og Skole.* Aarhus: Danmarks Lærerforenings Forlag, 1909.

Boëthius, Ulf. *När Nick Carter drevs på flykten. Kampen mot "smutslitteraturen" i Sverige 1908-1909.* Stockholm: Gidlunds, 1989.

Bruhn Jensen, Klaus, ed. *Dansk Mediehistorie,* Vol. 2. 1880-1960 Copenhagen: Samleren, 1997.

Chudacoff, Howard P. *How Old Are You? Age Consciousness in American Culture.* Princeton, New Jersey: Princeton University Press, 1989.

de Coninck-Smith, Ning. *Øregaard Gymnasium og Gentofte kommunes Gymnasiehistorie.* Upubl. manuscript 1996.

de Coninck-Smith, Ning. "Overlærer Jens Olsen Varde – praktiker og pionær. En skolehistorisk biografi". *Historiens kultur. Fortælling, kritik, metode.* Eds. Ning de Coninck-Smith, Mogens Rüdiger and Morten Thing. Copenhagen: Museum Tusculanum, 1997a, 117-140.

de Coninck-Smith, Ning. " …paa den mest ryggesløse Maade." Et kapitel af gadedrengenes historie i Esbjerg og det øvrige Danmark 1880-1914." *Den jyske historiker* 56 (1991): 71-90.

de Coninck-Smith, Ning. *For barnets skyld. Om byen, skolen og barndommen 1880-1914.* Unpublished manuscript. Odense 1999.

de Coninck-Smith, Ning. "The struggle for the child's time – at all times. School and children's work in town and country in Denmark from 1900 to the 1960s". *Industrious*

Children. Work and Childhood in the Nordic Countries 1850-1990. Eds. Ning de Coninck-Smith, Bengt Sandin and Ellen Schrumpf. Odense: Odense University Press, 1997b, 129-159.

Dinnesen, Niels Jørgen, & Edvin Kau. *Filmen i Danmark*. Copenhagen: Akademisk Forlag, 1983.

Drotner, Kirsten. "Modernitet og mediepanikk." *Kulturanalyse*. Eds. Trine Deichman-Sørensen and Ivar Frønes. Oslo: Norsk Gyldendal Forlag, 1990, 131-159.

Engberg, Marguerite. *Dansk stumfilm – de store år*. Vols. I-II. Copenhagen: Rhodos, 1977.

Goode, Erich, & Nahman Benh-Yehuda. *Moral Panics. The Social Construction of Deviance*. Oxford UK, Cambridge USA: Blackwell, 1994.

Hall, Stanley G. *Adolescence: its Psychology and its Relations to Physiology, Anthropology, Sociology, Sex, Crime, Religion and Education*. Vols. I-II. New York: D. Appleton & Co., 1904.

Johansen, Hans C. *Danmark i tal*. Ed. Olaf Olsen. Vol. 16. Copenhagen: Gyldendal og Politikens forlag, 1991.

Maase, Kaspar. "Die Strasse als Kinderstube. Zur ästhetischen Säuberung der Städte vor dem 1. Weltkrieg". *Dialektik* 2 (1994) 49-78.

Maase, Kaspar. "Kinder als Fremde – Kinder als Feinde. Halbwüchsige, Massenkultur und Erwachsene im wilhelminischen Kaiserreich." *Historische Antropologie*. Kultur. Gesellschaft, Alltag. 4. Jahrgang. Heft 1 (1996): 93-126.

Neuman, R.P. "Masturbation, Madness, and the Modern Concept of Childhood and Adolescence". *Journal of Social History* 3 (1974-75): 1-27.

Rasmussen, Albert. "Biografdreng i 1910". *Historiske Meddelelser om København* (1961): 146-149.

Sandfeld, Gunnar. *Den stumme Scene. Dansk biografteater indtil lydfilmens gennembrud*. Copenhagen: Nyt nordisk forlag, 1966.

Schytte, Jacob. "Filmcensur er et fyord … men filmcensuren i Danmark blev alligevel over 80 år". *Pråsen, Tidsskrift om film for børn og unge* No. 83. (1996): 29-47.

Infancy and Old Age as Causes of Death

Anne Løkke

During the last decades of the 19th century death in infancy ceased to be a natural occurrence. The untimely demise of infants moved from the realm of inevitable, naturally-ordained phenomena that humans were obliged to endure into the category of solvable problems. A social, hygienic and medical problem. This was achieved when physicians and statisticians gradually challenged the century-old conviction that children could die simply due to their tender age, just as the elderly die due to old age. This new perception of death in infancy as something unnatural was part of a more general change in the view of childhood brought about in the latter half of the 19th century. The entire perception of infancy underwent a fundamental change. New ideas on good child care arose. These were expounded within an entirely novel frame of reference, encompassing words and concepts originating in medical science and giving the doctor ultimate authority. This process could be called the *medicalization* of child care. Concurrently, changes in social norms were moving towards a *biologizing of motherhood*. Where wet-nurses, nannies, grannies, foster-mothers, elder siblings, etc. had previously been widely accepted as surrogate mothers, taking care of babies was gradually becoming the right and obligation of the *mother*. At the same time, infant mortality rates were in fact showing a rapid decline. These mutually interconnected processes, the infant welfare movement, medicalization of infant care, biologization of motherhood and the decreasing birth rate along with the decreasing infant mortality rate were phenomena common to all of Western Europe and North America and are fairly well described.[1] As regards Denmark between 1800 and 1920, it has for some years been a project of mine to investigate the subject matter "death in infancy" from social, cultural and demographic perspectives. The purpose of this paper is to present that part of the project which is about the changing categorization of death in infancy as it appears in the official population statistics and in the cause-of-death registration. Where it has been possible without being too heavy a burden I have added observations concerning the categorization of death due to old age.[2]

POPULATION STATISTICS

Population statistics and statisticians played a major part in the denaturalization of death in infancy. The observation of very different levels of infant mortality in different populations gave rise to the argument "no difference without a cause". In all cases where there was a difference between the infant mortality rate of two groups of the population, it was argued, the determing cause could not be God, Nature or Fate. Statisticians and doctors argued that it must be possible to reduce the highest rates to the lowest level and thereby let humans gain influence over infant death.

To obtain statistical knowledge of death in infancy requires a fairly reliable and uniform registration of births and deaths. At the start of the 1830's the Danish authorities managed after many attempts to achieve sufficient consistency and reliability in the reporting of marriages, births, and deaths to arrive at reasonably useful nationwide population statistics. The actual registration was the responsibility of the Church which had started to record these events around 1600. This was required by law from 1646. From the end of the 17th century there were attempts to compile annual lists based on the clergymen's reports. These lists, however, have not been systematically preserved, and what has been preserved is inconsistent in the manner of recording stillbirths and births out of wedlock to such an extent that the overall results are compromised. From 1835 the statistics can be reckoned to be reasonably trustworthy, and they are available in print as an uninterrupted series of *Statistisk Tabelværk*, with tables of marriages, births, and deaths in Denmark.

THE INFANT MORTALITY RATE

Availability of material which can serve as a basis for modern calculations of mortality does not mean, however, that such calculations were actually performed. The mere counting of deaths does not bring much knowledge with it apart from the commonplace fact that people die. To arrive at a different kind of knowledge requires concepts which allow the making of comparisons. The statistical concepts which make it possible to compare the frequency of child deaths in different places and different population groups today are known as the child mortality rate and the infant mortality rate.³ In official Danish statistics, calculations of infant mortality began in 1842, although the actual term was not used until much later.

The very idea of classifying deaths according to age and calculating mortality has roots going back to the 17th century. In the 18th century statisticians in different countries worked to find laws for mortality according to age, but it was only in Sweden that the basic material was compiled so systematically that it is still of use for modern purposes. In 1766 Per Wargentin (1717-1783) used this material to calculate mortality according to age, and hence also what we should call infant mortality. These calculations had great impact in Sweden where as early as the 18th century the authorities began a major campaign to reduce infant mortality.⁴ However, Wargentin's work has left no trace in Danish statistics.

In Denmark it was the physician and later politician, C. E. Fenger (1814-1884), who first undertook such calculations. He did so after a study trip which aroused his keen interest in the latest developments in science, medicine and statistics. Fenger was not especially interested in child mortality. His aim was to detect by close observation the natural laws of mortality. He hoped that this should enable him to clear the calculations for probable life expectancy of the confounding influence of high infant mortality, so that the new life insurance companies could have a rational basis on which to work. Using these calculations, Fenger formulated:

> "the general law that mortality immediately after birth is very high but falls thereafter until roughly the fifteenth year; it then begins to rise again, at first slowly then faster, and it continues to rise through all the subsequent age periods".⁵

Fenger's method was to compare the number of deaths in the course of a year in a particular age group with the number of living people in the same group. By this means he calculated mortality in the first year of life per 1000 births. He thereby arrived at what later statisticians call the "total infant mortality per calendar year", the only difference being that he included both live births and stillbirths among the births and deaths, whereas infant mortality rates today do not include stillbirths. This, however, makes no difference to the method, which has ever since borne Fenger's name in Denmark.⁶

DEAD CHILDREN IN 19TH CENTURY STATISTICS

The interest in infant mortality in 19th-century Danish statistics was an integral part of the growing concern in the mortality of all age groups. This can be traced back to the desire of the State to keep population statistics for administrative and military purposes, and the 18th century idea that it was possible to discover the laws governing God's creation. It would benefit mankind to understand and act according to these laws, since this would lead to greater happiness and prosperity in society. Ideas like this gave Sweden highly modern population statistics as early as the mid-18th century and led to the many partially flawed attempts in Denmark.

In Denmark it was, as I have said, not the interests of the state but the desire in the 1840's for a rational basis for life insurance operations that gave the impetus for statistics that were needed to calculate age-related mortality rates. The primary aim was to free calculations of average adult lifetime remaining from the confounding influence of the high child mortality. Once they were calculated, however, the infant mortality rates gave rise to deliberations about how extensive normal/inevitable mortality in childhood was. The subject had been discussed in the Age of Enlightenment when the thought probably occured in Denmark that not all child deaths were inevitable, but there were no precise ideas about the magnitude of infant mortality and how much it could possibly be reduced. In 1773 doctor Johan Christian Lange expressed the contemporary view in the subtitle of his book on child care: "Containing information about the question: What are the principle cause of death during infancy".[7]

What was new in Denmark in the 1840's was that the vague impression of "most people" was replaced by a figure for infant mortality that fluctuated between about 10 and 25% and gave a national average of 14-15%. This result immediately demonstrated that the 30-35% Icelandic[8] rate was abnormal and led to state initiatives to reduce it. In the 1850's the hygiene movement placed all kinds of preventable death on the public agenda, including that of illegitimate children. The movement here was the reverse. On the basis of a general unproven assumption that there was high mortality among illegitimate children and foster-children there rose the demand to have this mortality studied statistically. This demand was fulfilled in the official statistics of 1860. The statistics revealed the expected abnormally high mortality and thereby helped to provide arguments for the legislation that obliged fathers from 1888 to pay half of the real costs of supporting illegitimate children, and introduced public supervision of foster-children.

Around 1860 we also see the first debate about how large a proportion of deaths among normal legitimate Danish children could be considered biologically conditioned and how much was due to social and cultural factors. In the 1870's, although they still expressed themselves cautiously on the subject, statisticians had no doubt that poverty exacerbated infant mortality because it prevented mothers from breast-feeding and looking after their children as well as they would have liked.

In the 1880's statisticians were able to show that a long series of other factors were significant for the level of infant mortality, and it was finally established that the normal level could no longer be regarded as the biological minimum. This view was expressed with increasing precision throughout the 1890's until the statistician, Harald Westergaard, in 1901 ventured that biologically necessary infant mortality was no more than 7% and was probably less.[9]

The view of infant mortality in 19th century Danish statistics shifted from interpreting the observed average as an expression of a law of nature, to calculating minimums under different conditions in order to separate more and more groups. 'Natural' infant mortality grew smaller and smaller while the proportion attributable to human agency grew steadily. It is worth noting that this change in the perception of infant mortality took place before the measured rate of infant mortality began to fall. Death in childhood ceased to be considered natural even before the real drop in infant mortality. This denaturalization did not take place of its own accord. It was presented in meticulous scientific studies which were able to test the significance of a given variable for infant mortality through calculations. The process in the statistical literature is like a spiral: the statisticians had to convince themselves that death in childhood was not solely a natural phenomenon before they tried to convince the rest of the world.

Cause-of-death registration as a source

Cause-of-death registration is always based on a subjective judgement. Doctors often disagree about how to classify a specific death. Is it more correct to write the disease which has debilitated the patient or the pneumonia which was the acute cause of death? Or both, referring to a system previously agreed upon. It is also a subjective judgement as to which symptoms qualify for a given diagnosis. This subjective aspect of cause-of-death registration is often perceived as a problem because it makes comparisons across time and space difficult. But for my purpose the fact that diagnoses, nomenclatures and judgements change present no problem. On the contrary, these changes are the very source of the doctors' conception of death in infancy and old age.

For this purpose cause-of-death registration in Copenhagen is an excellent source. From 1829, vicars were forbidden to officiate at the graveside ceremony without a death certificate issued by a doctor.[10] From 1832 the certificates had to specify the cause of death. We have then an uninterrupted series of cause-of-death registrations issued by doctors in Copenhagen from 1832 until now.

From the beginning cause-of-death registration was published according to a standardized list negotiated by the city's superintending medical officer and the Royal Board of Health. But in its earliest years the list was not taken too seriously. From year to year there were changes both in the use of numbers and the mentioned diagnoses. The list was re-negotiated in 1848 and 1860. In 1875 a brand new terminology was adopted, worked out with inspiration from the English statistician William Farr. This one was strictly adhered to in the publication of figures.[11]

For my purpose it is a problem that the first year of life is not published separately before 1850. From 1832 to 1849 the two first years of life are published in aggregate. I do use the figures anyway, but it is not possible to compare figures directly from before and after 1850.

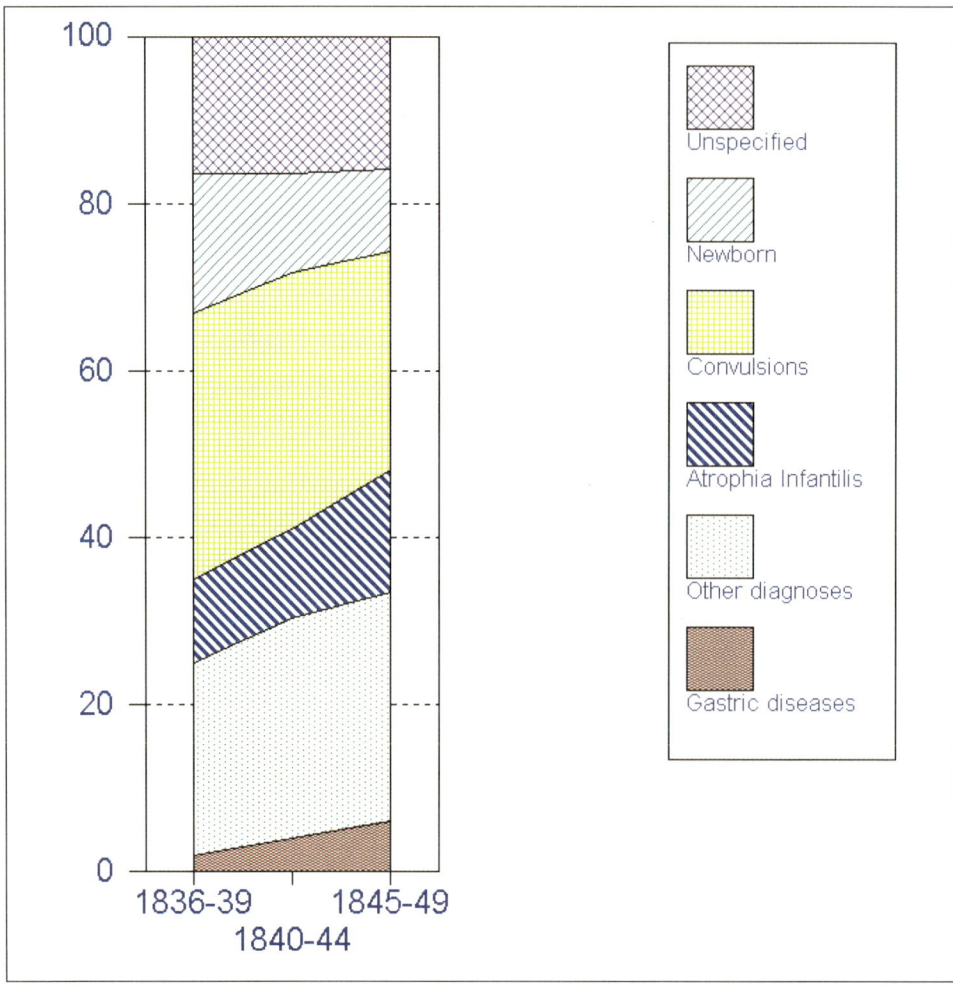

Fig. 1. Deaths during the first two years of life distributed as causes of death in percent of all deaths in the age group. Copenhagen 1836-49.

INFANCY AND OLD AGE AS CAUSES OF DEATH

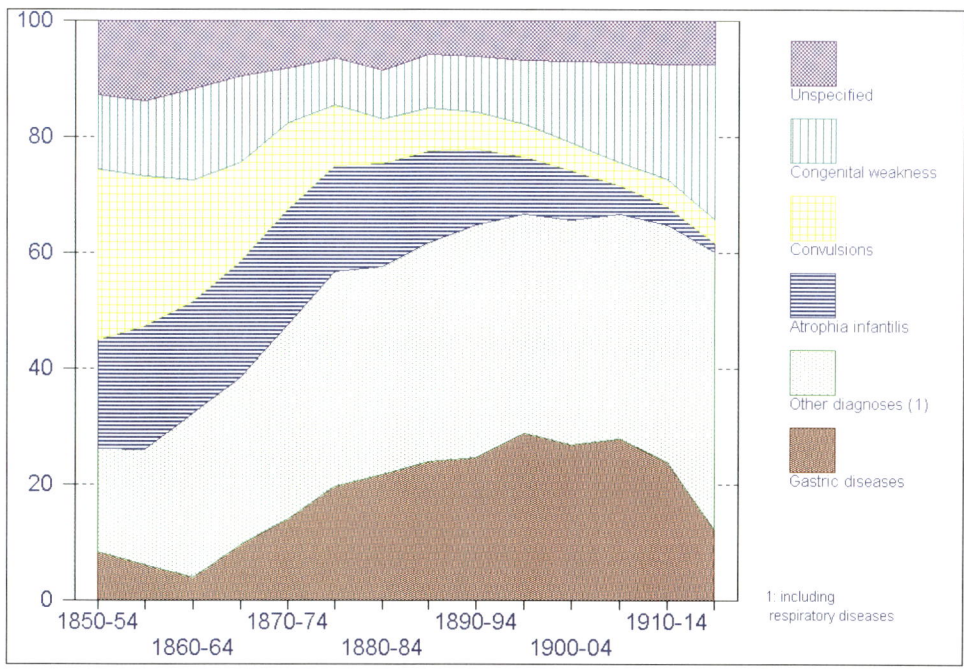

Fig. 2. Deaths in infancy distributed as causes of death in percent of all deaths in infancy. Copenhagen 1850-1919.

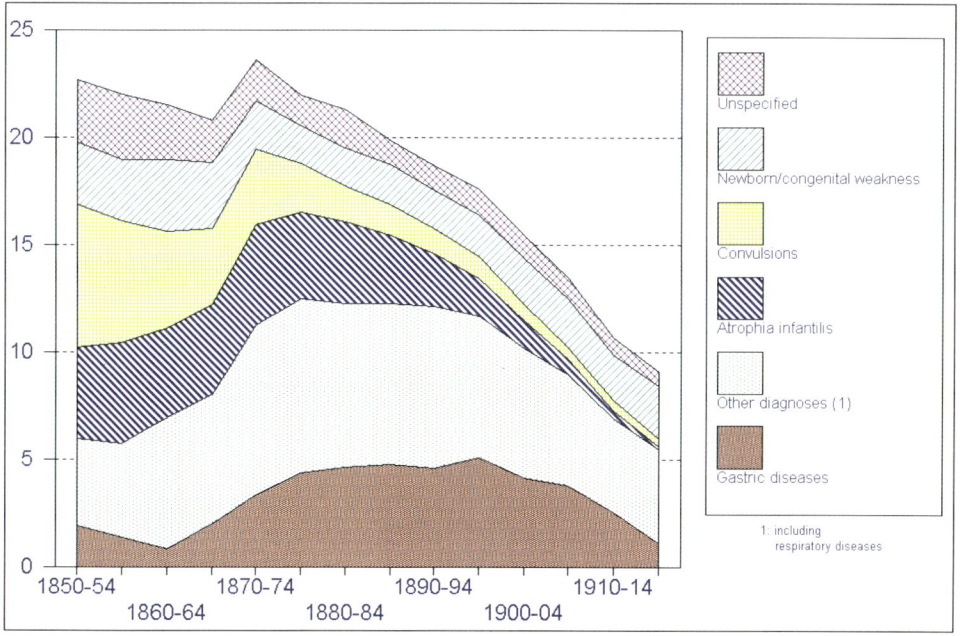

Fig. 3. Deaths in infancy per 100 liveborn distributed according to the causes of death. Copenhagen 1850-1919.

THE MOST FREQUENT CAUSES OF DEATH

The figures 1, 2 and 3 show the six most frequently noted causes of death in the years 1836-1920. In the 1830's 'convulsions' (kramper) was the most frequently noted single cause. A third of the deaths were categorized as such. From 1865 the most popular was 'Atrophia infantilis' (spædbørnstæring). From 1876 diarrhoeal diseases[12] were the major cause of death, exceeded after the turn of the century by congenital defects and respiratory disease. Before 1850 there was a considerable number of 'newborn' (nyfødte) and 'unspecified' (uangivne) and as time went by an increasing number of deaths were categorized under what I call 'other specific diagnoses'. By this I mean diseases which were then perceived as being capable of bringing about death. From 1836-39 to 1915-19 the proportion of specific diseases resulting in death rose from a quarter to just under two thirds.

It can be seen that of these categories only diarrhoeal diseases, respiratory diseases and other specific diagnoses were proper diseases. "Newborn" is an age. "Atrophia" means that the infant will not thrive but will fade slowly away. "Convulsions" is not a disease but a symptom which does not tell us anything about the aetiology. "Not specified" tells that the doctor has not found a specific cause of death or that he did not find it worth the bother to look for one. This category was decreasing throughout the period showing that doctors tried increasingly to find a cause of death to write at the certificate.

"Not specified" was used for a greater proportion of the deaths in all age groups at the beginning of the period compared to later, but it diminished most slowly for infants. In the period 1876-84 it was used in 10% of all infant deaths and in 1-2% of the deaths in the age group 15-35 years. Even among the over-65 group, it was used more seldom than among infants i.e. 5 % of the deaths. It can be shown that the use of the category "unspecified" among infants was more common in provincial towns than in Copenhagen.

"Newborn" and "old age" as causes of death

The category "newborn" occurs as a cause of death in the terminology from 1836-1874. The category had a pendant in the category 'old age' during the same years. That a term for an age can function as cause of death means that the death is perceived to be expected in that age group without further explanation.

The use of "newborn" was most frequent at the start of the period and the new nomenclature of 1875 changed the category to "congenital weakness" (medfødt svaghed). Old age was modified to "decrepitude" (alderdomssvaghed). The new categories can be interpreted as signs of a changing conception of death in these age groups. It was no longer a sufficient explanation of death that a person was very young or very old. The person had to be in a state of weakness too, – a weakness which separated him from his contemporaries, but on the other hand still needed no further explanation than age. When "congenital weakness" replaced "newborn" in the termonology, a number of specific diseases and deformities with newborns surfaced, with their own classifications, so they should not be included under congenital weakness.[13] Therefore, fewer instances were to be classified under congenital weakness than under newborn. Conversely, one must assume that congenital disease could be used far into the first year of life while newborn was restricted to a period close to birth.

While the term newborn in the old terminology referred to death as a risk for all newborns, "congenital weakness" is not a normal state for newborn babies, but only present in a few of the cases. With the classification "congenital weakness" a special group was separated, and the other newborns were freed from dying from 'newbornness' without further explanation.

The transition to the classification "congenital weakness" in 1876 does not immediately manifest itself as a change in the number of the cases which was noted here. From 1880-84 there is a gentle rise which gathers momentum from 1900, so that 26,8% of all deaths in infancy in 1915-19 were classified as "congenital disease". In the prefaces to the decade reviews of causes of death, editors were from 1914 aware of this rise and explained it as an increasing tendency among doctors to classify deaths in this area rather than "atrophia infantilis".[14] Due to the fact that infant mortality, as we know, was dropping during the period, a constant number of children dying of congenital weakness compared to live-born would gradually be more significant compared to the other causes of death. Table 3 shows that this was to a certain degree the case, but that congenital weakness actually also rose slightly compared to live-born. So there was both an increasing tendency with for doctors to use this classification, while the number of deaths due to congenital weakness was more significant due to a reduction in deaths overall. I have not followed figures for "old age" and "decrepitude" as closely as "newborn"/"congenital weakness", and have only made calculations for selected years.[15] From 1845-49, 27% of all deaths among people over 60 in Copenhagen were classified as "old age". The distribution according to age is shown in fig. 4. Here it can be seen that in only very few cases was it considered possible to die of old age as early as the 50s-60s, but the classification gained significance in the group over 60 years of age. Frequency of use rose with the age at death. About 2/3 of all deaths in the age group over 80 years were thus classed in this category.

During the period 1876-89 just under 22% of deaths among people over 65 in Copenhagen and provincial towns were categorized as "decrepitude", compared to 19% during the period 1890-1901.[16] During the period 1921-60 the number of all deaths (all ages in the entire country) classified as old age and apoplexy dropped from 18% to 15%. This happened at the same time as average life expectancy rose, so that the number of deaths occurring over the age of 65 rose steeply, so more people died at an age where they could have been included in the category "decrepitude".[17] Due to the fact that the various registrations cover different population groups both geographically and by age, it is sadly not possible to make direct comparisons over time. On the other hand it can be concluded that among the same population section there was a waning tendency to use decrepitude during the whole period from 1846-1960, without, however, it becoming insignificant or going out of use entirely.

Convulsions

"Convulsions" was the grand old explanation for death among children. Almost one third of all deaths during the first two years of life were classified as convulsions in 1836-39 and a couple of percent lower in 1840-44. It was believed that children could suffer from convulsions without prior illness. It could happen if, for example, the mother or wet-nurse breast fed after a strong emotional outburst. It was also believed that the child could suddenly contract convulsions and die in conjunction with teething.[18]

The number of deaths which were classified as convulsions dropped, however, rapidly and fairly evenly throughout the period, and amounted to about 10% in 1876-79 and stabilized at 4-5% after 1900.

Atrophia infantilis

At the end of the 1800's "Atrophia infantilis" did not have anything to do with tuberculosis regardless of the label atrophy. It was the description of a condition in which the infant never thrived, or its condition declined so it finally wasted away and died. In the terminology there was only one rubric for "atrophy" until 1860 when "Atrophia infantilis" was added in parentheses, and adults disappeared from the rubric. Like the category "congenital weakness" atrophy was not a specific illness, but it was not as nonspecific as "newborn" or "convulsions". The label was a comprehensive description of the infant's state, without conveying any notion of the aetiology. In relation to convulsions as cause of death, this was a clarification and an extension with regards to the course of the disease. "Convulsions" focuses on the moment of death without any awareness of what came before. "Atrophy" points towards a longer period where something has been wrong prior to the time of death. One might say that even though the diagnosis "atrophy" did not contain any built-in treatment or preventive measures, it made the condition abnormal. Attention was directed at the fact that languishing was a pathological state which could lead to death. The newer diagnosis "atrophia" meant that the many healthy infants were not expected to contract convulsions and die from one moment to the next.

Doctors classified a rising number of deaths under the term "atrophia" during the period from 1836 the greatest number being about 21% at the end of the 1850's. The usage fluctuated at 19-20% until a drop set in at the end of the 1870's. Only 1,5% were classfied in this manner in 1916-19, which is 0,1% of all live-births. To summarize, the use of the diagnosis rose steadily until 1850 and was in general use until 1875 whereafter it rapidly disappeared from use, scarcely being used at all around 1920.

The increase during the middle of the century took place at the expense of "newborn" and "convulsions". The editor of the cause-of-death statistic thought, as I have said, that the drop around 1900 was due to the fact that many deaths which earlier had been classified as "atrophy" were gradually being classed as those to "congenital weakness". This probably includes those infants who never thrived. On the other hand it is probable that children whose condition began to decline later during their first year, are at the middle of the century registered under atrophy, and at the end under digestive diseases.

Gastric diseases

During the period 1895-99, 29% of infant deaths were registered as gastric diseases, most of which were acute enteritis and acute epidemic diarrhoea. Gastric diseases counted for the majority of all causes of death at this time. That epidemic diarrhoea should play a leading role as the cause of death was fairly new. When the terminology was renegotiated in 1847, the physician O. Bang, who was a member of the Royal Board of Health and responsible for the first terminology, suggested that 'Diarrohea' should be removed, as it rarely was epidemically lethal.[19]

If one adds all the illnesses which have anything to do with 'the stomach', only 2% of deaths during the first two years of life were registered here in 1836-39. In the 1850's and 1860's, where the number for the first year of life alone is known, the number was between 4% and 10%. During the 1870's the rapid rise began taking the number of deaths due to acute diarrhoea alone up to almost 30% in the 1890's. The usage culminated here and dropped steeply after 1910. Also in relation to live-births, the gastric diseases peaked in the five-year period from 1895-99 (fig.3).

This rise is most likely the result of a transfer of deaths formerly categorized as convulsions and atrophy, alongside an actual increase of gastric diseases due to the rapid growth of Copenhagen. During the 1870's, the attention paid to digestive diseases in the medical literature began to increase. This attention exploded in the years between 1900 and 1920, when the aetiology and treatment of acute diarrhoea was one of the most important topics of discussion among pediatricians, not only in Denmark, but in the entire Western world.[20] That the number of deaths related to gastric disorders fell during the period when so much attention was focused on this diagnosis and when there was a widespread willingness on the part of doctors to use it as cause of death is no doubt due to the fact that around 1900 measures preventing such disorders had been succesful that the total number of infant deaths had been considerably reduced. A dual process is visible here. First a transfer of cases from the fate-ridden categories "convulsions" and "newborn" and the descriptive "atrophia" to "gastric illnesses", followed by a targeted effort to understand and fight gastric diseases with specific means.

Respiratory diseases

Respiratory diseases did not attract as much attention as gastric diseases at the end of the 19th and the beginning of the 20th century, but as the total number of infant deaths and deaths due to gastric diseases fell, the proportion of respiratory diseases resulting in death grew in relation to the total number of deaths, so that they were the largest group of specific illnesses in 1915-19.

Respiratory diseases and gastric diseases are, however, not independent variables, but form together an interdependence. Death following a weakness due to gastric diseases often occurs in the wake of an acute lung infection.[21] Fashion and chance decides what is written on the death certificate. The numbers from Copenhagen seem to support this interpretation. Already in 1836-39 almost 6% of deaths during the first two years of life where diagnosed as respiratory diseases. With regard to the first year of life the number grew slowly and irregularly until it reached 19,2% of the total number of deaths for the period 1915-19.

However, if one looks at the relationship with the live-born, the number fluctuated at around 2-3% until 1895 after which the quotient fell, so that from 1910 it was under 2%. Nationally, however, from 1920 when the cases started being registered, the number was still 2-3% until between 1930 and 1940 after which the quotient was halved.[22]

Other diagnoses

Under this heading I have included all the diagnoses which at the time were considered to be specific, even those which medical science later did not recognize as possible causes of death. The number of deaths categorized as the result of a specific diagnosis increased constantly from 1850. This is probably because the tendency to look for an illness as the cause of death increased and because the relative weight of individually rare diseases grew as the IMR declined. The latter group includes diseases which must be considered not to be influenced by factors which generally made infant mortality drop, e.g. congenital heart disease.

"The real cause of death"

In general, the cause-of-death statistics for Copenhagen show a development from their beginnings in the 1830's when only about 25% of infant deaths were registered under causes which could, with some good will, be termed specific diseases, to a point where in 1915-19 almost two-thirds were atributed to specific diseases. A similar development was also visible in the other age groups, but from the very beginning the share of infant deaths which were not related to a disease, was far greater than in other age groups. Likewise, the increase took place faster in the other age groups.

Doctor J. Carlsen (1850-1919), who was the editor of the cause-of-death statistics from 1890, was aware of the relatively large number of infants whose deaths were categorized under causes which were not specific diseases. Since his point of departure was that an illness preceded every death, no matter the age of the deceased this posed him a problem. He thought that death could not occur by itself without discernible cause. He wanted a cause-of-death statistic which provided information about the aetiology of the diseases, which could be applied to the prevention of deaths due to specific diseases. Therefore, he wished, if possible, to stop or at least minimize the use of the categories he called 'uncertain'.

He found the classifications "unspecified" and "sudden death without known cause" to be the most uncertain. Almost as insignificant he found "atrophia infantilis", "decrepitude", "convulsions" and "congenital disease". In his opinion most of these classifications covered 'Ignorance about the real cause of death'; when physicians used these classifications it must be because they had not bothered to seek out the real cause. The classifications Carlsen found useless covered about one-third of all deaths during the first year of life in the 1890's, and included four of the seven most used cause-of-death groups mentioned above. The, in Carlsen's words, 'uncertain' causes were also found to have been used often in the ages over 65 years. In the age groups from 5-65 they were, however, used rarely.[23]

Carlsen thought that in his colleagues' defence it could be stated that in the first and final chapters of life 'The difficulties in finding the cause of death are greater than in other age groups'. But he was not satisfied. He condemned the mortality rates for infants and the old as of 'very little worth'.[24]

As shown above Carlsen's views were gaining ground. 'Uncertain' causes of death were on the retreat, even for the infants. As time went on still more infants received a specific diagnosis for the disease which caused their death. But the age distribution where the ages between 5 and 60 years were classified under specific causes of death, suggests that there was more at stake than the colleagues' ignorance and indolence. The causes that Carlsen rejected as 'uncertain' because they were not specific diseases, implicitly describe death as a natural occurrence one could expect in childhood as well as old age. This interpretation is supported by the fact that in far fewer cases was a doctor consulted regarding infants and old people than in the age groups between. Carlsen noted that in 1890-99 about 9% of the entire population died without prior treatment by a doctor: 'That such cases will mostly be found in earliest infancy and old age does not require further proof'.[25]

C.E. Fenger already observed this tendency in 1846, when the population generally much more rarely called for doctors in connection with the illness which led to their death, but did, however, call for one about 5 times more often for 20-50 year olds than for children in their first year.[26]

When hospitalization became available to a larger portion of the population the same movement can be witnessed, first the young and adults, later infants and the old. In the years after 1890, more residents from rural areas died in hospitals situated in provincial towns, which muddled up the statistics. In this connection, however, it is interesting that while approx. 20-30% of deaths in provincial towns in the age groups from 15-45 years were country dwellers who died in hospital, this was only the case for 1-5% of the infants.[27]

At the beginning of the period there was apparently an agreement between doctors and the population that death could occur at the earliest stage of life without further explanation, just as the same could happen during old age. In the 'vigorous' ages[28], however, there was a greater tendency to provide a reason for death by way of a specific diagnosis. During the 1800's, disease as the cause of deaths was adopted increasingly to account for infant mortality and seems to have originated in Copenhagen, spreading into provincial towns and finally to rural districts.

Conclusion

The analysis of the cause-of-death statistics for Copenhagen has shown a development in classification. At the beginning of the period "convulsions" was the most used cause of death, followed by "newborn" and "unspecified". None of the three categories indicates a disease, and therefore none points at possible treatment which could have been instigated. One could call them ascertaining or resigning categories. The application of these categories was, however, in decline from the beginning of the period. Perhaps they were used more often earlier, but in any case there is a constant movement towards assigning the cause of death of more and more infants to diseases. "Atrophy" wedges itself in as an intermediate category. It was the most applied single category in the 1860's and the beginning of the 1870's. "Atrophy" is not a specific disease, but a condition. In contrast to "convulsions" and "newborn" it is, however, a visible condition which continues for some time, and therefore it is possible to intervene with treatment. Likewise, "atrophy" suggests that death can be prevented by means of correct treatment and nourishment. "Convulsions" could be avoided if, for example, the mother or wet-nurse remained even-tempered, but the view was that "convulsions" could appear in fine and healthy children from one moment to the next.

A similar movement could be witnessed with the change of name from "newborn" to "congenital weakness" in 1876. The undetermined idea of a dangerous period for all children after birth was substituted for a pathological state with some children. A definition which eventually opened up for prevention of a social, medical or eugenic kind.

However, most spectacular was the development in the use of "gastric diseases", especially "acute diarrhoea" as the cause of death. From being a rarely used cause which was almost discontinued as a category in 1850, "acute diarrhoea" was used increasingly from 1860, so that the acute gastric diseases around 1900 were registered as the cause of death of 27-29% of infants, – a development which cannot solely be viewed as an actual rise in gastrointestinal diseases. It is possible that urbanization had led to an increase in the occurrence of the disease all over Western Europe, which helped bring it into the consciousness of physicians. In addition to this, one may talk about a recategorization of infant death from cramps and atrophy to gastric disease, – a recategorization which took place alongside the invention of a terminology and institutions to prevent stomach diseases. One could say that the recategorization was part of the same movement which developed the means to fight these diseases. Copenhagen's milk supply was founded in 1878; philanthropic societies which worked for better nourishment for poor and illegitimate children picked up speed in the 1880's, standardized equipment for sterilizing milk for artificial feeding could be purchased from the end of the 1880's.

In this article I have only made a few spot tests concerning the causes of death among old people. The conclusions must therefore be preliminary and cautious. However, one thing can be concluded with certainty. A more comprehensive investigation of the categorization of the causes of death among old people would contribute to an understanding of perceptions of ageing and death in older ages as they have developed down the years. It would be possible to chart the changes in how old one must be in order to die of old age, as well as the diseases which at different times were most used as the causes of death. My random calculations based on surveys reveal that the use of the category "old age"/"decrepitude" as a cause of death has been on the decline since the 1840's, but it still played a considerable role in 1960. Since then "old age" has nearly disappeared as a cause of death. The category now called "senility without mention of psychosis" was in 1995 only applied to approximately 2% of all deaths among over 70 years olds. 80% of the causes of death among old people are now categorized as malignant tumors, cardiac diseases and respiratory diseases.[29]

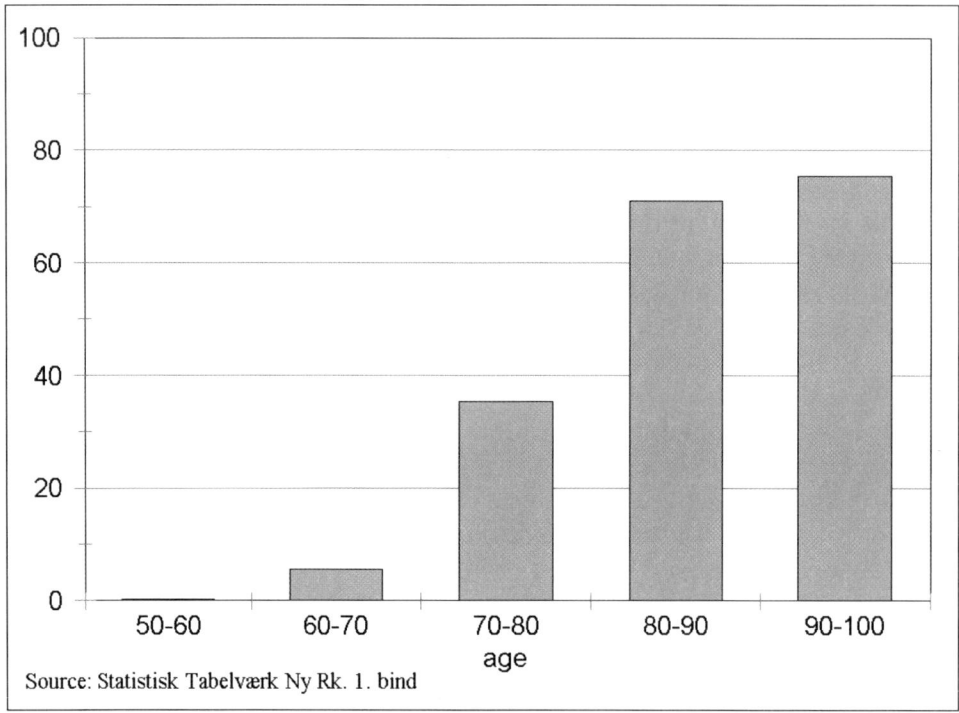

Fig. 4. Deaths from old age per 100 deaths in the age group. Copenhagen 1845-49.

There is a parallel between the categorization of deaths among infants and old people. In both groups a shift has occurred from nonspecific categories or categories whose cause is age to specific diseases. But contrary to contemporary wisdom which holds that it is still possible to die of old age, but certainly not of childhood, the category "old age" has almost disappeared while half the infants who in 1995 died during their first year died of no. 43 "certain causes of perinatal mortality". That means death from reasons connected with the transition from foetus to infant, i.e. to be newborn. Paradoxically, the probable reason for this is that while old people still have to die if not sooner, then later, death among infants is almost non-existent. The recategorization and denaturalization of death in childhood has taken part in a successful battle, so that only about half a percent of the live-borns in Denmark die during their first year of life. Around 1900 it was 12%. Among the few that die as infants, premature babies count for quite a few, and in these cases it is in fact age which is the problem.[30] Among old people no one seriously believes that death can be fought successfully, but it can be postponed and life over the age of 70 can consist of years with good health for more people. That "old age" as a cause of death has fallen into neglect can perhaps be seen as part of the battle for a longer life with less illness. The logical development would then be that, after a period of changes and research, old age will return as a cause of death, but not as an excuse for not being able to find the disease, but as a description of the condition in which death comes, as the whole body has aged to death and not because an illness has raged in a single organ.

1. Often the processes are dealt with separately. For an overwiev see C. A. Corsini & P. Viazzo (eds.)1997; V. Fildes, L. Marks & H. Marland (eds.) 1992.
2. The full version of "death in infancy" has been published in Løkke, 1998b. The part covering the population statistics, which is summarized here is published in full in English: A. Løkke 1995. The part here concerning the cause-of-death registration has not been published before. Other parts of the project are published in preliminary versions in A. Løkke 1997; A. Løkke 1998a.
3. The child mortality rate usually refers to the number of deaths during the first five years of life per 1000 live births, while the infant mortality rate (IMR) usually refers to the number of deaths during the first year of life per 1000 live births.
4. A. Brändström1984.
5. Introduction to Statistisk Tabelværk, oldest series, 6th fascimile, pp. XXII.
6. Nowadays the total generation-related infant mortality is usually calculated as a more precise expression, but calculation by calendar year can still be used under certain conditions.
7. J.C. Lange 1773.
8. Iceland was part of the Danish state until 1944. No other parts of the state reached IMR over 30%.
9. H. Westergaard 1901, p. 403.
10. The law distinguished between urban areas where doctors were in the neighbourhood. Here the certificate had to be filled out by a doctor. In rural areas where only very few doctors lived, laymen were empowered to issue death certificates. Not until 1920 did rural certificates have to be issued by a doctor.
11. For problems and use of cause-of-death registration in England and Wales, see A. Hardy 1994. German classification: H.J. Kintner 1986.
12. Infant diarrhoea or cholera infantum (kolerine no. 11, tarmbetændelse no. 87). For my categorization see Løkke 1998b.

13. Nomenclatures no.56 and 58-60.
14. Oversigt over Dødsaarsagerne (1914) p. 89* and (1921) p. 100*.
15. For a discussion of the categories old age and decrepitude in medical literature, see H. Kirk 1995.
16. Statistisk Tabelværk 5. Rk. Litra A nr. 5, Befolkningsforholdene, Copenhagen 1905, pp. 150.
17. Statistiske Undersøgelser no. 19, Befolkningsudvikling og sundhedsforhold 1901-60, Copenhagen 1966, p.104-105.
18. Tetanus was also known at the beginning of the period and was classified separately. With infants it was most often called lockjaw. The rubric convulsions only includes the non-specific convulsions.
19. B. Johansson 1946.
20. Monrad (1900), "Den akutte Gastro-enteritis hos spæde Børn", Bibliotek for Læger; Ørum (1908-09), "Kolerineepidemien 1908", Nordisk Tidsskrift for Terapi; Monrad (1908-09), "Kolerinen og dens behandling", Nordisk Tidsskrift for Terapi; Ørum (1909-10), "Kolerinestatistikken", Nordisk Tidsskrift for Terapi; Ørum (1910), "Undersøgelser vedrørende Børnekolerinens Ætiologi", Bibliotek for Læger; Lendrop (1910), "Om Patogenesen af særlig de akutte Gastro-entiriter hos Smaabørn", Ugeskrift for Læger; Bahr (1910), "Undersøgelser over Børnekolerinens Læge II", Bibliotek for Læger; Ørum (1911), "Serumterapi ved Kolerine", Ugeskrift for Læger; Bahr (1912), "Fortsatte Undersøgelser vedrørende Børnekolerinens Ætiologi", Bibliotek for Læger; Bloch (1912), "Børnekolerinen og dens Behandling", Ugeskrift for Læger; Bahr (1912), "Om Tarmens Bakterieflora", Skand. Veter. tids., Bloch (1920), "Ætiologien til de akutte Fordøjelseslidelser hos det spæde barn", Ugeskrift for Læger. For a treatment of the entiritis-debate in England and USA see: Dwork 1987 and Meckel 1990.
21. See a treatment of the illnesses' synergy in Sundin 1993.
22. Oversigt over Dødsaarsagerne (1937), p. 20 and Matthiessen 1964, p. 9. A quick glance at Aarsberetning angaaende Sundhedtilstanden i København from the 20's suggests that the numbers for Copenhagen stayed under 2% of live-borns, which means that the drop at the beginning of the century must be considered reliable, and the deaths due to respiratory diseases dropped in Copenhagen before the rest of the country. This is a phenomenon which could be interesting to investigate more closely due to the fact that there was no form of treatment once the illness had broken out, and that mortality was considerable for those children who were receiving treatment. The early drops in Copenhagen can almost only be explained by the fact that fewer children fell ill due to better housing and improved resilience due to improved care and nourishment.
23. J. Carlsen 1905, p. 5, table D.
24. Ibid. p. 4.
25. Ibid. 1905.
26. According to this investigation approximately 2/3 in rural areas and 2/5 in the towns died without receiving aid from a doctor. B. Johansson 1946, p. 86.
27. Oversigt over Dødsaarsagerne (1921), p. 2* table B.
28. This term is used in Ugeskrift for Læger's publication of the weekly lists of deaths in Copenhagen. See e.g. Ugeskrift for Læger 1876, p.159, where the vigorous ages from 5-60 are presented independently, deaths during the first year are presented both independently and with children up to the age of 5 and old people over 60.
29. 79,9% of the men and 83,3% of the women over 70 years of age are registered under these causes of death. Calculations based on 'Befolkningens bevægelser 1995'. Danmarks Statistik, table 42.
30. In 1995, a total of 353 children died during their first year, of which the 207 died during the first week after birth. In the same year, 400 children were born with a birth weight below 1500g of which 129 were below 1000g.

Bibliography

Brändström, Anders. *"De kärlekslöse mödrarna", Spädbörnsdödeligheden i Sverige under 1800-tallet med särskild hänsyn till Nedertornea.* Acta Universitatis Umensis, Umeå – Studies in the Humanities 62. Stockholm: Almquist & Wiksell International, 1984.

Carlsen, J. *Oversigt over Dødsaarsagerne.* Copenhagen,1905.

Corsini, C. A & P. Viazzo (eds.). *The Decline of Infant and Child Mortality,* Hague: Martinus Nijhoff Publishers, 1997.

Dwork, Deborah. *War is Good for Babies.* London: Tavistock, 1987.

Fildes, V, L. Marks & H. Marland (eds.). *Women and Children first, International maternal and infant welfare,* 1870-1945. London: Routledge, 1992.

Hardy, Anne. "Death is the Cure of all Diseases" *Social History of Medicine* 7:3 1994.

Johansson, Børre. *Den danske Sygdoms- og Dødsaarsagsstatistik.* Copenhagen: Munksgaard, 1946.

Kintner, H.J. "Classifying Causes of Death" *Historical Methods* 19:2, 1986, pp 45-54.

Kirk, Henning. *Da alderen blev en diagnose. Konstruktionen af kategorien "alderdom" i 1800-tallets lægelitteratur.* Copenhagen: Munksgaard, 1995.

Lange, Johan Christian. *Børnevennen,* Copenhagen 1773.

Løkke, Anne. "No Difference Without a Cause. Infant Mortality Rates as a World View Generator". *Scandinavian Journal of History* 20:2. 1995, pp 75-96.

Løkke, Anne. The "antiseptic" transformation of Danish midwives, *Midwives, Society and Childbirth, Debates and Controversies in the Modern Period.* Hilary Marland & Anne Marie Rafferty (eds.). London/New York: Routledge, 1997.

Løkke, Anne. "Philanthropists, mothers and doctors. The philanthropic struggle against infant mortality in Copenhagen 1866-1920" *Charitable Women-Philanthropic Welfare 1780-1930.* Birgitta Jordansson & Tinne Vammen (eds.).1998a Odense University Press.

Løkke, Anne. Døden i barndommen. 1998b Gyldendal, Copenhagen.

Matthiessen, P.C. *Statistiske Undersøgelser* no. 11. Copenhagen; Det statistiske Departement, 1964.

Meckel, Richard A. *Save the Babies* Baltimore; Johns Hopkins University Press,1990.

Sundin, Jan. "Spädbörnsdödlighet och kulturella faktorer". *Bibliotek for Læger* (dec. 1993) p. 384-99.

Westergaard, Harald. *Die Lehre von der Mortalität und Morbilität* Jena 1901.

Fashioning Agehood:

Lifestyle Imagery and the Commercial Spirit of Seniors Culture

Stephen Katz

The term "gerontology" was coined by Elie Metchnikoff (1845-1916), the celebrated and popular scientist who worked at the Pasteur Institute in Paris from 1888 until his death in 1916. He wrote two influential books on the subject of aging: *The Nature of Man* (1903) and *The Prolongation of Life* (1907), respectively subtitled "Studies in Optimistic Philosophy" and "Optimistic Studies". Thus Metchnikoff helped to launch gerontology not only as a science of aging, but one inspired by a discourse of optimism; in particular, an optimism that the pathological ravages of the aging process could be contested, and even eliminated. Over half a century later in 1968 in the United States, Robert N. Butler introduced the term *ageism* during a housing dispute while he was Chair of the District of Columbia Advising Committee on Aging.[1] While Butler went on to become the first director of the American National Institute on Aging in 1976 and remains a pioneer in the gerontological field, ageism has become a valuable way of putting a name to the widespread bigotry faced by older persons. Today, ageism joins racism and sexism as terms that identify the prevailing forms of injustice and inequality in Western societies.

From Metchnikoff's optimistic gerontology to the legacy of Butler's critical ageism, researchers and practitioners in aging studies have attacked negative medical, cultural and political characterizations of old age as a time of illness, decline, poverty and unproductivity. In their place, gerontologists have promoted a new perspective on later life in an era where changing demographic patterns are set to transform social relations amongst all age groups. This perspective includes, on the one hand, the empowerment of 'gray' political movements, through which retiree organizations lobby to reform pension policies and social security provisions; and on the other hand, the promotion of positive images that resignify aging in terms of activity, independence, resourcefulness and wellbeing. Thus, gerontologists and their associates, and communities of elderly citizens and groups, are together challenging both representational politics and the politics of representation.

However, it is the politics of representation and the call for positive images which I address here, with the help of visual illustrations from popular culture. Before proceeding, let me add that not all gerontologists are uniformly sanguine about their profession's positive turn. Indeed, some gerontologists have castigated overly positive frameworks for constraining the freedom of older individuals by imposing unrealistic expectations on them. For example, David Ekerdt sees the construction of an active 'busy ethic' in retirement to be a form of moral regulation akin to the work ethic: "It is not the actual pace of activity but the preoccupation with activity and the affirmation of its desirability that matters".[2] Likewise, Harry Moody criticizes the professions for sometimes ignoring the material realities of aging that include poverty, loneliness and poor health. As well, the "frenzy of activity" in old age can actually mask, rather than diminish, the emptiness of meaning.[3] Martha Holstein also points out the sexist implications of new models of *productive* aging.[4] Most importantly, as historian Thomas R. Cole concludes, is the probability that positive attacks on ageist perspectives tend to reproduce, rather than overturn, the intolerance and disrespect generated by such perspectives.[5] In other words, the *positive* is not necessarily or naturally the opposite of the *negative*, but part of a continuum of images that differentiates old age and culturally configures the lifecourse.

While this internal critique begins to contest the positive construction of aging, and draws our attention to the vacuousness of much popular anti-aging literature, it doesn't fully elucidate how positive images intersect the radical impulses of gerontologists and gray politics with the growing consumerist industries around old age. One way to understand this intersection is to borrow from sociologist Arlie Hochschild's examination of the commercial spirit of feminism in women's advice literature.[6] According to Max Weber, the historical commercial "spirit" of capitalism" drew on the revolutionary wellsprings of Protestantism; likewise, says Hochschild, a commercial "spirit" of domestic life in the late twentieth century is drawing on the revolutionary wellsprings of feminism. Thus, according to Hochschild's focal analogy, "feminism is to the commercial spirit of intimate life as Protestantism is to the spirit of capitalism".[7] And perhaps what is occurring in our case is similar: the political energies of the gray movement overflow it, and are dispersed and redeployed in the service of a commercial spirit of seniors culture.

A second and related way of analyzing the positive economy of aging is advanced by cultural theorists such as Zygmunt Bauman, Mike Featherstone, Mike Hepworth, (the late) Glenda Laws, Bryan Turner and Kathleen Woodward, who, in different ways, note that the foundational characteristic of what they term the postmodern lifecourse is the de-differentiation of modernist life stages. Rigidly chronological and generational boundaries that formerly demarcated childhood, middle age and old age are eroding under pressure from cultural directions that have accompanied the profound changes in labour, retirement and the welfare state, and the globalization of Western consumer economies and lifestyles. Inspired by these writers, several recent academic projects have emerged: *Images of Aging: Cultural Representations of Later Life* 1995 (eds. Mike Featherstone and Andrew Wernick), a collection based on a conference held at Trent University in Canada in 1992; *Images of Aging in Western Cultures* 1995 (eds. Cornelia Hummel and Christian D'Epinay), based on a second conference in Sierre, Switzerland, in 1993; and *Figuring Age: Women, Bodies, Generations* 1999 (ed. Kathleen Woodward) based on a 1996 conference of the same name held at the University of Wisconsin-Milwaukee, sponsored by the Center for Twentieth Century Studies. Further, the editors of the journal *Body and Society* are planning a special issue on Aging Bodies/Images of Aging. Hence, cultural studies of images of aging seem to have come of age and it is to these studies that I hope this essay can contribute. My purpose here is not to question the optimism of those images that attempt to rescue aging bodies, identities and memories from their social ostracism at the edge of life and restore them to the world of the living, but to question the expanding consumerist spaces where, in the commercial spirit of seniors culture, such images circulate, acquire representational validity and obscure our view of the material realities – both positive and negative – around living, aging and dying.

LIFESTYLING THE LIFECOURSE AND POSTMODERN TIMELESSNESS

Figure 1, taken from the Apocalypse Manuscript (Latin & German, c. 1420), contains a typical wheel of life image in the lower right corner. Wheel of life motifs are numerous in medieval literature; they shape the human lifecourse as mobile and spiritually rich with numerous beginning points. As Mary Dove states in her fascinating study *The Perfect Age of Man's Life*, the concept of "the perfect age" in medieval literary and artistic representations referred not to a stage of life, but to a state of it; a point of contact between the time of the body and the timelessness of the soul. Furthermore, the prominent wheel of life figures associate the perfect age with "kingly status because it is not an age in the way in which the other ages are ages: it turns the sequence of the ages into a wheel, and changes our understanding of the movement of time".[8] Thomas R. Cole concurs:

Figure 1.

"In the late medieval countryside, only the bells of the monastery or parish would have broken the natural rhythms of daily life. An individual life cycle corresponded to the cycles of the seasons, of day and night. Seasonal and diurnal time, in turn, were part of the world's time, which began with Creation and would end with the Apocalypse. Ultimately, all time belonged to God. It was, therefore, not for sale, nor was it precisely divided into linear segments."[9]

Similarly, death and dying were depicted in medieval society not as an ending of the lifecourse, but as a process intrinsic to it, communally symbolized and universally harmonized.[10] This perspective is evident in the medieval practice of the Ars Moriendi or the 'art of dying', that required the dying person to participate in a ritualized series of steps – last rites, confession and visits from members of the public – in order to die properly and with dignity.

Figure 2.

By comparison, if premodern lives were spun through spiritualized wheels that orbited gracefully in accordance with the ritualized arts of living and dying, and modern lives eventually were configured by industrial models of productivity, then postmodern lives unfold according to consumer categories of successful and timeless aging. But postmodern, consumer timelessness shares little with premodern, spiritual eternity. As Zygmunt Bauman says, in contrast to "traditional ways of dabbling with timelessness" the "postmodern strategy of survival "does not allow the finality of time to worry the living – by slicing time (all of it, exhaustively, without residue) into short-lived, evanescent episodes. It rehearses mortality, so to speak, by practicing it day by day".[11] I think that this characterization of postmodern life can be clearly seen in the following examples.

Figure 2 is from a special article on 'growing up' for women in Mirabella magazine (May/June 1996). Growing up in this case is predominantly a fashioned and fashionable enterprise, however. As the copy reads: "Everyone is born. Everyone dies. All the rest is aging". But what stays the same throughout the lifecourse here is the commodity-form, the red dress. Thus commodities restrict individual growth and development to the fashioned realm of activity, control, beauty and mobility. In turn, commodities reshape the sequencing of the lifecourse itself within the confines of this realm.

In addition to lifestyling the lifecourse, consumer industries reconstruct aging through representations of generational relations and nostalgia. Again, to cite Bauman's reflections on postmodern time: "Instead of trying (in vain) to colonize the future, it dissolves the future in the present".[12] Figures 3 and 4 both exemplify how commodity culture recasts and collapses the chronological span of generations into a single present. The Motorola advertisement for cellular phones (figure 3) displays a fifty-year history as a generational connection, showing a male line of toughness and legendary durability. Hence, the line says, "Like father, like son". More fantastical is the British Airways image (figure 4) that mixes young and old selves and bodies in a montage of two different points in the lifecourse. The advertisement, in order to convey the idea of airline comfort, superimposes the head and shoulders of an adult man, photographed in colour, onto a child's body cradled in its mother's arms, photographed in black and white. Thus the innocence of childhood and the stress of adulthood are juxtaposed into one generation-jumping image. The photographic trick of using black and white to represent the past in a nostalgic way, along with colour to distinguish the present and future, is effective here and commonplace in other advertisements that attempt to package generational time as part of the progress of a commodity form.

ANTI-AGING AND THE SCIENCES OF DEFENSE

In his analysis of positive images of aging and the attack on ageism, Mike Hepworth concludes that, "the chief characteristic of prescriptions for positive ageing should be an ironic acceptance of the natural ending of one's

Figure 3.

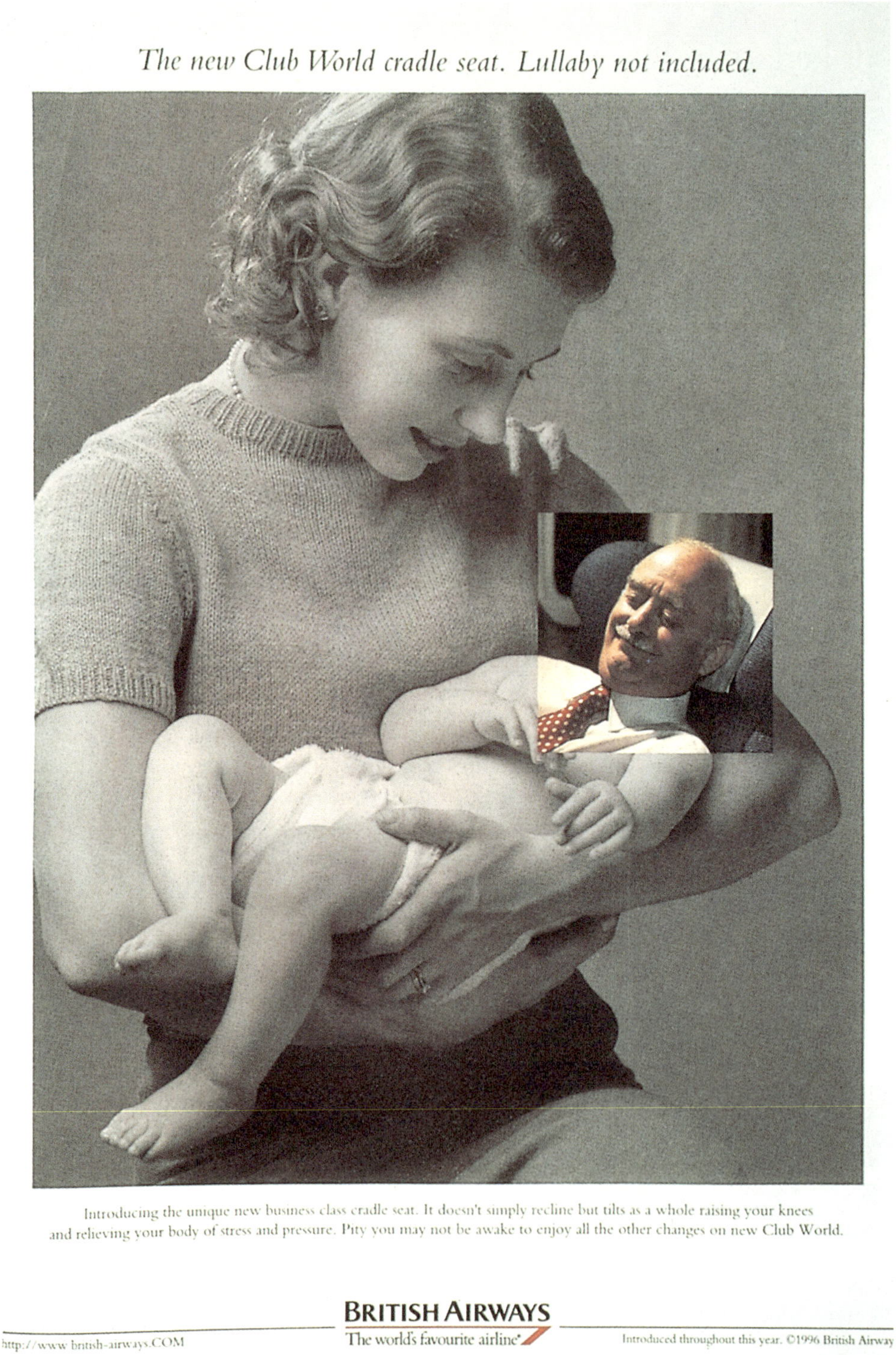
The new Club World cradle seat. Lullaby not included.
Introducing the unique new business class cradle seat. It doesn't simply recline but tilts as a whole raising your knees and relieving your body of stress and pressure. Pity you may not be awake to enjoy all the other changes on new Club World.
BRITISH AIRWAYS
The world's favourite airline
http://www.british-airways.COM
Introduced throughout this year. ©1996 British Airway

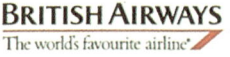

Figure 4.

Figure 5.

life";[13] however, the mass-mediated narrative of the lifecourse has produced just the opposite. In fact, it has forged a disciplinary link between positive aging and anti-aging. The proliferation of techniques around exercise, cosmetic surgery, diets and beauty products has created an anxiety-riven culture where, as Kathleen Woodward points out, "at precisely the historical moment that the elderly are appearing on the historical stage in record numbers, many are vanishing into the crowd, no longer visibly marked as old".[14]

Skin – with its wrinkling, cracking and sagging – is feared as the most obvious betrayer of aging, especially for women. So masking skin-effects is a major offensive in the war on aging. Often advertisement campaigns employ military metaphors and simulated scientific vocabularies to lend authority to these products. Examples are Estée Lauder's "Skin Defender", Ponds' "Age-Defying System", or L'Oréal Plenitude's anti-wrinkle "revitalift". As a Nivea Visage advertisement for its "anti-wrinkle creme" proclaims, "The Problem isn't Aging. It's Wrinkling". A most demonstrative and sophisticated example of the science of beauty is "the V.P. Box system" and the "Tua Viso" device in Figure 5. The accompanying anatomical portrayal of the face is a key legitimating feature in this instructional narrative on how to maintain facial youthfulness.

Anti-aging techniques and products create an illusion of consumer democracy by projecting a world in which everyone can have age-resistant, beautiful bodies. However, it is the elite celebrities of Hollywood to whom homage is paid for their anti-aging heroism. Mike Featherstone has noted that one of the characteristics "demanded of celebrities is to have personality" which replaces "the more traditional virtues of character".[15] And part of having personality, today, is the adoption "of a positive attitude towards the aging process", and an ability to "remain 'forever young' in … work habits, bodily posture, facial expressions and general demeanor".[16] Often before-and-after type images of Hollywood stars, whose bodies have been transfigured by expensive dietary, cosmetic and surgical procedures, become the standards by which members of the public are encouraged to calculate the effects of the aging process on their own bodies. Before-and-after images have been around since 1860, linked to treatises on physical education, and were generally gender neutral. In the 1920s, Charles Atlas's advertising agency created a new imagery that dissociated physical culture from health, and promoted muscularity as a virtue in its own right[17]. Today's popular images go much further to accentuate not only the drama of the distance between the two states – before, and, after – but also to minimize this distance in order to show the extent to which aging heroes succeed in staying young. In short, aging heroes appear to mark time not by how they age, but by how they manage to grow older without aging.

MARKETING ALCHEMY: TURNING GRAY INTO GOLD

As the lifestyle ideals of consumerism fashion the postmodern lifecourse, real estate, cosmetic, financial, pharmaceutical and recreational industries are awakening to the fact that there is "gold in gray",[18] and are targeting the elderly as a newly prosperous group of consumers. The titles of books such as Stephan Buck's *The 55+ Market* (1990) and Jeff Ostroff's *Successful Marketing to the 50+ Consumer: How to Capture One of the Biggest and Fastest-growing Markets in America* (1989) say it all. Indeed, marketing agencies are "imagineering" – to use Glenda Laws's suggestive term[19] – later life into a simulated seniors culture segmented according to spending behaviours and taste profiles.

One of the fastest growing consumer industries is tourism. As more geographical landscapes and locations suitable for elder-travel become available, more marketing resources are poured into making seniors culture mobile. For example, the Canadian company ElderTreks is a travel organization devoted to elderly people that takes into account those with special needs, yet exotic trips are still the mainstay. Elder-tourism is also part of the global leisure economy that transforms fixed places into transferable commerce-spaces such as MacDonalds, Holiday Inns, theme

FASHIONING AGEHOOD

ADVERTISEMENT

Club Med - "Life as it should be"

Almost 45 years ago, an idea was born in Europe that was to revolutionize the world of leisure and vacationing in the 20th century. A simple concept of worry-free, pre-paid vacation with friends developed into Club Med which is now a global company with over 113 holiday villages in 35 countries around the world and welcomes over 1 million guests annually.

Club Med built its reputation in North America during the '70s as an international haven for active, sports minded singles and couples. As those same career crazed singles hit parenthood, Club Med kept pace with the introduction of the special "Family Villages" that provide supervised programs for children 4 months - 12 years of age.

Now that the Baby Boomers are approaching their 50s, Club Med has offered a new dimension to their holiday offerings and introduced a special program called "Forever Young" for guests 55 years and over. This program offers savings at selected Club Med villages where mature travellers' love of freedom, food, fitness and fun is all brought together with a pre-paid fixed price that covers almost everything except drinks at the bar and optional excursions.

The Club Med village concept ensures all services are close at hand in a safe, secure environment. Daily programs including water exercises, stretching, archery, golf, juggling, kayaking, tennis, scuba diving, rock climbing, windsurfing and sailing are offered with free lessons from Club Med's international team of instructors.

Club Med caters to a wide range of clientele – while the average age of a Club Med guest is 37 and 40% travel with their families, already over 4% of the guests qualify for the Forever Young savings. A Family Reunion at a Club Med "Family Village" is a very popular stress free way of bringing three generations together. Everyone is free to find their own combination of activity and relaxation.

One great way to maximize "Forever Young" savings is to travel during "Kids Free" periods. Why not take the grandkids off to experience the thrill of joining the circus at either Eleuthera, Sandpiper or Ixtapa? Learning a second language?

What fun to practice in the truly international atmosphere of Caravelle (Guadeloupe). Perhaps you've always wanted to learn to play tennis? No better place than Paradise Island in the Bahamas.

As a mature single traveller, a truly memorable experience can be found at the newest Club Med in Columbus Isle the Bahamas. Forget single supplements; this exceptional upscale village has uniquely designed rooms for singles that are priced 50% below the normal twin share rate.

Whether on your own, or with a friend or relative, Club Med is truly for the young at heart.

PAGE 12 JULY/AUGUST 1995

Figure 6.

Figure 7.

Figure 8.

parks, etc. where, as Graham Rowles says, "every place can be anyplace in an essentially placeless world".[20] Even Club Med, whose traditional appeal is geared more to younger cohorts, profiles "mature" travellers in its advertisement in Figure 6, whose copy reads, "Forever Young, At Club Med life begins at 55". The mobilization of seniors culture also features in the recreational vehicles market. The RoadTrek advertisement in Figure 7 idealizes life on the road with its beautiful surroundings and gourmet picnic. Along with new touristic spaces, new residential communities are springing up and publicized as retirement "escapes", "villages", "havens" and "parks". These terms geographically isolate such environments from real communities which are occupied by a diversity of age groups.[21] However, life in a retirement "village" can also mask the aging process by recasting retirement living as continuously active and problem-free. Hence, new retirement developments, like new touristic landscapes, can have the ironic effect of presenting agehood as an ageless and timeless experience, while making it a separate segment of the lifecourse at the same time.

Often the marketing of seniors culture can best be observed at commercial conventions and trade shows, where retirement and financial consulting, and pharmaceutical and leisure industries, are jointly promoted. One such event I attended in Toronto, The Great Canadian Maturity Show (Toronto

Convention Centre, Fall 1992), was a colourful affair celebrating the democratizing of "seniors" as active and acquiring consumer citizens. (See Figure 8). The bringing together of industry, consumers and images in one place makes these events illuminating indicators of the scope of elder-marketing today.

AGING BY OTHER MEANS

Thus far, this essay has reflected on the commercial construction of seniors culture as a process whereby the interactions of life and lifestyle are shaped by the larger agendas and discourses of consumer society. However, seniors culture is also an opportunity to go beyond the disciplining bounds of consumer practices and ideals – not to defy aging, but to defy positive ageism, subvert its spaces, temporalities and subjectivities and cultivate an alternative politics of representation and living in time, rather than against it. If space permitted, this essay could look at those studies where subversion is the norm rather than the rule, such as the ethnography by Counts and Counts[22] on recreational vehicle usage that demonstrates how a growing number of retirees "on the road" live a rewarding nomadic existence and develop complex social networks. Equally significant are those radical images of aging, such as the powerful photograph of an older woman proudly posing in a bikini found in Brigid Keenan's *The Women We Want to Look Like*,[23] that defy Western society's stereotypes of the aging body. Such images counteract, as well, mainstream ones which Mike Featherstone criticizes for depicting the "elderly as subhuman or para-human beings [who] comprise a suppressed minor strand within consumer culture".[24]

To foster the radical potential of seniors culture, however, we might also consider how innovative metaphors about human aging come from aging in other areas, such as architecture or nature. A text on buildings, for instance, begins with the statement: "Finishing ends construction, weathering constructs finishes".[25] Weathering, while destructive of buildings, also adds to and enhances them by slowing revealing their finishes. Finishes, in turn, do not signify an ending, or an "unending deterioration", but are intrinsic to "the continuous metamorphosis of the building itself, as part of its beginning(s) and its ever-changing 'finish'".[26] The aging of buildings thus inspires us to contemplate not only the beauty and profundity of "weathering" and "finishing" in everyday environments, but also to expand our understanding of human aging by seeing it in other material contexts where time is governed by different movements and meanings.

This reflective exercise prompted me to look around my house to see what kinds of aging (outside of myself) existed. There is my African drum; its outer skin slowly being worn through my years of playing it to reveal

Figure 9.

another skin underneath, a drum-skin that will wear as well and constantly produce new sounds to the drum in the process. There are the cast-iron frying pans in the kitchen that, with use, oiling and care, become better cooking utensils. Aging, again, augments beauty and utility. In my yard, gardening composting bins are reminders that it takes time for compost to age and become the organically powerful and historically vital material that it is. Looking at firewood curing and weathering beside the fireplace encourages thinking about the place of wood in our everyday products and environments, and how we respect its aging and celebrate its endurance. Even a Chicago peace rose in my flowerbed, Figure 9, so-named for the ending of World War II but whose original stock dates from before the war, signals that rose stock has a history and is understood as such by gardeners. A rose is not just a rose, but a gateway to the dynamics between material culture and the contingencies of time; dynamics that, in turn, lead us to confront the commercial spirit of seniors culture and its postmodern timelessness with an eternity of possibilities on how to live and age.

Acknowledgements

I thank the following companies and agencies for their assistance and permission to allow illustrations and extracts to be reproduced in this essay: The Wellcome Institute for the History of Medicine (Figure 1); Mirabella Magazine (Figure 2); Motorola Canada (Figure 3); British Airways (Figure 4); Vupiesse Italia S.A.S (Figure 5); Club Med Sales Inc. (Figure 6); Home & Park Motorhomes (Figure 7); and Patricia Stamp for her photograph of Figure 9. A special thanks is owed to my research assistant, E. Suzanne Peters for her valuable work in locating and collecting images of aging.

---

1. R. N. Butler 1969; 1990.
2. D. Ekerdt 1986, p. 243.
3. H. Moody 1988, p. 238.
4. M. Holstein 1992.
5. T. R. Cole 1986, p. 129; 1992, pp. 227-233.
6. A. Hochschild 1994.
7. Ibid p. 12.
8. M. Dove 1986, p. 98.
9. T. R. Cole 1992, p. 14.
10. See Ph. Ariès 1981; N. Elias 1985.
11. Z. Bauman 1992a, p. 29.
12. Z. Bauman 1992b, p.187.
13. M. Hepworth 1995, p. 190.
14. K. Woodward 1991, p. 161.

15. M. Featherstone 1992, p. 177.
16. M. Featherstone 1995, p. 227.
17. S. During 1997, pp. 828-830.
18. M. Minkler 1991.
19. G. Laws 1995.
20. G. Rowles 1994, p. 122.
21. See also G. Laws, 1996.
22. D.A. Counts and D.R. Counts 1996.
23. B. Keenan 1977, p. 197.
24. M. Featherstone 1995, p. 227.
25. M. Mostafavi and D. Leatherbarrow 1993, p. 5.
26. Ibid p. 15.

Bibliography

Ariès, Philippe. *The Hour of Our Death* (Tr. Helen Weaver). New York: Alfred A. Knopf, 1981.

Bauman, Zygmunt. "Survival as a Social Construct". *Theory, Culture & Society,* 9 (1992a): 1-36.

Bauman, Zygmunt. *Mortality, Immortality & Other Life Strategies.* Cambridge: Polity Press, 1992b.

Butler, Robert N. "Age-Ism: Another Form of Bigotry". *The Gerontologist,* 9 (1969): 143-146.

Butler, Robert N. "A Disease Called Ageism". *Journal of the American Geriatrics Society,* 38 (1990): 178-180.

Cole, Thomas R. "The "Enlightened" View of Aging: Victorian Morality in a New Key". In Thomas R. Cole, & Sally A. Gadow (Eds.), *What Does it Mean to Grow Old? Reflections from the Humanities.* Durham, N.C.: Duke University Press, 1986.

Cole, Thomas R. *The Journey of Life: A Cultural History of Aging in America.* New York: Cambridge University Press, 1992.

Counts, Dorothy Ayers & David R. Counts. *Over the Next Hill: An Ethnography of RVing Seniors in North America.* Peterborough, Ont.: Broadview Press, 1996.

Dove, Mary. *The Perfect Age of Man's Life.* Cambridge: Cambridge University Press, 1986.

During, Simon. "Popular Culture on a Global Scale: A Challenge for Cultural Studies". *Critical Inquiry,* 23 (1997): 808-833.

Ekerdt, David J. *The Busy Ethic: Moral Continuity Between Work and Retirement.* The Gerontologist, 26 (1986): 239-244.

Elias, Norbert. *The Loneliness of the Dying* (Tr. Edmund Jephcott). Oxford: Basil Blackwell, 1985.

Featherstone, Mike. "The Heroic Life and Everyday Life". *Theory, Culture & Society,* 9 (1992): 159-182.

Featherstone, Mike. "Post-Bodies, Aging and Virtual Reality". In Mike Featherstone & Andrew Wernick (Eds.), *Images of Aging: Cultural Representations of Later Life*. London: Routledge, 1995.

Hepworth, Mike "Positive Ageing: What is the Message?" In Robin Bunton, Sarah Nettleton & Roger Burrows (Eds.) *The Sociology of Health Promotion: Critical Analysis of Consumption, Lifestyle and Risk* London: Routledge, 1995.

Hochschild, Arlie Russell. "The Commercial Spirit of Intimate Life and the Abduction of Feminism: Signs from Women's Advice Books". *Theory, Culture & Society,* 11 (1994): 133-149.

Holstein, Martha. "Productive Aging: A Feminist Critique". *Journal of Aging and Social Policy* 4 (1992): 17-34.

Keenan, Brigid. *The Women We Want to Look Like*. London: MacMillan, 1977.

Laws, Glenda. "Embodiment and Emplacement: Identities, Representation and Landscape in Sun City Retirement Communities". *International Journal of Aging and Human Development,* 40 (1995): 253-280.

Laws, Glenda. "A SHOT OF ECONOMIC ADRENALIN": Reconstructing "The Elderly" in the Retiree-Based Economic Development Literature". *Journal of Aging Studies,* 10 (1996): 171-188.

Metchnikoff, Elie. *The Nature of Man: Studies in Optimistic Philosophy*. New York: G.P. Putnam's Sons, 1903.

Metchnikoff, Elie. *The Prolongation of Life: Optimistic Studies* (Tr. P. Chalmers Mitchell). London: William Heinemann, 1907.

Minkler, Meredith. "Gold in Gray: Reflections on Business' Discovery of the Elderly Market". In Meredith Minkler & Carroll L. Estes (Eds.), *Critical Perspectives on Aging: The Political and Moral Economy of Growing Old*. Amityville, N.Y.: Baywood, 1991.

Moody, Harry R. *Abundance of Life: Human Development Policies for an Aging Society*. New York: Columbia University Press, 1988.

Mostafavi, Mohsen & David Leatherbarrow. *On Weathering: The Life of Buildings in Time*. Cambridge, Mass.: The MIT Press, 1993.

Rowles, Graham D. "Evolving Images of Place in Aging". In Dena Shenk & W. Andrew Achenbaum (Eds.), *Changing Perceptions of Aging and the Aged*. New York: Springer, 1994.

Turner, Bryan S. "The Postmodernisation of the Life Course: Towards a New Social Gerontology." *Australian Journal of Ageing*. Vol. 13, (1994): 109-111.

Woodward, Kathleen. *Aging and its Discontents: Freud and Other Fictions*. Bloomington: Indiana University Press, 1991.

Memories, Age and Biographical Discourse

Lene Otto

The problem that gave rise to this article is the way almost all research dealing with age concepts, aging and age relations describes ages of life in general terms without having an eye for different cultural meanings of age. I find it impossible to interpret the historical development in age relations without recognizing the fact that concepts like childhood and old age have completely different life-historical meanings for different cultural groups. We cannot decide whether the general tendency is childhood to become shorter or longer or whether age has become more or less important without paying attention to cultural differences. Rather than searching for general age norms in past and present, one should try to understand how different cultural meanings of age, life-cycle and identity are expressed and maintained.

My thesis is that age should be viewed not as a biological fact but as a discursive construction. In the debate over essentialism almost all forms of knowledge and feelings have been questioned, but it is still very common to maintain that all life ages are endowed with universal characteristics which distinguish them from each other. Here, I will defend an anti-essentialist view and propose to understand age identity as constituted by a 'biographical discourse'. In so doing, I am inspired by the notion of discursive structures which forms the basis for the french scholar Michel Foucault's concept of discipline and which actually constructs objects submitted to discipline. The 'biographical discourse' is my concept for the historical way we deal with and express our personal identity – the historical construction of the life course. My thesis is that biography was invented as an instrument-effect in the spread of bio power; that biography emerged as a central component in a strategy of power which created the individual life course during the nineteenth century. The new historical self-reflection meant a dramatic rise in discussing, writing, and thinking about age and the life-cycle. It became a common belief that, in accounting the story of one's life, one constitutes oneself.

Since the very experience of being a subject across a lifespan and during different ages is an outcome of discursive workings, life stories are an important source for understanding the structure of the modern biographical discourse. In my own research I have explored how age identities are presented in life stories. Specifically, I was interested in how notions of age and the life course were inscribed in identity constructions and reconstructions. I used the narratives as a kaleidoscope through which to reflect on some central questions of autobiography, identity and age.

Since I find discourse just as important to examine as its putative referents, I will start by elaborating on this concept.

THE CONCEPT OF DISCOURSE IN FOUCAULT'S TRADITION

The starting point for the following considerations is the supposition that the concept of life-history has two different cultural meanings:

* life-history as the history of the course of life, that is, as a product of knowledge and power. This perspective implies a historical analysis of age categories within the development of Western society, and

* life-history as stories about the experienced lifetime. This perspective implies an analysis of how individuals structure the self in their written life stories.

My theoretical point is emphasizing that this *does not* imply two different analytical approaches; the reverse is the case. I find it more reasonable to approach them as two sides of the same coin – the same discourse. You may say that cultural order is created and sustained through discursive practices.

So, I want to argue in favour of a method by which people's life-worlds are studied without any assumptions of a dichotomy between what is experienced and what is constructed. Discourse analysis is such a method if we avoid seeing a dualism between the discourse and its reception. I want to avoid the view that experiences of age are one thing and age discourse something else. In contrast, I take the view that people's experiences are not outside discourse but part of it. Accordingly, in Western culture at least, we are living for the first time in a period in which people of different ages are regarding themselves as young, adult, old etc., that is, as possessing a problematic 'age identity'.

This stands contrast to the widespread view, that common people's lives and conceptual worlds are in opposition to the state and professional discourse. The Durkhemian dichotomy between the individual and society, in which the individual's behaviour is subjugated to society's systems of classification, die hard. I will argue that it is a false dualism to distinguish between the concept and its supposed effects. Individual identity is not formed in *contrast* to societal knowledge; rather, identity *presupposes* societal knowledge. Accordingly, 'popular concepts' and 'professional concepts' are not independent opposites. I find it more reasonable to approach them as two sides of the same question. The experience of individuality *presupposes* concepts, and they are used to express experiences and feelings of identity. In this way the concept and the content is not separated. Concepts chart out and help shape reflexivity and feelings of self-identity and personal autonomy. The concepts of ages of life order life and time, at the same time both representing and changing life. They are discursive. New kinds of subjectivity are produced through discursive practices, the way Foucault has analysed it in several books.[1] He argues, that knowledge and power directly imply one another. Accordingly, the exercise of power itself creates and causes to emerge age differences as new objects of knowledge.

One more point has to be made clear; discourse are not artefacts, but an analytical tool used by the researcher. When I refer to a 'biographical discourse' in the following, it is my concept of the growing concern about the life course. This discourse can be traced in memories, in scientific works as well as in everyday practice. Discourse is everywhere, in our thinking as well as in the organization of our society.

Biographical discourse

Both scientific knowledge about people's life-times and their personal experiences are part of what Michel Foucault viewed as the imperative to tell the truth. Foucault argues that specialists producing discourse within institutional settings are a manifestation of a 'will to truth' constantly growing stronger and deeper.[2] Scientific knowledge and peoples initiating urge to understand themselves and to deal with their own life – the autobiographical consciousness – are not oppositions, but part of the same discourse. As I see it, biographical practices create and control subjects because the "turning of real lives into writing"[3] from the beginning was a disciplinary method in that the child, the patient, the madman and the prisoner were the objects of individual descriptions and biographical accounts. With the growth of the technology of control and observation, a new curiosity arose about the ordinary individuality[4] which had been entirely unknown at the beginning of the eighteenth century.

Biographical discourse trained people to acquire a "hermeneutics of experience" and in that way to become a the self-contained individual, which now is the standard of psychology. Consequently, experiences, age consciousness and memory are topics we ourselves feel to be located at the level of the individual. It seems to us that they are private events – private in the sense of originating within us and being available only to us by introspection. It is a new phenomenon, that occupation with one's own life – one's biography – has become an obligation and not just an opportunity. We construct reality biographically, and we live our lives biographically. The personal narrative has replaced the former identification with family, class, rank or political ideology.

BIOGRAPHICAL DISCOURSE AND THE STATE

It is possible to locate the origin of biographical discourse in the state. What is characteristic of modern power is the construction of a subjectivity we may term individualism, in which we search for meaning of life in our own life. The interest in biography – ages and the life cycle – do not grow out of the individuals themselves, on the contrary, individuality is constituted by biographical discourse. I do not believe in the existence of a universal psychological incentive, a basic need to know oneself. On the contrary, the need to know one's inner self is created by Christianity and fully developed by state government during the nineteenth century. At that time the individual not only became a possibility but also a necessity. People were forced to become free individuals and were expected to make something out of life. The reflexive project of the self is both emancipatory and coercive. One fulfils oneself as subject and is constituted as object.

Foucault himself, contrary to his teacher Louis Althusser[5], was not willing to admit the state a determining role in the development of ideology. Actually, he was not at all concerned about the state as an institution, but rather with what he terms governmentality – tactics which allow the state to survive. Without it the social world would not and could not exist. Although he agrees that power relations historically have become increasingly linked to state control, he refuses to accept that they can be reduced to state apparatuses, the way Althusser sees it.

Following Foucault, I understand biographical discourse as part of a tactic which allows the state to survive. It is a manner in which the political structures of the state relate to the construction of definite forms of individualization, and this type of governmentality does not simply command subjects, but rather looks after each individual during their lifetime. In Foucault's words, it is a kind of power dependent on knowing people's minds and exploring their souls[6]. This pastoral power has, according to Foucault, ramified and spread into secular forms of the modern state.

The modern way of government is total compared to the absolutist state. The actual power of the monarch over the daily lives of the subject population in the absolutist state was in one respect total: power over life or death. On the other hand, its degree of effective penetration throughout the population remained relatively low. The kind of subjectivity produced by sovereign power was essentially one based on ritual and commemoration of the type found in family trees, portraits, statues, noble tombs, etc. In such a manner the rich and the powerful were subjectified, the great mass of the population remaining anonymous unless transgressing the law. In contrast, discipline, the manner in which the emerging industrial societies of the capitalist West provide subjection, creates subjects of everyone. Power does not just operate on a few tortured bodies to serve as an example but radiates throughout the entire society, creating subjects and simultaneously subjecting. A insidious process producing subjects who will make the most of their lives.

Looking at relationships between the formation of the modern state in the 19th century and the individual life course, it becomes clear that the state creates conditions which single out the individual both as the object of state activity and as a distinctive, self-reliant actor. Legal rationality establishes the individual as the prime holder of rights and duties and as the prime target of bureaucratic acts. The individual person as a subject is different from other subjects in the state (families, guilds or corporations), because the individual has an existence limited in time. This makes biological existence an important condition of modern subjectivity. The state must produce individuals, whose lives become worthwhile. We are obliged to fulfil our political role as individual subjects through different phases of the life course as if we were seeking to realize our own desires. So, in the modern state, age becomes a necessary part of the concept of person. Actually, personhood can be viewed as synonymous with life-course. The individual, independent of age, is recognized by the state and incorporated in society as a life course.

The concept of age is therefore related to the concept of personhood, meaning recognized as a person. I do not think, that the modern preoccupation with chronological age is a way of separating groups which are not recognized as persons; rather, age-grading is an element in the construction of individual life stories that recognizes personal identity, independent of age. This way all ages of the life course are implicated in the concept of person. Subsequently, age differentiation is a process in which individuals of all ages become subjects. Children are not the property of their parents alone; they have a right to survive, granted by the state. Today all age groups are recognized as subjects with civil rights, even the unborn foetus. The discursive construction of age is a way of extending the concept of person; you are recognized as citizen independent of age, and all age groups have the right to be under protection of the state. Hence, biographical discourse played an important part in the creation of a new form of subjectivity, or new dimensions of subjectivity, especially 'personality' and 'ages'. This new 'biographical subjectivity' was grasped in thought and utilized in practice. With the development of new languages for speaking about subjectivity, and new techniques for inscribing it, measuring it, and acting upon it, individuals as well as society came to perceive life as consisting of a sequence of phases which are different from each other in some important respects.

THE BIOGRAPHICAL DISCOURSE AND LIFE STORIES

Different forms of written self-reference, referred to as personal memories, autobiographies and life stories should not just be regarded as individual, but also as cultural products. Due to my method of analysis, I regard written memories not as private recollections, but as representations of biographical discourse. Individual life stories at the same time reflect and shape biographical discourse.

The concept of 'classical' autobiography is based on the idea of a unified self, but there are other forms of self-reference that are not so oriented toward the inner personality. This is the case with popular biographies, still I regard them as representations of the biographical practice – the duty to be the biographer of our own life, to understand it, order it and create meaning and sense and relate life events which are otherwise isolated. By interpreting life stories, we learn about 'the biographical discourse' and about the ways in which discourse makes sense in the author's different cultural worlds.

The following reflections are based on my study of life stories from an archive in the Danish National Museum called Ethnological Surveys (Nationalmuseets Etnologiske Undersøgelser). The archive was founded in 1939. It contains several hundred 'popular autobiographies' or autobiographical accounts from individuals from all social groups. Most of the life stories are written independently of any requests from the museum.

The authors of my sample of life stories are all born between 1890 and 1920 and they wrote their life stories sometime between 1960 and 1980. That means that they reconstruct their lives from the perspective of old age. Central among the various motivations for writing is its therapeutic value in the face of the crisis and the isolation of old age, and its fulfillment of a need to see one's life as part of the great chain of generations. The primary criterion for selecting my sources was the extent to which a particular account comprised a 'total' life story.

DIFFERENT CULTURAL MEANINGS OF AGE AND THE LIFE COURSE IN POPULAR BIOGRAPHIES

It is common knowledge that it is impossible for anyone to give an accurate account of their own past existence or the development of their personality, because memory is both selective and deforming. Such accounts should be understood as authentic rather than 'true', since the process of bringing to mind the lived life in a written form is, of course, a selective one. Out of the endless play of experiences, the author is selecting and establishing only certain connections.

It is generally recognized that our view of our own life history is determined by the way we perceive our present. Our own prehistory is constructed by concepts and problems provided by the present. I assume that such concepts and values are a product of cultural life-modes[7]. The ethnological study of life-modes is wellsuited for analysis of the ideological conceptions and everyday practices of various groups. It takes its point of departure in the assumption that society contains distinct cultural life-modes, each of which constitutes its own mode of existence and universe of concepts, with a Hegelian inspiration called praxis. This theory operates with three distinct basic life-modes: the self-employed life-mode, the wage-earner life-mode and the career professional life-mode.

As individual persons we operate in our praxis with different conceptual systems which determine how life is understood and which blind us to each other's way of seeing. Even though we may speak the same language, we use it to make sense of and express fundamentally different conceptual worlds. Since individual words are used with quite different cultural meanings, you need theoretical concepts to apprehend, that apparently identical words do not have the same semantic meaning. They reflect the differences in life-modes.

Understanding these different cultural conceptual worlds has proved important when analysing personal memories to find out how people divide life into culturally relevant units, and what specific meanings are attributed to different life phases. In the following interpretation I will highlight contrasts in ways life and age are perceived in different life-modes.

The Life-Mode of the Self-Employed is the core of a simple commodity production unit like a family farm or a small artisan shop. It is not structured according to economic relations but rather according to ideological social relations often in the form of family ties[8]. In a family enterprise, the prime concern is to keep production going and assure a future in self-employment for the children. There is no clear distinction between time of work and free time. Free time has no meaning. You are never free from work, because you are never put to work. Personal involvement is the prerequisite for and indeed the essence of being self-employed. It is not an old-fashioned life-mode, even though it is undoubtedly the case that this life-mode was more wide-spread in the period when the authors of the memoirs went through their life course which is in the first half of this century.

In this life-mode, life, like work, is conceived of as a whole, not as a succession of phases with new beginnings. In a way life is not divided in past, present and future. The future is part of the present, because life is part of a much bigger generational project. The meaning of life transcends individual life, in family and kinship. A common form of expressing the close relationship of one's own life to genealogical and regional structures is represented in a model of autobiographical writing, which in the literature is often called 'family chronicle'. This type of life story is known to be typical of nineteenth-century autobiographies but I have found that they are very common in this century too, especially among the self-employed. The life story is not created around the 'self', but rather stories of the family, the village of birth and the personal life are interwoven. The individual 'self' is integrated into, and completely subordinated to, a kind of collective family memory. Often the narrative of the author's own life story starts late in the document, sometimes even expressed grammatically in the third person.

In one of the life stories in my material representing this life-mode, a former farmer writes about his life as if life was laid out before him, he does not view his life as a result of choices.

> "When one gets old and look back upon life as it was lived over seventy years, I'm not actually able to identify any sharp corners or cross roads, at which it was a matter of choosing the right way to go".

His view of life is almost holistic, not divided in phases. Consequently, childhood is not remembered as being 'another country', which is typical for this life-mode, but in contrast to other life-modes in which the meaning of childhood is it's otherness. It is related to the fact that the life-mode of the self-employed implies that children from their earliest years are involved in its practical functions, so childhood is not one's personal property.

I find that people in this life-mode remember (or construct) two major transitions in life in this life-mode. The first is the transition from childhood to youth, the other is from youth to adulthood. The reason for this could be that it is only in this life-mode that we find a well-defined period of youth, with its own end and concerns. Youth, in this life-mode, is a transition period where full adulthood is gradually obtained. You are not able to have a household of your own until knowledge in many different areas is acquired. In the life stories you rarely see the actual words 'my youth' expressed, but still a period characterised by working for others and gradually learning what is needed is distinct in many life stories. Even though they were away from home and economically independent on their parents at an early age, nobody recognized them as adults. They were young and therefore had their own tasks and social relations. Furthermore, their income was not their personal property, it was used to pay for brothers' and sisters' education etc. In this period young people were free of surveillance but not at all living an independent life in a modern sense. The author mentioned above is one of the very few writers from this generation who identify a stage called youth, lasting from his 20th to his 28th year. He recalls these years as a period of restlessness. He was waiting for his father to retire and decide who was to take over the family farm. Brothers and sisters were dependent on each other, they could not plan their own future life course independently of each other.

Although incorporation into adult life in this life-mode is successive, adulthood is not fully accomplished until marriage. That is why marriage is considered the other major transition in life, often combined with having own property. When self-employment is the aim of life, marriage is at the same time the means to become self-employed and part of the purpose. One author, who is a farmer, express it this way: "Now we were two persons, who wished to work together, and the road we wanted to take was given".

Old age is not a sudden break of working life, but rather, like youth, it is a transition period with slow withdrawal. A substantial part of life is concerned with chosing the right time to retire and make room for the next generation. To retire and become 'former' is the object of all efforts, not a traumatic experience of being redundant. Identity in this life-mode is not dependent on age. Consider the following passage from an author, who always signs himself 'former farmer'.

> "From July 1st, 1959, I was not a farmer any more, but life at the farm went on as usual. Now it was my son who had the income and had to meet the expenses, but my wife still did all the housework and prepared the meals as usual".

In *the Life-mode of the Wage-earner* the meaning of life is not found in work, as in the case of the self-employed; the 'good Life' is outside of work, during time off. This way, work is merely a means for earning free time. Consequently, life is in a way divided into a work-life and a family-life. Work doesn't presuppose an overall perspective and this is also characteristic of the life-view in this life-mode, which is more divided in phases and ages.

For people representing this life-mode, whose existence is primarily dependent on their manual labour and therefore their body, life stories are often preoccupied with their physical existence. Identity is bound up with the body. In opposition to the self-employed the use of 'I' is common in life stories written by people of working-class and lower-peasant background. I will argue, that the grammatical use of 'first person' has to do with this physical identity rather than a psychological identity. This is further supported by the extensive use of chronology in these life stories, which I interpret as establishing a kind of order and coherence, different from the order of the development of a personal self.

It seems as if changes in life are related to the body, not to personal development. This is expressed in the way childhood is described. It is as if the child is another person independent of the person who is telling the life story. The concept of childhood in this life-mode can be summarized not as a phase of preparation, but as a *contrast* to adulthood, as a period of life symbolizing the real life of free time, free of obligations. Because this early phase has no biographical meaning, childhood narratives are often filled out with myths and narrative conventions.

In life stories, written by people representing this life-mode, 'youth' was hardly a distinctive stage in the beginning of this century. It was undistinguishable from adulthood. Confirmation plays an important role in these life stories. I think this is because the ritual is both a symbolic and a real transition to adulthood, meaning the ability to support oneself. Since the meaning of adulthood depends upon neither qualifications nor personal development, confirmation as a ritual transformation from child to adult is meaningful in this life-mode.

> "My confirmation day was one of the most beautiful experiences I had… But the next day the rules were tightened: Remember now, you are an adult! No more trying to get around things. Well, I had looked forward to leaving home, to earn my own living, everything would be a lot better".

Since the essence of adulthood seems to be self-support and hard work, to become an adult is knowing the value of one's own labour and to be able to negotiate one's wage.

> "My father wanted me to stay home over the summer to help out… But I wanted a wage for it, which he couldn't promise, but by now I knew exactly what my work was worth, and that whetted my appetite. He had to ask my younger brothers".

In many life stories the first wage is remembered as a point of transition because of the strong feeling of self-dependence it caused. I have quite a few examples embodying careful descriptions of the feeling of equality generated by the ability to pay for a sister's new dress or his mother's coffee and cake in a restaurant.

In this life-mode old age is similar to childhood in the way it is viewed in contrast to adulthood. In old age time is again your own and can be filled with leisure activities. This view of old age is used as a general definition of old age, but I am convinced that it is specific for this life-mode. For a wage earner who is not very engaged in his work, old age is not conceived as marking a stop but rather a new beginning. One writer puts it this way.

"Three years later I was old enough to become 'employed by the state', I mean to receive pension. That is all there is to say about that. I don't understand how I got the time to go to work before".

It is characteristic for *the Life-Mode of the Carrier Professionals* that they are not paid for the time spent at work. Rather they are individually hired on the basis of their particular qualifications and loyalty to the firm. Statistically speaking, this life-mode is steadily increasing, but it was not very common in my period of study. The essence of life is to strive to make demands on oneself, improve qualifications and surpass colleagues, who at best are competitors on the way up through the hierarchy.

The concept of life in this success-oriented life-mode is advancement. The aim of life is neither self-employment nor extensive leisure time. The concept of leisure time is rather fictitious, because work is an involvement. In life stories the personality and personal abilities are in focus. Life is regarded as a task and the actual life course is viewed as a result of personal choices. Accidental occurrences have no meaning; you take responsibility for your own life. If life is a failure, it is because of your own short-comings, because you didn't make the right choices. Just as success is your own doing, so is failure.

Identity is inseparable from personal abilities. The phases of life are regarded as stages of development. You are an adult when your personal abilities defy competition, when your qualifications are optimal. To be an adult is to be unique. Life is conceptualized as divided into many stages but with only one major transition, namely from childhood to adulthood. In this life-mode it is a problem knowing *when* you are a grown up. This comes about because, since neither functional age nor biological age has any meaning, you expect an inner transformation or fulfilment.

I see a tendency in the memoires to remember being a child not as being different but rather as being incomplete. As a result, childhood is the period of life in which the future is sketched and life takes a direction. This way childhood is closely related to adulthood. As a child you were already you. In life stories told by people with carrier jobs it seems important to draw attention to the continuity between the child and the grown up. All activities are part of the same plan. Retrospectively all events are interpreted teleologically, leading in one direction.

Differentiating between biographical meaning and chronological meaning, I will argue that youth is inseparable from childhood in this lifemode and consequently, confirmation has no biographical meaning, because it is not a transitional event. Looked at from the outside, you can argue that youth in the life mode of the carrier professional is a long period, because the nature of unique qualifications is that it takes a long time before you are recognized as 'one among equals'. On the other hand, I will argue that youth as a distinct stage has no meaning, because it has no biographical meaning. The same is true regarding old age, which is not different from adulthood. Even when you retire you continue to do what you have always done, that is to acquire new skills.

To sum up, even if we see life stories as part of biographical discourse creating subjectivity, it is not in opposition to cultural analysis aimed at understanding different cultural meanings of age and the life course. In the generation born early in the 20th century, people from the self-employed life-mode identified two life-historical important transitions, namely when they entered the stage of youth, and years later, when they became adults. Marriage was equivalent to entering into adulthood. In the wage-earner life-mode there was not a stage of youth which was distinct from adulthood. The transition remembered was from childhood to adulthood, which merged with confirmation. Thus, confirmation was not a symbol, but rather a real mile-stone. The next important transition was retirement. Pensions were a new benefit for this generation, and made old age an attractive stage of pure leisure time. In the carrier professional life-mode, where life is conceptualized as a career, people do not remember youth as seperated from childhood, which is due to the fact that in this life-mode, the only important transition is from non-adult to adulthood.

Theoretically, I have been concerned about the manner in which individuals turn themselves into subjects. In a sense, this is the opposite side of the coin and complementary to those external practices analysed by Foucault as discipline. My point was, that popular biographies do not just describe an individual's personal experiences. The concept of biographical discourse enables you to understand experiences of life and age not just as psychological phenomenon, but rather as cultural constructs.

---

1. See e.g. M. Foucault 1982.
2. M. Foucault 1970.
3. M. Foucault 1977.
4. Until then the chronicle of a man, the account of his life was a privilege, a procedure of heroisation, rather than a procedure of subjection.
5. L. Althusser 1972.
6. M.Foucault 1982.
7. For an introduction to the ethnological concept of life-modes see T. Højrup 1983.
8. This means that family has a very distinct meaning, it has an economic function.

Bibliography
Althusser, Louis. *Politics and History*. London: New Left Books, 1972.

Foucault, Michel. "The Order of Discourse" (1970), repr. in: R.Young (ed.) *Untying the Text*, Boston: Routledge & Kegan Paul,1981.

Foucault, Michel. *Discipline and Punish: The Birth of the Prison,* London: Allen Lane, 1977.

Foucault, Michel. *The History of Sexuality.* Vol. 1: An introduction, Penguin, Harmondsworth, 1979a.

Foucault, Michel. "Governmentality" in *Ideology and Consciousness* 6 (1979b): 5-21.

Foucault, Michel. "The Subject and Power" Afterword to H. Dreyfus and P. Rabinow *Michel Foucault: Beyond structuralism and Hermeneutics.* Brighton: Harvester 1982.

Højrup, Thomas. "The Concept of Life-Mode. A Form-Specifying Mode of Analysis Applied to Contemporary Western Europe". *Ethnologia Scandinavica,* 1983.

Meyer, C. "The Self and the Life Course: Institutionalization and its Effects". in A. Sørensen, F. Weinert, and L. Sherrod (eds), *Human Development and the Life Course,* Hillsdale, NJ: L. Erlbaum, 1986.

Otto, Lene and L. Pedersen. "Collecting Oneself. Life stories and Objects of Memory". *Ethnologia Scandinavica,* 1998.

Rose, Nicolas. "Calculable minds and manageable individuals". *History of the Human Sciences* 1 (1988).

II

Age in Practice

A World of Their Own Making:

Families and the Modern Culture of Aging

John R. Gillis

Since the middle of the nineteenth century western societies have been living with not one but two kinds of time, one quantifiable and linear, the other qualitative and cyclical. Objectified and externalized in the ticking of the clock and the turning pages of our calendars, linear time is divided into standard units, each with its own distinct beginning and ending. Cyclical time also has its moments, but they cannot be standardized. While linear time is irreversible and is forever lost to us, cyclical time can be slowed, stopped, and even reversed.[1] Linear time is the product of the imperatives of the modern economy and the nation state; and nothing is beyond its reach, including families. But families have learned to live with linear time by creating their own kinds of cyclical time to compensate for ephemerality and fragmentation that has resulted from what David Harvey has called modernity's "time-space compression", that acceleration in the pace of life that has resulted in what is now commonly referred to as "time famine".[2]

I have come to think about these two dimensions as the time we live *with* – reified and objectified – and the time we live *by* – internalized and subjective.[3] Aging is subject to the same duality. On one hand, age is subject to externalized and objectified standards generated by the the imperatives of a modern consumer economy and the bureaucratic nation state. Yet, aging is also a subjective process, which everyone tries to accelerate, slow, even reverse. When we tell children "act your age", we are implicitly recognizing the dual dimension of the aging process. The fact that children cannot demand the same of adults suggests that there is a micro-political, as well as a social dimension to aging.

During the past decade or so, our understanding of time has been dramatically altered. Once a given, against which social scientists and historians clocked and calendared their subjects, time has been significantly problematized and shown to be constituative of social relations of all kinds. As Barbara Adam puts it, time is "simultaneously abstracted and reified, experienced and constituted."[4] We can observe a similar shift in our understanding of aging, which is now also seen as something which, while reified, is also experienced subjectively. It is possible now to speak about the ages we live *with*, abstracted and reified, and those we live *by*, experienced and culturally constructed.

I want to focus here on the role that families have in the constituting both the ages we live *with* and those we live *by*. Family birthdays and anniversaries number our days, providing us with very precise beginnings and endings that get us through our tightly scheduled modern lifetimes. But even as these occasions remind us of the inevitability of the aging process and the ultimate finitude of our lives, they are also rituals which connect us with others, even the unborn and the dead, providing us with what David Cheal has aptly called "convoys" of persons with whom we share the seasons of our lives, who help us through the best and the worst of times.[5] Those convoys are constituted for the most part by family members, or by close friends who are treated as family. As Kerry Daly has noted: "Individual time and family time are closely synchronized, for most individual transitions are related to family transitions."[6]

In this respect, the aging of children and older people are inseparable. Children do not come by aging naturally. As the history of age will show, children are endowed with ages, increasingly refined and precise, by adult society. Nor is aging a natural phenomenon for older people. Adults age with children. In modern society, parents sense how old they are in relationship to the age of their offspring. The transitions to and within grandparenthood are similarly dependent. Just as the histories of old age and childhood are inseparable, so are the identities of the young and the old. The ages we *live by* are the product largely of the symbolic interaction among family members, as these are enacted through a variety of family times.

Even as they acknowledge the finitude of time, family times shield us against its terrors by convincing us, despite the evidence of clock and calendar, of a certain permanence and continuity in all things human. The same is true of all family occasions – confirmations, bar and bat mitzvahs, weddings, graduations, and retirement parties – which mark the passing of linear time but also connect past, present, and future, slowing, stopping, even reversing time, if only for a moment.

Ironically, modern families teach the very linear notions of age and generation which are the cause of so much discomfort to themselves. Other modern institutions manage to survive the aging and death of their members by treating them as replaceable, but families do not operate according to the same principles.[7] The aging and death of its members represent losses for which families have developed compensatory rituals – anniversaries and memorials – illustrating T.S. Eliot's observation that "only through time, time is conquered."[8]

Yet, none of these rites, as currently practiced, are more than a hundred fifty years old. I will be arguing that in the course of the nineteenth and twentieth centuries family has displaced religion and community as western culture's chief creator of times out of time, giving us the set of hidden rhythms that we now live by. So accustomed have we become to thinking of family times as a natural part of our cultural landscape that we are not even aware of their functions or their origins. We think of them as old when in fact they are relatively new. In order to put the record straight and to understand our own complex relationship with aging, we need to think of family time(s) not as an immutable part of nature, but as the product of history, changing even as we speak.

I

Virtually all of ways we number our days are relatively recent. To be sure, the real time that people in the preindustrial past had at their disposal was very different from the time we have available today. Before the middle of the nineteenth century, Europeans and Americans lived on average only two thirds the number of years we do, but, equally significant, they never knew when to expect the grim reaper, for mortality came to every age group and not just preponderantly to the elderly as it does today. While their lives were shorter and more uncertain, they did not necessarily hanker after the longevity that we have come to crave, for the understanding of time they had available to them allowed them to live with their allotted time, gave meaning to lives which seem to us nasty, brutish, and short. They imagined the end to be near, yet death did not hang over them as it does over us, for they accepted mortality and could imagine an immortality beyond time itself, while we, unable to accept mortality, have substituted longevity for eternity. "The price of exchanging immortality for health", Zygmunt Bauman has pointed out, "is life lived in the shadow of death; to postpone death, one needs to surrender life to fighting it. "Modernity", he notes, "deconstructed mortality one cannot overcome into a series of afflictions one can".[9]

Able to imagine something beyond time, something eternal, preindustrial society was able to disconnect aging and death from biology as such. Aging meant to them something very different than it does for us.[10] It was understood that one could age spiritually at a rate quite different from that by which one aged biologically. "Just as we speak of bodily age, whereby we proceed from infancy to boyhood … and so forth … so spiritual age is a progress from virtue to virtue, from grace and grace, from good to better, from perfection to greater perfection" wrote one fourteenth century English bishop.[11] We have great difficulty imagining aging apart from the physical body, but preindustrial generations had no difficulty accepting the miracle of the *infantia spiritualis*, the holy or wise child, or the child prodigy. For the same reasons, they were prepared to believe stories of persons living hundreds of years.[12]

All peoples attempt to form temporal convoys, groups sharing a common sense of time, sustaining one another through the difficulties of life's journey.[13] In the preindustrial past, temporal convoys were provided largely by church and community. The models of aging that people lived by were not provided by their relatives or even their friends, but by religious archetypes and communal exemplars. Church and community also provided the rites of passage between one phase of life and another, as well as the models of the good life and the good death. They launched the temporal convoys that allowed earlier generations to pilot through the rough seas of time to the safe harbor with God in an eternity beyond time itself.

Preindustrial families did not celebrate their members' births, mark anniversaries, or commemorate in the way we do. It was not that they were less caring, but they found themselves in convoy with a larger circle.[14] The Catholic church provided a huge repertoire of saintly aging and dying. Believers remembered the birthdays of saints, and ignored their own. Protestants abandoned the saints and organized their convoys of mere mortals, but not necessarily of members of their own families. The life transitions – birth, marriage, and death – that we think of as family occasions, were conducted communally. Individual and family were not yet synchronized, for, before the 1840s, there was as yet no concept of family time.

In the seventeenth and eighteenth centuries, the masters and mistresses of godly households were providing most of the images of the good life and the good death for Protestant Europe and North America. This put a great burden on a relatively few persons, but as long as they were willing to act out their assigned roles in the great public passages of life – birth, marriage, and death – this gave the rest of the population reassuring images to live by.

The understanding of time that premodern Europe and America lived with was very different from our own. It did not stretch infinitely into past or future, but has been described as a "closed medium in which events in succession were dominated by the specter of human mortality." Sir Thomas Browne, whose own life spanned almost seventy years in the seventeenth century, understood time in the following manner:[15]

"Think not thy time short in this world, since the world itself is not long. The created world is but a small parenthesis in eternity: and a short imposition, for a time, between such a state of duration as was before it and may be after it."

It was God's, not man's time that Europeans and Americans lived with and by before the nineteenth century. Its image was that of the wheel, endlessly turning. Life was also seen as a cycle from womb to tomb, not as a linear development through a fixed set of ages ending with death as we would conceive it. Imagined as a wheel of fortune, life was perceived as being unpredictable, as "nothing so endless, nothing sooner broke."[16] No matter how old you were you were equidistant from death, that unpredictable event which broke the cycle to open the way to eternal life.[17] Birth and death were things that simply happened. In an era before anyone had the power to control birth or postpone death, both could be awaited but not anticipated. Time was not man's to give, and any attempt to do so was a challenge to the divine will. By and large, people were content to live in what Saint Augustine called the "present of things present."[18]

Numerical age had little meaning for most people before the nineteenth century. Time, measured out in quantitative units of years, months, weeks, and days mattered less to both the individual and the community.[19] Time and age had not yet separated themselves from place, so that, while most rural people could not tell their numerical age with any great precision, they could make rough calculations of how young or old a person was by his or her relationship to certain remembered events – a saint's day, a flood, a harvest. In rural England time was still be counted in the same way as late as the First World War, where children, asked to give their birthdays, replied:[20]

"Our Charlie's birthday is when they cuts the corn, and Alice's is when they ears the corn."

For most of humanity prior to the industrial era age was never an absolute, but always relative to a person's place in the world. Birthdays and anniversaries were something that only the aristocracy were entitled to. The rest of mankind had their ages defined for them. Ages of entry into work and school varied enormously; and even the lives of children of the same family followed very different paths.[21] The middle years had no set pattern either; and the age of retirement varied hugely, ranging from the from the 30s through the 80s.[22] Numerical age also had very little effect on the decision to marry. None seemed nervous about precocity before the nineteenth century; and, while access to power and wealth was generally regulated by rules of seniority, nobody objected when prodigies stepped out of line of succession.[23] People "aged" suddenly as they changed places in the social order. A young man or woman automatically became an adult upon marriage regardless of years, just as retirement from the head of a household brought sense of loss that had nothing to do with physical capacity as such. Children were taught to prepare for their deaths at very early ages, but they also learned to be ready for any contingency. Junior members of a family found themselves instantly transformed into elders upon the death or retirement of their parents. Prematurity was a condition of existence that did not unduly bother contemporaries. "In a culture that valued eternal life rather than eternal youth, this preference is not surprising," writes historian Thomas Cole, "Transcending one's age allowed a person to triumph over secular time, to enter into the timeless world of eternity."[24]

II

With the onset of the industrial revolution, the chronotype of the small parenthesis bracketed by eternity was displaced by the notion of a fleeting present, located along an arrow of time between a vanishing past and a looming future. In the course of the nineteenth century, western societies underwent a process of temporal standardization that Martin Kohli has called chronologization.[25] The imposition of numerically standardized linear times and ages was partly the result of capitalist industrialization, with its emphasis on mechanization and synchronization, but no less important was the emergence of the modern nation state, which constituted its identity by creating a uniform timescape as well as a uniform territory.[26]

Numerical age consciousness became the signature of modernity, first with the middle classes and later with the rest of European and North American society. Infants were taught their age almost as soon as they were able to speak. Knowing one's age became the earliest sign of comprehension, while forgetting it became a sure sign of dementia.[27] Historical demographers have been able to show how the ages of going to school, entering work, getting married, and establishing families became ever more standardized in the period 1870-1970.[28] Variations in the retirement ages of men also tended to narrow as people internalized certain ages as the standard for their own behavior. Not only were the ages in which people did things becoming more standardized, but so too were the sequences in which they did them. In earlier periods, young people thought nothing of moving back and forth between school and work, but by 1900 the flow was going all in one direction.[29] Science and medicine had taught western society to think of aging as part of nature's laws. In order not to appear unnatural, everyone did their utmost to act their age from birth to death.[30]

The ideal of living a long, productive life ceased to be a vehicle for spiritual journey and became an end in itself. In the second half of the nineteenth century longevity replaced eternity as primary goal of life; and acting one's age took precedence over the spiritual quest. Previously, old age was a sign of sanctification; now longevity itself was sanctified.[31] By the beginning of our century western civilisation was no longer running on God's time, but man's. Age, like time, was no longer seen as a gift of God, but now both time and age were seen as a kind of private property, capital which, when used well and invested correctly, would produce more time and better aging, but when used badly could bring failure and humiliation.[32] By 1900 science and medicine were called in to assist individuals in aging properly.[33] Consistent with the needs of a capitalist economy and the nation state, new norms of aging began to affect actual behavior, so that in this century what was the product of history came to be seen as an imperative of nature. Until the 1960s, age was endowed quality with the same quality of giveness as time itself, obscuring but by no means eliminating the contradictions and problems it created.

III

In fact, the Victorian middle classes were first to experience the acceleration of the pace of life, and the accompanying sense of "time famine" that is so much on everyone's mind today. The very people who invented industrial time were finding it impossible to live with it. Work time removed men from the household; school time removed children. Even as families grew rich materially, they found themselves time poor. And the less time families had together, the more certain times came to matter to them. As time grew scarce, symbolic time loomed ever larger. Victorian families were the first to feel the need for what we now call "quality time." In response, they invented a wholly new repertoire of daily, weekly, and annual occasions which we now regard as "family time," ritualized occasions through which family members not only synchronized their time, but created unique temporal convoys. By 1900 the middle class calendar was crowded with family times – birthdays, weddings, graduations, anniversaries, Christmasses, and memorial services – rituals which had not even existed a half century earlier.

The anthropologist Barbara Myerhoff reminds us that "by stating enduring and underlying patterns, ritual connects past, present, and future, abrogating history and time; ritual always links participants one to another and often beyond, to wider collectivities that may be absent, even to ancestors and those yet unborn."[34] The convoys that church and community had once created were now provided by family. Baptisms initiating a series of birthday celebrations focused on the child, but also determined the parents' sense of their own aging. Weddings took on the same cultural function, with the result that the life transition of one family member affected the life experience of every other. As death rates declined and more parents survived to see their own children grow up and have their own children, intergenerational connections became stronger than ever. By the mid-twentieth century, families were generating connections with both the dead and the unborn, creating for themselves a sense of collective immortality that effectively replaced older religious notions of eternity.

The family occasions the Victorians created were an ingenious effort to cope with the fleeting sense of time that families themselves were complicitous in generating. We still rely on these rites to create the time we live by, turning each birthday and anniversary into moments of premonition and memory. Earlier generations could find reassuring images of the good life beyond time in eternity or in the timeless archetypes provided by community, but, because we insist on thinking of ourselves as linear beings, each with his or her own biography, each with a unique family history, we can never escape our finitude and are tempted to turn all events into ritual and image, all history into myth in order to give ourselves a little of that sense of permanence and connection that linear time denies us.

IV

By the late twentieth century, families have become central agents in the creation of both the time we live *with* and that we live *by*. Families not only teach time, but manage it. This vital work is largely unpaid; and not surprisingly delegated to women, whose time is thought to be less valuable than men's and thus at the disposal of the family. Women are not only modernity's kinkeepers, they are also its timekeepers, subject to greater stress than men when it comes to time and aging. For while men may spend time with family, women spend time on it. Not only are they assigned the tasks of managing the diminishing amounts of time families live with, but they are also the chief creators of the time families live by – meal times, birthdays, weddings, holidays. For men, these times are leisure, but for women they are work, work disguised as an activity that is supposed to come naturally to women.[35]

In the last two decades, families have had to live on ever shorter time rations. Rising female employment takes time from family; and, in America at least, the employed are working ever longer hours. The reappearance of child and adolescent labor is another cause of time scarcity.[36] Even the best time management techniques leave families feeling they have lost control over the time of their members, a situation reflected in conflicts between parents and children, and between spouses.

V

And as goes time, so goes age. The past two decades have experienced what might be call a dechronologicization, a loosening of the previously tight standards and sequences of aging. There is no longer any consensus about right ages to do things. Surveys showed agreement over the '"best" age of first marriage dropping from 90% in the 1960s to only 40% in the 1980s.[37]

The fact that due to growing divorce rates there was so much more marriage in the form of remarriage from the 1970s onwards only made the matter of timing more ambiguous. Middle age, which previously had been associated with a stable marriage and a houseful of children, had become a period of painful divorces and empty nests, no longer a timeless state, but a period of frantic changes. According to surveys done in the 1980s, the years designated as the prime of life had shifted from middle age to young adulthood.[38]

The age of retirement was also coming unstuck, as more and more people, especially men, began opting to retire before 65.[39] Women, who previously tended to subordinate the timing of their lives to men's schedules, were now both entering and exiting employment in much larger numbers, with the result that, when there were two retirements to be considered, the timing became a matter of negotiation.[40] Leaving, like entering employment, had become a conditional rather than a final decision, which found many older people in part-time employment. Like mid-life, old age ceased to be a state of being and became a stage of becoming. This is partly attributable to the remarkable increase in longevity, but also to the improved circumstances of the elderly, who since the 1960s had enjoyed better incomes, better living conditions, and better health than any previous generation. By 1980s it was possible for Peter Laslett to declare that old age was not one stage but two, which he called the Third and Fourth Ages. Laslett's Third Age included the "young-old," those in their sixties and seventies, able and eager to live active, independent lives in retirement. To his Fourth Age belonged the "old-olds", those who fit the traditional stereotype of old age, dependent and inactive.[41] Yet even this distinction now seems too rigid for those like Gail Sheehy, who talks about a "Second Adulthood," emphasizing the creative possibilities open to all older people.[42]

We have reached that point where numerical age is no longer a reliable predictor.[43] But it is not just the timing but the sequencing of the times of our lives that have become uncertain. The life cycle has become more fluid in the last two decades, even to the point of losing its linear quality. In the future, people will have not just one career, but several. High divorce rates offer more than one opportunity at marriage. It is common to talk about second and third families as providing an opportunity to try again; and, just as the children of divorce seem to grow old before their time, the parents feel reborn through the same process.[44]

People are ceasing to act their age, with the result that the apparent natural laws of aging are being called into question in the social as well as the medical sciences.[45] Now that the word is out that age is a poor predictor of the mental and physical capacities, this self-fulfiling prophecy generates even more discrepancy between the old images of age and actual behavior. One of Gail Sheehy's most consistent findings is how much disparity there is between people's numerical age and how old they feel. She found that both adult men and women feel eight to ten years younger than their birth certificates would indicate.[46]

VI

Many would label this the post-modern moment, but there is something very familiar about the "time-space compression" that has intensified as a result of the current globalization process. Even as time is further separated from place, and people are forced to live with time they can neither control or even understand, we see a whole set of new times and ages to live by emerging. We are currently experiencing a proliferation of age-related rites the likes of which we have not seen since the mid-nineteenth century. We are in the process of reinventing the times of our lives.

Rites and symbols of aging which once clustered toward the beginnings of life are now shifting to older age groups. As age of schooling, marriage, and employment, and parenthood are detached from their moorings, age boundaries blur. Midlife loses its timeless quality to become one of the most rapidly changing, most ambiguous periods in women's as well as men's lives. Changes in the length of life, career patterns, and familial relations are causing women as well as men to reach for symbols that would give meaning to the flux of middle age. Most adults would no doubt like to forget their annual birthdays, but they find themselves fixated on years like forty, fifty, or sixty fashioning these into collective observances of ever greater significance.[47] As the anthropologist Stanley Brandes explains: "To take forty as representing middle age has enabled people to situate themselves with reference to other, more clearly defined age groups. It has provided a kind of anchor point, a frame of reference, which we seem to require in the increasingly age-differentiated society in which we live."[48]

Even those in the Third and Fourth Ages, who previously denied their ages, are now celebrating them, though in entirely new and creative ways. Elizabeth Colson calls our attention to new rites of age solidarity, exemplified by the collective birthday parties organized by senior citizen centers, where members celebrate not their individual ages but the all encompassing symbol of "good old age." In these popular ceremonies, attended by families and friends, all those having a birthday in the month celebrate it together. Each celebrant receives a round of applause, but the celebration is more of the community than of the individual, of a season of life rather than of specific ages present. By combining birthdays the senior citizens have "celebrated their distinctive status and reassured themselves, and told outsiders, that it is good to be old."[49] Age is thereby transformed from something that divides and isolates to something that unites and comforts. Old age becomes, something extending across space as well as time, reaching backwards and forwards to encompass people from their sixties through their nineties. Together, elders of quite different ages form a convoy which will see them through the rough seas of time, providing a model for others to imitate.

VII

Rituals which we once largely identified with family are finding new venues, yet family continues to create new times to live *by*. Modern communications now allow family members to form temporal convoys at a distance. Birthday parties by phone or e-mail are now common; photographs and videos create a presence even in absence. This record of family occasions provides a sense of togetherness that is often lacking in the event itself. In an era of time famine, with family members so widely dispersed, it is imaginative acts of anticipation and memory that increasingly substitute for real time together.

But such times require the investment of time; and families can no longer rely on their traditional timekeepers, for women's time is now torn between work and family in the ways that men's time has been. Clearly, it is time for men to begin to do their fair share of the cultural work of aging. But the current time famine requires something more than a redress in the gendered division of labor. The fact is that family, society's smallest unit, is no longer able to sustain the burden that modernity has placed upon it. In this crucial moment, both women and men need to become more conscious of the history of time and aging, a precondition to the questioning of both the reified notions of time and age we live *with* and the magical times and ages we live *by*. Rethinking aging means rethinking family, which, in turn, means rethinking society. This is not something that, in this conservative political climate, is particularly popular, but I believe we have no alternative. The task of cultural reconstruction before us requires the joint effort of all members of society, young as well as old, for aging is today everyone's problem and must be everyone's business.

---

1. E. T. Hall 1983, *passim*. Also E. Zerubavel 1981.
2. D. Harvey 1989, chapter xvi.
3. On the general theme of the families we live *with* and the the families we live *by*, see J. Gillis 1996. On the concept of time, see J. Bender and D. E. Wellbery 1991, p. 4.
4. B. Adam 1989, p. 468.
5. D. Cheal 1988, p. l0l; also G. Hagestad 1986, pp. 679-94.
6. K. J. Daly 1996, p. 23.
7. A. J. Weigert and R. Hastings 1977, pp. 1175-76.

8. Quoted in D. Harvey, p. 206.
9. Z. Bauman 1992, pp. 142, 163.
10. T. Cole 1992, p. 5.
11. Thomas, Bishop of Brinton, 1380, quoted in Cole, p. 6.
12. *Ibid*, pp. 7-8.
13. D. Cheal 1988, p. 101.
14. Weigert and Hastings 1977, pp. 1175-76.
15. Quoted in D. Gifford 1991, pp. 71-72.
16. Quoted in Cole 1992, p. 4.
17. *Ibid*, p. 15.
18. St. Augustine, *Confessions*, XI:20 (26); on the presence of the presence in the past, see R. Muchembled 1985, p. 48.
19. C. Cipolla 1957; Cole 1992, p. 11.
20. *Reports and Transactions of the Devonshire Association*, 1917.
21. On the variation of life courses, see H. J. Graff 1995, chapters iii; on Europe, see I.K. Ben-Amos 1994, *passim*.
22. T. Held 1982, pp. 227-54.
23. J. Kett 1977, pp. 191-4
24. T. Cole 1992, p. 8.
25. M. Kohli 1986.
26. J. Gillis 1994, pp. 3-24; also M. Kammen 1991; M. Ozouf, chapter vii; Zerubavel, chapter iii.
27. J. Kett 1977, Part II; J. Gillis 1975, chapters ii, iii.
28. J. Modell, F. Fustenburg, T. Herschberg 1976; M. Anderson 1985, pp. 69-87.
29. M. Anderson 1985, pp. 85-87.
30. T. Cole 1992, Part III.
31. T. Cole 1992, chapter v.
32. T. Cole 1984, pp. 332-4; G. J. Gruman 1978.
33. T. Cole 1992, chapter ix.
34. B. Myerhoff 1984, p. 306; also C. J. Rosenthal and V. Marshall 1988, pp. 669-84.s
35. K. Daly 1996, chapter vii.
36. *Ibid*, pp. 92ff.
37. Neugarten and Neugarten 1986, p. 37.
38. M. Martel 1958, p. 56.
39. Neugarten and Neugarten 1986, p. 35; D. Stannard 1978, p. 18; also G. Sheehy 1995, p. 72.
40. "Conflict for Working Couples: When He Retires, Must She?" *New York Times*, Nov. 9, 1993.
41. P. Laslett 1991, chapter vi.
42. G. Sheehy 1995, pp. 137-8.
43. Neugarten and Neugarten 1986, p. 36.
44. Neugarten and Neugarten 1986, pp. 37-38; J. Meyrowitz 1985, chapter six, xiii.
45. G. Lebouvier-Vief 1982, pp. 151-82.
46. G. Sheehy, pp. 61-62; Neugarten and Neugarten, pp. 37-38; also M. Buchmann 1989, chapters ii, viii, and conclusion; and S. Kaufmann 1985.
47. H. P. Chudacoff 1989, chapters vi-vii; E. Colson 1977, pp. 189-189; B. Myerhoff 1978, chapter vi.
48. S. Brandes 1985, pp. 105-6.
49. E. Colson 1977, p. 189.

Bibliography

Adam, Barbara. "Feminist social theory needs time: Reflections on the relation between feminist thought, social theory, and time as an important parameter in social analysis". *Sociological Review* 37 (1989).

Anderson, Michael. "The Emergence of the Modern Life Cycle in Britain". *Social History, x*, nr. l (January, 1985), pp. 69-87.

Bauman, Zygmunt. *Mortality, Immortality, and Other Life Strategies*. Stanford: Stanford University Press, 1992.

Ben-Amos, Illana Krausman. *Adolescence and Youth in Early Modern England*. New Haven: Yale University Press, 1994.

Bender, John and David E. Wellbery (eds.) *Chronotypes: The Construction of Time*. Stanford: Stanford University Press, 1991.

Brandes, Stanley. *Forty: The Age and the Symbol*. Knoxville: University of Kentucky Press, 1985.

Buchmann, Marlis. *The Script of Life in Modern Society: Entry into Adulthood in a Changing World*. Chicago: University of Chicago Press, 1989.

Cheal, David. "Relationships in Time: Ritual, Social Structure, and the Life Course". *Studies in Symbolic Interaction* 9 (1988).

Chudacoff, Howard P. *How Old Are You? Age Consciousness in American Culture*. Princeton: Princeton University Press, 1989.

Cipolla, Carlo. *Clocks and Culture 1300-1700*. London: Collins, 1957.

Cole, Thomas. "Aging, Meaning, and Well Being: Musings of a Cultural Historian." *International Journal of Aging and Human Development*. 19: 4 (1984) pp. 332-4.

Cole, Thomas. *The Journey of Life: A Cultural History of Aging in America*. Cambridge: Cambridge University Press, 1992.

Colson, Elizabeth. "The Least Common Denominator". *Secular Ritual*. Sally Moore and Barbara Myerhoff (eds.) Assen/Amsterdam: Van Gorcum, 1977.

Daly, Kerry J. *Families & Time: Keeping Pace in a Hurried Culture*. Thousand Oakes, CA: Sage Publications, 1996.

Gifford, Donald. *The Farthest Shore: A Natural History of Perception*. New York: Vintage, 1991.

Gillis, John. *A World of Their Own Making: Myth, Ritual, and the Quest for Family Values*. New York: Basic Books, 1996 and Oxford: Oxford University Press, 1997.

Gillis, John. *Commemorations: The Politics of National Identity*. Princeton: Princeton University Press, 1994.

Gillis, John. *Youth and History: Continuity and Change in European Age Relations*. New York: Academic Press, 1975.

Graff, Harvey J. *Conflicting Paths: Growing up in America*. Cambridge: Harvard University Press, 1995.

Gruman, Gerald J. "Cultural Origins of Present-Day 'Ageism': The Modernization of the Life Cycle," *Aging and the Elderly*. S. Spicker, K. Woodward and D. van Tassel (eds.) Atlantic Highlands, N.J.: Humanities Press, 1978 pp. 365-70.

Hagestad, Gunhild. "Dimensions of Time and the Family," *American Behavioral Scientist*. ixxx, nr. 6 (July/August 1986).

Hall, Edward T. *Dance of Life: The Other Dimensions of Time*. New York: Anchor Books, 1983.

Harvey, David. *The Post-Modern Condition: An enquiry into the origins of cultural change*. Oxford: Blackwell, 1989.

Held, Thomas. "Rural Retirement Arrangements in Seventeenth to Nineteenth Century Austria". *Journal of Family History*, vol. 7, nr. 3 (Fall, 1982), pp. 227-54.

Kammen, Michael. *Mystic Chords of Memory. The Transformation of Tradition in American Culture*. New York: Knopf, 1991.

Kaufmann, Sharon. *The Ageless Self: sources of meaning in late life*. Madison: University of Wisconsin Press, 1985.

Kett, Joseph. "Curing the Disease of Precocity". *Turning Points: Historical and Sociological Essays on the Family*. John Demos and Sarane Boocock (eds.) Chicago: Chicago University Press, 1977.

Kett, Joseph. *Rites of Passage: Adolescence in America 1790 to the Present*, New York: Basic Books, 1977.

Kohli, Martin. "The World We Forgot: A Historical Review of the Life Course." *Later Life: The Social Psychology of Aging*. Victor Marshall (ed). Beverley Hills: Sage, 1986.

Laslett, Peter. *A Fresh-Map of Life: The Emergence of the Third Age*. Cambridge: Harvard University Press, 1991.

Lebouvier-Vief, Gisela. "Individual Time, Social Time, and Intellectual Aging," in *Aging and Life Course Transition*. Tamara Hareven (ed) New York: Guilford Press, 1982.

Martel, Martin. "Age and Sex Roles in American Magazine Fiction (1890-1955)". *Middle Age and Aging*. Bernice Neugarten (ed.) Chicago: University of Chicago Press, 1958.

Meyrowitz, Joshua. *No Sense of Place: The Impact of Electronic Media on Social Behavior*, New York: Oxford, 1985.

Modell, John, Frank Fustenburg and Theodore Herschberg. "Social Change and Life Course Development in Historical Perspective". *Journal of Family History*. i (1976), pp. 7-32.

Muchembled, Robert. *Popular culture and elite culture in France, 1400-1700*, (trans. Lydia Cochrane). Baton Rouge: Louisiana University Press, 1985.

Myerhoff, Barbara. "Rites and Signs of Ripening: The Intertwining of Ritual, Time and Growing Older". *Age and Anthropological Theory.* David Kertzer and Jennie Keith (eds.) Ithaca: Cornell University Press, 1984.

Myerhoff, Barbara. *Number Our Days.* New York: Simon and Schuster, 1978.

Neugarten and Neugarten. "Changing Meaning of Age in Aging Society". *Our Aging Society: Paradox and Promise.* A. Pifer and L. Bronte (eds.) New York: N.W. Norton, 1986.

Ozouf, Mona. *Festivals and the French Revolution.* Cambridge: Harvard University Press, 1988.

Rosenthal, Carolyn J. and Victor Marshall. "Generational Transmission of Family Ritual". *American Behavioral Scientist*, xxxi, nr. 6 (July/August, 1988), pp. 669-84.

Sheehy, Gail. *New Passages: Mapping Your Life-Across Time.* New York: Random House, 1995.

Stannard, David. "Growing Up and Growing Old: Dilemmas of Aging in Bureaucratic America". *Aging and the Elderly.* S. Spicker, K. Woodward and D. van Tassel (eds.) Atlantic Highlands, N.J.: Humanities Press, 1978.

Weigert, Andrew J. and Ross Hastings. "Identity, Loss, Family, and Social Change". *American Journal of Sociology,* 82, nr. 6 (May, 1977), pp. 1175-76.

Zerubavel, Eviatar. *Hidden Rhythms: schedules and calendars in social life.* Chicago: University of Chicago Press, 1981.

Complete Motherhood:

The Mother-Infant Relationship in the First Few Days of Life, 1920 to 1950

Maxine Rhodes

Historians have tended to look to popular childcare manuals to develop theories about childrearing practices in the past and have seen them as being of primary importance in shaping the mother-infant relationship. Indeed, popular childrearing manuals have been used to chart the development of childcare practices[1] and to identify shifts in models of knowledge and parental practice.[2] Whilst these manuals were an important influence upon parental attitudes in some cases, their contribution in shaping the mother-infant relationship should not be over-emphasised, especially if this detracts from an examination of other, equally (or more) significant influences. Little attention has been paid to other factors such as the differing experiences between women having their first and subsequent babies, or to the networks through which women learnt to be mothers (family/friendship, educational, community and work). This is partly due to a lack of sources, although some researchers are beginning to address these issues through oral history methodology.[3] In addition, there has been little discussion of the influence of the maternity services, with which increasing numbers of British women were coming into contact, and in particular of the effect of the place of birth and of the relationship between a mother and her midwife in the first few days of the baby's life.

The transformation to 'mother' (itself an important phase in the female life-cycle) involved a complex set of inter-related factors and was not completed in a few short weeks. The way in which a woman developed as a mother had implications for the first stage of life, influencing the construction and experience of infancy. As a result, the first few days of life were an important time in defining the basis of the mother-infant relationship for all mothers and for mapping the landscape of babyhood.

Mothers were not the only factor in this relationship and whilst the process of becoming a mother was influenced by the system of health care offered to pregnant and childbearing women and was also a product of social, cultural and economic forces, infancy itself was defined by a range of influences. By focusing on the interpersonal relationships which resulted from women's interaction with the maternity services in a local setting (in this case, Kingston upon Hull – a city in East Yorkshire, England), a greater understanding can be gained of how ideas of infant needs and norms of behaviour were dictated and disseminated and the consequences of this for the relationship between mother and baby.

The inter-war years saw increasing interest in the psychology of infants and its relationship to later mental health and both European and American psychologists (who were investigating the first year of life) concluded that what happened in infancy was important to emotional as well as physical development. Historians have commented on this shift in knowledge and the growing interest in the infant, but have argued that it is not until the end of the inter-war years "that the infant emerged as having particular psychological as well as physical needs, dictating parental priorities."[4] In Britain the scientific management of children (promoted by such experts as Truby King) tended to dominate the childcare literature of the period, and this method, which focused on good habits and regimentation rather than the need for parental love, illustrated the dangers of the 'old ways' and the benefits of the new methods based upon scientific research. But mothers still had to be convinced; for example, *The Motherhood Book* published in the 1930's commented that despite the widespread propaganda of "simple yet scientific methods of baby rearing, it is only too apparent that, even today, thousands of babies are starting life sadly handicapped because of the seeds of ill health sown during the first month of their existence through the ignorance and prejudices of those in charge."[5] The remedy was simple: good habit-forming was to be promoted and even maternal love was to be regulated. *The Lady's Companion Women's Book of Health* (again published in the 1930's) provided a clear example of this when it advised: "between tea-time and the 6 p.m. feed is a good time for mother to devote to her baby, taking him on her knee, and giving him all her attention. This should be baby's hour."[6] Although some psychologists had expressed opinions about the infants' emotional needs, these needs usually came low down on a list of priorities, and affection, whilst recognised as important, was to be limited to avoid 'spoiling' the child. Some exploration of the psychological aspects of babyhood was also taking place within the infant welfare movement (which had begun with a concern for the physical well-being of infants), and this debate usually took place through professional journals, amongst professional bodies and at specialist conferences. In 1925, for example, the National Association for the Prevention of Infant Mortality included a discussion of child psychology in its programme of lectures.[7] Similarly, the

Child Study Movement had from its inception been interested in infant mental development and had published as early as 1902 a pamphlet on 'Baby and How to Understand Him'.[8] However whilst it is clear that some debate was occurring about the psychological (as well as the physical) needs of infants, such professional discourses were often distinct from the majority of parental practices and the models of knowledge used by midwives.

Most women in Britain were cared for during and after the birth of their children by midwives – whether they had a hospital or home confinement. In 1919 midwives attended 51 per cent of all births in London and 69 per cent of all births in the county boroughs.[9] By 1946 midwives were still the most usual attendant, being present at 64 per cent of home and 51.4 per cent of hospital births.[10] However the care of new mothers was not confined to the actual birth itself but also extended to the fourteen days after the birth (the puerperium) and it was midwives who provided day-to-day care, gave information and monitored mothers and their babies during this time. It is therefore particularly pertinent to focus upon the patterns of infant care taught to and practised by midwives – these appear in some cases to have been two different things – for an indication of how the mother-infant relationship was encouraged to develop.

The potential for extreme influence in shaping patterns of infant rearing is obvious, given midwives' contact with mothers and babies in the first weeks of life. The maternity services embodied a particular form of medical knowledge and provided the criteria for becoming a 'good mother' but the way this was presented to, and interpreted by, the midwife had significant consequences for the nature of the interaction between mother and infant. Midwives did not simply pass on the information they gained from formal training; rather midwifery knowledge was a more flexible entity essentially based on a combination of what was taught in training and experienced in practice. Interviews with midwives in Hull during this period reveal further complexities and illustrate how the application of this knowledge was very much dependent on the midwife's own personality and interaction with tutors and patients.[11] Although never a simple or consistent relationship, the nature of training and practice had a great influence on the relationship between mother and baby.

Midwifery textbooks provide a useful illustration of how the infant was to be cared for and how the midwife could encourage the mother to follow her example and become a 'good mother'. Midwifery educators themselves realised the important place of the midwife within the maternity services and incorporated an educational function into her role: "she has a very important part to play in seeing that the baby has the best possible start in life, and in teaching and advising the mother as to the care of her baby."[12] One midwifery text-book which remained popular throughout the inter-war years and was commonly used as an instruction manual for pupil midwives was John Fairbairn's *A Text-Book for Midwives*. John Fairbairn himself was President of the midwives' regulatory body, the Central Midwives Board (C.M.B.) during the period 1930-1936 and his book went through several reprints. This text reaffirmed the important role of the midwife in the first few days of life, both as a protector of infant health and an educator in infant rearing. As part of this, much emphasis was placed upon the promotion and establishment of breast-feeding with a routine based on regular 3 or 4 hourly feeds and no night-time feeding. Much of the rationale for encouraging breast-feeding was based on its impact upon infantile and maternal health (in reducing infantile infection and helping the womb to shrink) although other important functions were recognised; indeed, it was seen (at least in the inter-war years) as vital to the personal and moral development of the child.

> "The careless, shiftless, and ignorant mother whose child is brought up without method, and given the breast whenever he cries for it, is injuring both the health and character of her child. Not only is he likely to have disturbed digestion and irregularities of the bowels, but he is acquiring the slipshod ways of his parents, and without discipline and self-control he grows up self-willed and unable to adapt himself to our social customs and is neither physically nor morally a credit to the race."[13]

Breast milk was regarded as the ideal food for babies and regulated breast-feeding was equated with good mothering. In addition, emotional benefits were also hinted at as breast-feeding was believed to provide a bond between mother and infant and promote greater closeness through "the more intimate understanding of her baby and its needs (which) comes from complete motherhood."[14]

Another text popular during the 1940's was produced by R. Christie Brown, Barton Gilbert and Richard Hobbs (who were all involved in some way with examining or training midwives/maternity nurses). Similar themes can be found in this text, with particular emphasis being placed once again on the midwife's educational role.

> "The nurse is looking after the mother and child and one of her most important duties is to encourage each partner to learn about the other, and to see to it that when she leaves them they have become a self sufficient unit, no longer needing or wanting her help."[15]

Here too breast-feeding was to be promoted, although there had been some change in emphasis on the issue of night feeds; now, the general attitude was that it was better to feed a crying baby than to allow the rigidity of a routine to result in the failure of breast-feeding after only a few weeks because of an unhappy baby or mother.

Whilst midwifery text-books give a useful insight into the content of training and the basis of midwifery knowledge, it must be remembered that they only reflect what was considered to be ideal practice. Research has shown that pupils underwent a period of great personal change during training as they became immersed in the values and attitudes of the midwifery profession. Training not only provided technical skills but was also important in locating midwives within a particular hierarchy and moral landscape and this affected their relationships with mothers. Once qualified, midwives went on to practice and used their experiences to further refine what they had been taught. They had to be adaptable, not least because those working for the local authority often found themselves caring for some of the poorest women. Whilst there was great variation in both the standard of housing and preparation for birth from street to street and neighbour to neighbour, midwives often remarked upon the poor domestic environments in which they worked and the lack of facilities.

> "Some of the houses were quite dirty… and you used to have a job to get them to provide a clean bowl or bucket. You used to have to boil all the water to boil your instruments… and then after you'd had the delivery you'd to dispose of the afterbirth on the fire."[16]

Poverty was often encountered and midwives recalled making do with whatever was to hand in the house. One remembered a delivery of twins where the woman had no blankets for the cot and so the midwife brought a blanket from home, filled a glass bottle with hot water and wrapped it in a laundry bag before putting the babies in the cot back to back.[17] Training had taught them to lay twins at opposite ends of the cot but this midwife (who was the only one married with children at the beginning of training) believed her method was superior and sensible as it provided warmth and, she believed, mimicked the position of the babies in the womb.[18] Such a common sense approach to domestic difficulties was encountered in many of the reminiscences. However, recollections were not always sympathetic to the situation in which many mothers found themselves.

> "They don't know how to clean, these people. That is what we were told to do, try and educate these people into a better way of life. I did my best… A little bit of praise went a long way."[19]

Midwives tended to feel a certain moral superiority to the women they cared for although whilst some tended to be judgmental and critical of domestic circumstances, others seemed to recognise the efforts made to prepare for the birth (given often difficult circumstances) and felt some sympathy.

> "The very first delivery I had on the District... the woman was in the little front room and her husband was away at sea... and I could see fleas on the bed jumping... there was nobody there to look after her."[20]

Such differing attitudes towards childbearing and nursing women resulted in very different levels of support during the first few days of motherhood.

The issue of breast-feeding is perhaps the most useful illustration of the important role of the midwife and her relationship with mother and infant. Throughout this period midwives were taught to equate breast-feeding with good mothering and despite the relaxation of feeding routines by the 1940s, midwives could do much to influence the self-image of the mother and her relationship with her baby depending on their attitude to breast-feeding. The potential for an authoritarian relationship with the mother is quite apparent, especially as midwives were duty bound by the rules of their profession to report bottle feeding to local health officials and to advise the mother to seek medical help.[21] Some women would have been caused distress by what was regarded as their failure to breast-feed whilst others would have been praised for their efforts. Inconsistencies in approaches to breast feeding were acknowledged in the interviews despite the emphasis placed upon it in training.

> "Some patients used to be scared of the midwives. Some of the midwives were, I don't know, so strict, so sergeant major type, you know."[22]

This midwife's own approach was dictated less by the requirements of the maternity and child welfare service (which promoted breast feeding) and more by the individual mother and baby.

> "I wasn't one that pushed breast feeding. If they could breast feed, yes, breast feed without any trouble, lovely; but I wouldn't have a baby crying for hunger... all I want is a happy mother and a happy baby."[23]

Whilst the midwife herself was obviously influential in helping to mould the relationship between mothers and babies, the place of birth would also have been important as the experiences of home and hospital birth differed quite substantially, particularly with regard to the mothers' (and to some extent the midwives') autonomy in the method of infant rearing and the time spent with the infant. During the inter-war years a maternity policy had been developed which supported the increased use of the maternity hospital and a particular regimen within it. As a result the proportion of hospital births in England and Wales more than doubled from 15 per cent to 35 per cent between 1927 and 1937[24] and had reached 65 per cent by the

1950's.[25] Women giving birth in hospital were closely monitored and were separated from their babies for the majority of their stay – which was usually fourteen days. They were given some instruction on infant care and were then expected to go home and take full responsibility for their child with support from the local health visiting department.

In Hull, the Municipal Maternity Home became more and more popular with local women during this period – detailed study of the hospital environment reveals something of the impact of the institutional environment on the culture of childbirth.[26] In the hospital, women were not allowed to get out of bed at all for the first eight days. After this, they were allowed to go to the bathroom but were usually only granted full mobility after the 10th day.[27] The babies were kept in a separate nursery and the midwives cared for them in every way – except for feeding which the mothers did themselves.

> "Every morning there were two of you had to go in the nursery... bath the whole nursery full of babies and then carry the babies out to the mothers to be fed. During the day after they had been fed, they were taken back to the nursery and then the nurses changed them."[28]

The rationale for such an arrangement was based on the popular notion that this gave mothers complete rest and ensured their return to health. Midwives and medics were also afraid of haemorrhage and maternal death and therefore implemented the system vigorously. Notes from pupil midwife casebooks clearly illustrate how women and their babies were viewed and treated. In the (not untypical) case of a 26 year old mother of one who had a normal delivery followed by an 'uneventful' puerperium, the notes give some idea of the very close observation under which women were placed.

> "Patient passed a normal amount of urine per day. Breasts and lochia remained normal. Lactation was established on fourth day. On the ninth day, patient was up for a bath and toilet with no ill effects. Vaginal examination by Medical Officer on tenth day revealed uterus involuted, cervix closed. Patient discharged home same day satisfactory on being advised to attend the post-natal clinic."[29]

Records from other maternity hospitals confirm that this system was not isolated to Hull; in Sheffield, for instance, women were treated in a similar way and were monitored in addition to see if daily post-natal exercises had been completed.[30] Such an arrangement obviously provided few opportunities for the mother to get to know her new baby and casenotes make no mention of the emotional condition of mother[31] and baby; however, it did allow for great control of maternal and infant behaviour by maternity hospital staff. The idea that the mother and baby might need to bond emotionally was not regarded as important; instead, more attention was placed on monitoring physical health. Psychological theories about the emotional needs of mothers and babies had not yet filtered through into the environment of birth.

Women giving birth at home attended by a midwife were also monitored by daily visits following the birth but had more control over their own behaviour; they were for example more able to take responsibility for the care of their own babies and could develop routines which fitted their existing domestic arrangements. Midwives were taught to treat women who had home births as if they were in hospital and mothers were expected to stay in bed for at least nine days. A routine similar to that found in the hospital was established – as this extract from a pupil's case book illustrates.

> "Vulval toilet was given twice daily up to the 5th evening and then once daily up to the 9th day inclusive. A bed bath was given on the 3rd, 6th and 9th mornings and linen changed. An aperient was given on the 2nd evening, bowels remaining regular afterwards. Lactation was established by the 3rd day and remained adequate… She was up for one hour on her ninth day with no ill effects… She was a very easy-going person and whilst in bed spent most of her time in supervising the running of her household and keeping an eye on her youngest child."[32]

However, the degree of control midwives could enforce varied as they were not present in the mothers' homes all the time. Research suggests that midwives suspected that women 'disobeyed orders': "I think at home after the midwife's gone the patients used to get out of bed anyway."[33] Whilst some believed in retrospect that this was a good thing (as mobility reduced the risk of thrombosis), others voiced disapproval – although they did acknowledge that domestic responsibilities had to be catered for: "I once delivered a patient and left her, went back again – because you always went back again after an hour later to see if she was all right – and she'd haemorrhaged and I know I was most cross because I said, 'You've been out of bed.' But what could you do if the child was coming home from school and wanted something to eat?".[34] Interaction between mothers and midwives, whether in home or hospital, had important implications for the mother-infant relationship and whilst these interactions were complex and operated on a range of levels, physical rather than emotional health remained the primary concern of the maternity services into the 1950's.

To fully understand the construction of infancy and the interaction between a mother and her new baby, the context of the birth needs to be examined and the impact of social relationships, especially those with midwives, formed in the first few weeks of life assessed. Whilst such interactions may have been influenced by childrearing theories popular at the time, what is clear is that the relationship between mother and baby cannot be viewed simply as a product of the downward dissemination of information from experts in infant psychology and rearing; there were many other forces shaping the architecture of motherhood and infancy. As important as the messages received from any childcare manuals were the messages coming from midwives about the need for complete motherhood and whilst these reflected some of the dominant childcare theories, some 'rules' appear to have been interpreted and applied more flexibly in the relationships built up between midwives, mothers and babies. Whilst there was one dominant framework for constructing infancy there were many variations in its application and it seems clear that the place of birth had some impact upon this by altering the level of autonomy both for midwives and for mothers in adapting information on infant rearing to the surroundings in which they both found themselves. As a result the nature of infancy was influenced by both formal and informal bodies of knowledge which shaped the understanding of infant norms and needs.

Much of the discourse amongst medical health care professionals seems to have focused upon the physical health of the baby with only some brief acknowledgement of the links between this and later mental health. There was little discussion of the emotional impact of childbirth, of becoming a mother, or of the impact of caring for a new infant on the mother or of the emotional needs of the infant herself. Whilst further research is needed to examine the impact of other factors influencing the first relationship in life, it is clear that the organisation of the maternity services (with its reliance on the midwife) and the nature of midwifery training and practice were more influential in defining mothers and infants than has previously been acknowledged.

1. See for example: C. Hardyment 1983.
2. See C. Urwin and E. Sharland 1992.
3. For example: E. Roberts who has addressed some of these issues in A Woman's Place: An Oral History of Working Class Women 1890-1940, 1986 and at the 1996 Annual Conference (London) of the Oral History Society, L. Tracy explored 'Ideas Surrounding Motherhood: Oral History and the Welfare State'.
4. C. Urwin and E. Sharland 1992, p.175.
5. *The Motherhood Book*, c.1930s London, Amalgamated Press Ltd. p.116.
6. G. M. Cox c.1930s, p. 99.
7. National Association for the Prevention of Infant Mortality Mothercraft, London, The National league for Health, Maternity and Child Welfare, 1925, p. 257.
8. British Child Study Association *The Paidologist*, Vol. 4, No. 2, July 1902.
9. Ministry of Health Annual Report 1920-192, London, H.M.S.O., 1921, p.24.
10. Committee of the Royal College of Surgeons and the Population Investigation Committee Maternity in Great Britain, Oxford University Press, 1948, p.66 and 71.

11. The influence of training on the development of the professional persona is discussed in M. Rhodes 'Births, Bedpans and Bugs: The Contribution of Professional Education and Training to Becoming a Midwife, 1938-1951' Forthcoming in J. Bornat et. al. *'Oral History, Health and Welfare'*, Routledge, 1999.
12. J. S. Fairbairn 1930, p. 256.
13. Ibid. p.267.
14. Ibid. p.264.
15. R. Christie Brown 1950, p. 672.
16. M. Rhodes Interview with Mrs S Tape 4.
17. M. Rhodes Interview with Mrs SY Tape 8.
18. Ibid.
19. Ibid.
20. M. Rhodes Interview with Mrs S Op. Cit.
21. Central Midwives Board Rules, London, Spottiswoode, Ballantyne and Company Ltd. 1928, Rule e12a and note.
22. M. Rhodes Interview with Mrs F Tape 3.
23. Ibid.
24. *Registrar General Statistical Review of England and Wales for the year 1927*, London, H.M.S.O., 1929 and Registrar General Statistical Review of England and Wales for the year 1937, London, H.M.S.O. 1940.
25. R. Campbell and A. Macfarlane 1994 p.13.
26. M. Rhodes 'Municipal Maternity Services: Policy and Provision 1900-1939 with particular reference to Kingston upon Hull and its Municipal Maternity Home', Unpublished thesis.
27. M. Rhodes Interviews with midwives.
28. M. Rhodes Interview with Mrs S Tape 4.
29. Mrs S Casebook 1947.
30. Mrs SW Casebook 1947-8.
31. Except if a woman was diagnosed as having puerperal mania/insanity. This was defined as a psychosis of the mind during the puerperium, usually triggered by pregnancy but capable of being brought about by other life events during this time. Treatment was initially usually given within the Maternity home with transfer to the local asylum at a later date if necessary.
32. Mrs S Casebook 1948-9.
33. M. Rhodes Interview with a midwife who wishes to remain anonymous.
34. M. Rhodes Interview with Mrs SW Tape 9.

Select Bibliography

Campbell, R. and A. Macfarlane *Where to be Born? The debate and the evidence.* National Perinatal Epidemiology Unit Oxford 1994.

Christie Brown, R et. al. *Midwifery: Principles and practice for pupil midwives, teacher midwives and obstetric dressers.* Frome, Butler and Tanner Ltd, 1950.

Cox, G.M. *The Woman's Book of Health.* The Lady's Companion London, c.1930's.

Fairbairn, J. S. *A Text-Book for Midwives.* London: Humphrey Milford for the Oxford University Press, 1930.

Hardyment, C. *Dream Babies: Child Care from Locke to Spock.* London: Cape, 1983.

The Motherhood Book. London: Amalgamated Press Ltd, c.1930's.

Rhodes, M. "Births, Bedpans and Bugs: the contribution of professional education and training to becoming a midwife, 1938-1951". Forthcoming.

Rhodes, M. "Municipal Maternity Services: Policy and Provision 1900-1939 with particular reference to Kingston upon Hull and its Municipal Maternity Home" (unpublished thesis).

Roberts, E. *A Woman's Place: An oral history of working class women 1890-1940.* Oxford: Basil Blackwell, 1986.

Urwin, C. and E. Sharland. 'From Babies to Minds in Childcare Literature: Advice to parents in inter-war Britain.' in R. Cooter (Ed.) *In the Name of the Child: Health and welfare 1880-1940.* London: Routledge, 1992.

When Men Are Made into Boys

Old Boys in the Danish Sports Movement – The Sporting Fellowship of Elderly Men in the Beginning of the 20th Century

Jørgen Povlsen

Time goes by when children sleep,
Then days are felt as years,
When man wakes and recollects,
Then years are felt as days[1]

Paradoxically the term "old boys" was adopted as a way to categorize elderly sporting contestants about the turn of the century by the Anglomanic Danish sporting movement. In its original English context, "old boys" was the name given to former pupils who returned to their boarding schools and played with their own team of "old boys" against the current school team in a five-a-side game or football match, often in connection with end-of term, or prize-giving celebrations. There are very few sources which refer specifically to the appropriation of the concept of Old Boys. There is no doubt, however, that the English phenomenon "old boys" inspired its construction in the Danish and the Nordic sports system – incidentally a construction which has not been used in the rest of Europe.

The Danish lawyer O. S. Winding refers in "Idrætsbogen" (1909) to the origin of the Old Boys concept in England:

> When the "old boys" left school they introduced the game wherever they went and they established the so-called "Old Boys' Associations" called after their respective old schools, for example "Old Etonians" – boys from Eton, "Old Rugbeians – boys from Rugby School. "Old Carthusians" – boys from Charterhouse etc. In 1855 football was already being played at Cambridge University, and in 1857 a club was founded in Sheffield which still exists today as "The Association Club

of Amateurs". In 1858 and 59 the Blackheath and Richmond clubs were founded which still exist today as rugby clubs. Matches between different clubs were difficult, however, as each played according to the rules that they had learned at the school of which they were 'old boys'."[2]

Around the turn of the century and onwards a specific cultural understanding of age and aging became visible in connection to the growing sports movement. This development was explicitly related to the emergence of Old Boys associations in the Danish sporting culture. On a micro level it contains the story of the plasticity of the age-concept, on a macro level it points further at the relativity and diversity of ways to grow old. This article will deal with this plasticity and focus primarily on the playing with age and embodiments of age in a framework of masculinity, aging and sport.

AGE IN SPORT

Sport seems to be one of the social and societal connections where age differentiation and categorisation appears most plainly and distinct.[3] Sport is, furthermore, one of the areas where this tendency to compartmentalize is implemented most clearly in modern society. Linear time, which became more conspicuous throughout the 19th century as a way of disciplining, controlling and coordinating the industrial work and work force, is deposited in a radicalised form in sport.[4] The linearity of chronologisation – understood here as a designation of numerical age – is one of the more important types of fulcrum in modernity, and perhaps the most decisive for achievement of justice and equality which crystallizes in sporting contest between competitors of the same age. From first childhood years to the final years of old age, sportsmen are classified, according to developmental psychological and physiological considerations, in limited chronological age categories and groupings.[5]

However, it is still characteristic that after the age of 30 there is very little differentiation between the various chronological age groups. In the majority of sports disciplines there are only the categories Old Boys/Old Girls, veterans or masters.[6] Paradoxically, two or more conceptions of age are in conflict here, as sporting age appears to follow a different logic than that of societal age. For example, there is apparently in most cases no difference between adult sport and elderly sport, as the Danish version of Old Boys is an age category which typically consists of all male adults over the age of 30. At the same time the particular age perception, which belongs to sport, makes it possible for us to speak about for example 18 to 20 year-old girls "pensioning" themselves off, that is they withdraw from their active sports careers in competitive gymnastics or swimming. This means that in sport one can be *labelled as old* very young, like the girls just mentioned, and one can belong to the younger set in an older age, as is the case of seventy or eighty years old "Old Boys". When it is about presenting oneself as younger than one's actual chronological age, sport constitutes a perfect stage for self-presentation, and thereby supports a positive image of old age.[7] But the other way around sports participants are also *labelled as old* long before they have become so in a broader societal sense, as is often the case when competing in one of the categories of veterans or masters.

In the view of others, elderly competitors in sport today are regarded in an equivocal way. On the one hand, for example, footballers who continue playing until their late 30's excite admiration, but on the other hand they may just as easily excite ridicule and be regarded as "old has-beens". This polarity creates a certain tension and leaves space for a playing attitude against age and age perceptions. Subsequently, attention will therefore be directed to the presence of older sporting contestants in the age hierarchy of sport.

In the light of the scientification of old age during this century, and especially the scientific knowledge about nutrition, training, health issues obtained during the last couple of decades, progress and outstanding performances of older athletes are more or less supposed to be contemporary phenomena. However, we ought not to forget that in the early 20th century and before, there had been remarkable elderly sporting athletes. The Danish writer Asmus Diemer refers, among others, to the Scot David Andersen who, at the age of 88, won a 100 metres race for veterans held at Celtic Park, New York, at the beginning of this century. At almost the same time the 95-year-old swimmer J. Classey beat 5 much younger competitors in a 55-yard race in London, and there is also mention of an unnamed 60-year-old who ran a 400-metre race in a time of exactly 1 minute.[8]

Age has clearly long been a theme in sport. What was new about the establishment of Old Boys associations in Denmark around 1913 was that they contributed in a decisive manner to the institutionalisation of the elderly athlete. Previously, elderly athletes had only appeared on the scene – as the above examples demonstrate – as individualists with special physical abilities retained at an advanced age. From the first decades of the new century, the experience of age in sport is collectivized and the participation of the elderly in sport subsequently organised and regulated by the sporting organizations.

THE OLD BOYS ATHLETIC ASSOCIATION OF 1913

On the 18th March 1913 the Old Boys Athletic Association of Copenhagen (Idrætsforeningen Old Boys af 1913, København) was founded. It was the result of a number of conversations between men, especially in Danish

Athletics circles, who missed the social get-togethers with old comrades from their sporting days. The association was to be for elder sportsmen, as they expressed it.[9] Age criteria for admission to the association were discussed at the founding meeting. 30 was proposed as a limit, but, as many of the prospective members were under the age of 30, the possibility of passive membership was discussed. However 30 was agreed as the lower limit for membership. At the association's 40 years jubilee in 1953, it was obvious that a shift in the age distribution of the members had taken place.[10] Over the years the average age of the members increased, partly because the original members had grown old in the association (15 members from 1913 still participated), partly because of a changed perception of age and sport in society combined with the increased life expectancy which had brought about a higher frequency of participation in sport in old age, than that of 1913. In 1953 the association had a total of 232 members with a majority of members between 41-75 years.

Before the association was founded in 1913 a search was made for members. The group of such potential members was no larger than that the initiators – the master-joiner Olaf Olsen, the book-keeper Carl Haller and the dispatcher Johannes Gunderman from the Copenhagen Athletic Association – considered that they were able to identify most of the prospective members from an old group photograph which had been taken in connection with the first athletics meeting that the track sports clubs took part in together.[11]

At first the formation of Old Boys associations was a phenomenon limited to Copenhagen, but in the following decades the idea spread throughout the country.[12] In 1921 "Idrætsforeningen Old Boys" was founded in Aarhus, Denmark's second largest city. Like the members of the Copenhagen association, the members of this association in Aarhus were mainly recruited from the middle classes. In fact, a majority of the first initiators and subsequent members of the two associations mentioned here were recruited from the upper middle class. They prevailed with their rationalism, belief in science and pursuit of progress. In the light of the expansive ideas of industrialisation dominating Danish society at the time, these men were fascinated by sport as a means of manifesting their vigour, vitality and efficiency.[13]

During the last decades of the 19th century and after the interest in different sports disciplines was growing in Denmark. In 1882 a book by Bowler on cricket was published under the Danish title, *Cricket. Et Par Ord til "de Ældre"* (Cricket. A few words for "the elderly"), and in 1913 a book appeared by Asmus Diemer entitled, *Sport i den ældre Alder* (Sport in Old Age). As early as in the 1880's informal groupings of elderly cyclists were formed in Odense, the third largest city in Denmark. In Copenhagen the old athletes' association, Valhalla, was founded in 1913. The name Valhalla refers to the old Nordic vikings who, in this connection, became a metaphor for manhood, vigour and vitality. A cyclists' association in Copenhagen was mentioned too – which also carried the name "Old Boys."[14] There even happened to be a heavy dispute about the right to wear this name between the two old boys associations in Copenhagen.[15] In 1913 old competitors were called to take part in an Elderly Athletics Association's meeting and tournament in Kristiania, Norway, and a corresponding meeting was subsequently arranged two years later in Stockholm. In December 1916, The Copenhagen Athletics Federation tried to form an Old Boys subgroup but without success.[16] In August 1918, former oarsmen from The Rowing Club of Copenhagen founded an association for elderly rowers. The aim of this association was to maintain interest in rowing among elderly members in the club.[17]

Similar to these other fellowships of elderly sportsmen which were established in Denmark in these decades, The Old Boys Athletic Association in Copenhagen was a comradely and social association, which also had sport as its main objective. But the first Old Boys associations, too, give the impression of being rather restrictive lodge brotherhoods. As one of the members of the OBAAC expressed it.

> "As far as I'm concerned, being together with compatriots who knew me as a young man is the best company I know. Being one of the Old Boys is, for me, the only sort of free masonry I want".[18]

New members were elected by ballot and strictly approved before being accepted as members of the association. This select and enthusiastic age fellowship of socially equal and ideologically like-minded men constituted the basic precondition for the playing out of embodiments, other than those determined by the distinct, normative perceptions of the relationship between age and the body at that time in society as a whole. Where the question of age, in a broader societal connection, differentiated and segregated people, age appeared to be the real ritualising and fellowship-forming experience for these Old Boys between 30 – 80 years of age.

When one of the initiators, J. Gundermann, in his opening speech at the initiation of the association on March 5th, 1913, continually described elderly sportsmen as Old Boys, the connection was made directly to English boarding schools, where former pupils, as mentioned above, were referred to as Old Boys, and who would typically be 17-18 years-old. "Old Boys" as a concept in its Danish and Nordic version covers sportsmen in age groups between 30-80 years, if not older.

In the speech a number of arguments, which underlay reasons for the desire to found an association for elderly sportsmen, were put forward. An important aspect was the lack of mutual opportunities for elderly sportsmen to talk about and revitalise their sporting experiences.

> "The first purpose of the association – to create pleasure and enjoyment – is a particularly attractive purpose which I hope every associa-

> tion may achieve for its members. If we presume that we can achieve this, it is because, in our youth in different ways and at different times, we have all been enriched by so many good and enjoyable memories – memories which, like bottles of vintage wine, which have matured for years, and are only waiting for a suitable occasion to be opened and transport us back to a time, when soul and body had not yet been attacked by the virus of everyday care and worry".[19]

Gundermann went on to speak, in nostalgic and moralistic terms, of the importance of retaining youthfulness as the unspoiled fulcrum and codex of sport and, seen through the eyes of the initiator Gundermann and other like-minded persons, of combating the degeneration that even sport had been subjected to.

> "We are gathered here today, all stout-hearted old Sportsmen from all the old clubs both defunct and dynamic, we are gathered here to try to discover whether the warm friendship which brought us together in our youth, and which gave us such wonderful memories still exists, and whether this friendship can still recreate those happy youthful hours for us, and if we can do this – and there is no doubt in my mind that we can – then we make our contribution to giving the sport of athletics that continuing tone of youthfulness, vivacity and vigour that it had, when we were young, and which we cannot do without".[20]

It was also the dream of health and rejuvenation that was referred to when putting the case for sport to the prospective association.

> "However, one of the methods we have considered is touring sport.[21] This most natural, most healthy and most enjoyable of all sports has been sadly neglected in recent years. We who know how this sport can make elderly into young and young into boys again will not neglect it".[22]

Age was experienced here by these men as a plastic concept. A person was no more bound up in his chronological age, than that he could feel himself rejuvenated, not only by comradely social gatherings through common memories, but also through the mere sensation of the body in sporting activities. Into the current search for health-reforming and health-promoting measures and directives, physical activity was introduced on a level with light, fresh air and cleanliness. Sport and physical activity became from now on important aspects of the incipient aestheticization of the aging body. Later on in the 20th century this aestheticization of the aging body became normatively closely linked to the socially acceptable.[23] One of the striking characteristics of the elderly sportsmen assembled here was their excess in relation to – and belief in – was the excessive nature of both their belief in and practice of measures to combat decay through physical training.

> "To resume training, yes, why should there not be one among us, of our age, who would like to compete in the sporting arena? Look at such a man as the Englishman Webb who was here last summer. What did he not achieve, even though he was older than several of us, and even though he did not appear to deny himself the pleasures of this world? With the present ideal conditions for training there are perhaps many who would like to try one more time to show their mettle. Or, after physical training, to regain their suppleness of body and resistance to the constant attacks of our changeable climate on our general health".[24]

Around the turn of the century declarations about health and hygiene were, to a large degree, based on the theme of all-embracing theories of degeneration and decay. The main enemy was the recently discovered bacteriological mechanisms. Against these threats the sovereign remedy was supposed to be fresh air, light, and cleanliness. It is remarkable, how this group of elderly sportsmen with great stamina were introducing progressive visions of the strong and healthy aging body, as they fought against the massive wide-spread fear of illness and degeneration, which first and foremost defined biological aging.

From the preceding quotation it appears that these men considered themselves as being in their prime, and for this reason they did not rule out the possibility of still being able to compete on equal terms in the field of sport. Another decisive factor may also have been that more systematic training based on scientific criteria was beginning to be introduced[25] into an otherwise almost entirely self-taught sporting movement, based on intuition and inherited experience.

In its first years the association reflected the pattern that was characteristic for Danish sport immediately before and shortly after the turn of the century. That is to say that associations and federations were not divided laterally and into disciplines, as they are today. Old Boys had a wide range of activities – walking, athletics and training were performed at the stadium, football and gymnastics took place at Randersgade School and handball[26] was played after gymnastics training at this school. Members of the association often entered competitions in the various sporting disciplines. On the 15th October 1913, members of the association won three events at an Old Boys athletic meeting arranged by the Copenhagen Athletics Federation, and there was lively competition between members and for members.

The social activities of the association also included frequent get-togethers where members' wives and children took part. In connection with certain sports meetings arranged by the association, for example the annual cross-country run, there was a tradition that a picnic for the members and their families was held at Kongekilden, before the race took place.

One of the centres of interest for the Old Boys association were the members' association meetings which took on considerable importance outside the normal playing season. Here the members would play cards, table tennis, skittles, but there was also time for a chat about old times.

> "As soon as winter has closed its cold hand on daily life, these members' meetings become the lungs of the associations. Here the old pike catch their breath. Remember this when the days grow short." [27]

INVOCATION, RITUALITY AND THE AGING BODY

As was the custom at the time, songs praising brotherhood and social fellowship were often sung in the Old Boys association of 1913. The following contribution – a translation or transformation of the opening verse of a four verse song – is typical of the pathos and aura which formed the framework of the fellowship of Old Boys.

Old Boys! Your goal!
Iron-hard memories converted to steel,
Hardened in friendship what once was contended.
Fellowship formed and always intended,
When and wherever life's contests flame out,
Old Boys! Your Goal![28]

The tribute to the association, in the symbolistic style of the era, evokes a picture of common experiences of age and character among men. Belief in the future and the opportunities afforded by industrial development are all in evidence here.[29] These are mature, modern and self-aware men who are being addressed here.[30] They are grown men, who play a patriarchal role in their businesses and families with autocratic authority. In the song, a picture is created of a male individual at the most powerful stage of his life course, almost as it is exemplified in the iconic "Stages of Life" of the late 19th century. There is much physicality and vitality in these verses. The human body and the creative power of the production process are united in a belief in freedom, growth, and survival based on male vigour and the friendships forged in sport. Vitality and health, will and youthful strength are in contrast to decline and degeneration present, albeit implicit in the verses. Experience of life – and thus age – are exemplified most clearly in the line in the second verse: "fortified by life's surging torrent". The song reveals an idealistic search for a lost companionship as the key to a type of ethical conduct, which does not seem to be so very far from the spirit of the Boy Scout movement.

The pretentious sentiments and self-glorification of these verses were, however, in direct contrast to the accusations levelled by the barrister Krenchel in his polemical letters on drunkenness in the newspapers in 1926.[31] The affair was due to some boisterous drinking songs in the association's song book and caused the temperance advocates of the time to rush into print. Krenchel, who himself was a former rower, tried over the years to influence the leadership of the Danish Sport Federation, to implement a policy on keeping sport and drinking apart. Once, in 1926, at the yearly meeting of the representatives of the Danish Sport Federation, he managed to persuade the president of the federation, general Carstenschiold, to present a resolution on the subject. While reading the resolution aloud at the meeting Carstenschiold became beware of the massive resistance among the representatives and in sheer confusion he forgot to put the resolution to the vote. The Old Boys association's excesses were not an outstanding phenomenon in the Danish Sports Movement of that time. But the reflexive playing of the Old Boys on the one hand being real dedicated sportsmen and on the other hand being men about town was characteristic of the good fellowship of these men.

INVENTING TRADITIONS – THE CELEBRATION OF SPECIAL BIRTHDAYS

Among these elderly sportsmen around the turn of the century a new cultural ritualising of life phases took place. The celebration of special birthdays had attained great importance in bourgois life style and this was also reflected among the Old Boys. They seized every opportunity to send telegrams – often in verse – to those with birthdays or anniversaries or even condolences. What appeared here as a part of the elderly fellowship was a confirmation of the movement away from the cyclic-rhythmic recurring celebrations of an agrarian society, towards the chronologically linear rationality of individual life and career courses.[32] But at the same time as rational order was being established by the logical structure of chronology, special birthday events were invented and implemented as a tradition, which gave room for excessive celebrations, as is mentioned below.

Accounts of the celebrations of special birthdays in the "Old Boys Association of 1913" show that, whereas in 1915, a celebration was arranged when a member reached the age of 50, – "Yes, at that time it was quite an event"[33] – by 1953 they had long gone over to celebrating the 75-year birthdays of members. This reflects the fact that these men, now reaching old age, were the first to age in a new sports movement, and thereby to be given the chance to celebrate their life-long sporting careers as something special. In this sense the celebration of special birthdays was a ritual, which helped to cultivate fellowship as an "age culture" because, as a person was being celebrated, his status as elderly among the elderly was also being confirmed. This is reported in an account of one of these special birthdays:

About 70 Old Boys members met at Søborg on the 30th June, 1929, and proceeded in a body to congratulate the association's co-founder and good comrade "Buller".[34]

> At this time "Wolle" - Oluf Rasmussen - had his summer residence close to that of "Buller". First of all we walked over to "Wolle's Park" where we left our packets of sandwiches, and here we were equipped with songs, hats (paper), the orchestra received their instruments (cardboard), and all the participants were instructed to proceed in high humour to "Buller's" summer residence at Bagsværd. After our decorous arrival with song and music, an accompanying rostrum was put up on the newly-mown lawn, a microphone was set up – appearances must be kept up – and all the time the orchestra played under their conductor "Pjæng".
>
> The speaker mounted the rostrum in order to outline the programme for the festivities. A cantata had been specially composed for the occasion and the first movement was sung by Joseph Hislop accompanied by a choir in the background under the leadership of Wilh. Rønnow singing, "For he's a jolly good fellow". After which the chairman of the Old Boys, Johs. Gundermann, mounted the rostrum and spoke in such glowing and eloquent words to "Buller" and his family, that he almost got carried away, and, in conclusion, presented "Buller" with a gold watch and chain from "His friends in the Old Boys".[35]

The boyish, comradely fellowship in the association is also demonstrated in the widespread use of members' nicknames – "Wolle", "Big C", "Little C", "Buller". In the association's 1953 jubilee edition, two of these are referred to as. "The Birthday Boys" – "Little C" and "Walther" became 70 - and 50 years-old respectively on the 6th February and 31st January".[36]

Criticism has been levelled – and with good cause – at the celebration of "children's birthdays" in old peoples' homes for even the very old. In contrast to this, in Old Boys associations it was a case of comradely banter, but with a solid basis in the cultivation of the childish element that physical and bodily experiences apparently gave them.

Sport makes boys into men – and men into boys

Again and again in sport we meet the phrase, "Sport makes boys into men – and men into boys". The first part of the assertion is well documented in the literature as a ritualised transition from childhood to adult life.[37]

The second part of the motto "– and make men into boys" has hardly been investigated at all. It is possible that the discussion about infantilizing practices has prevented a closer study of this phenomenon. A deeper definition of the empirical character, together with a closer analysis of the phenomenon will be carried out in the following discussion. Let us begin with an analysis of a micro example.

When a little notice in an official report of a dinner party in "The Old Boys Association of 1921" in Aarhus says: "And nobody dribbled",[38] then, in spite of its laconic and abbreviated character, this statement contains the core of the dilemma, that basically there was a spirit of ambivalence among Old Boys with respect to the question of age. On the one hand boyish mentality was admired, and on the other hand an ironic and humorous attitude was maintained towards the same phenomenon. It is symptomatic for the old boys that during socializing events as well as in sport they drift from formalized behaviour to informalized and vice versa. As is pointed out by Elias, the civilizing process among other things is a matter of turning a not civilised subject child into a civilised adult. During this process of discipline and rationalization the individual learns to control emotions and spontaneous expressive behaviour. The symbolic codes of behaviour, which are the fundamentals of being accepted as a member of society, must thus be learned if boys shall be made into men. This learning process is also penetrating modern sport. The interesting thing about sport is that it constitutes a field of controlled decontrolling of emotions,[39] which means that sport play a remarkable role in the developing of civilized bodies and at the same time represents a space, where one can give way to one's emotions and simultaneously be reflexive (controlled) about it.

After their active sporting careers were over, elderly men again cultivated youthful and boyish activities. And, behind the cultivated veneer, behind the seriousness of work, duty and discipline, which was typical of the bourgeoisie as well as for these white-collar workers and tradesmen, the wild and exuberant suddenly appeared, especially during convivial gatherings with sporting friends, when fun was made of age and potential regression as exemplified by the remark, "And nobody dribbled – down his shirt etc."

This observation that "Nobody dribbled – down his shirt" is especially interesting, when we consider that these middle class sportsmen's ideal of physical prowess was concerned to a high degree with physical control, as an expression of strength of character – which was, of course, one of the most important formative aspects of sport at that time.[40] In the image presented there is a play on the loss of self-control and the loss of physical control which are assumed to be a natural consequence of the aging process. The "old boy" was facing a dilemma with on the one hand the image of an old man who really spills food on his clothes and on the other that of the physically uncontrolled child, who does not even know how to avoid it. The real excitement of the old boys' fellowships lay in this controlled decontrol, which allowed them to maintain a balance delicate enough to establish an equilibrium between the old man and the boy.

Previously in this book[41] we have seen how the perception of childhood, the childish body and childishness in a "second childhood" can be extremely stigmatizing for an elderly person. On the other hand, we must not disregard the fact that a certain boyish mentality among the elderly men gives an opportunity for other embodiments and aspects of the self to emerge which are apparently connected with physical experiences generated through exercise, sport, bathing etc. Elias as well as Goffman and Shilling[42] speak about physical control as a fundamental basis for the maintenance of self-identity. But with Old Boys it is a question of living with declining physical control – even in relation to the high level of bodily control that they as sportsmen formerly possessed. For them the contest between the fixation of bodily control and the relaxation of bodily control is of great importance, which is why the biological conditions of aging are played out in a symbolic form. This can contribute to an explanation of the marked focussing on age and life phases, which characterises former, as well as current activities of "old boys".

BOYISH SPIRIT – AGE AND MALE CULTURE AT THE TURN OF THE CENTURY

Bourgeois culture at the turn of the century contained a special nostalgic-romantic and sentimental interest in childhood. Childhood was regarded as a pure and idyllic period, where everything was characterised by innocence and clarity. The emphasis placed by Old Boys on the "boyish spirit" as the source of rejuvenating experience can be seen as an extension of this perception of childhood. But active Old Boys were at that time not the only exercising old men who experienced these changes in the perception of different corporealities. Other male fellowships existed, alongside and sometimes pre-dating Old Boys associations, outside the usual institutionalised and organisationalised sports fellowships. One of these will briefly be described here – which has its roots in bathing – and in particular winter bathing.[43]

On the 25th May, 1825, Rysensteen[44], one of the oldest Nordic public bathing establishments was founded in Copenhagen, with in the beginning apart from the sea bath only steam baths and whirl baths. The steam baths were closed before the turn of the century, due to the expansion of the city and the development of the street system. But Rysensteen continued to offer seabathing. It was Rysensteen – and after 1885 also at the public baths "Helgoland" – the winter bathers frequented. Rysensteen's winter bathers were given the name "Sørøverne" ("Sea Robbers") in 1915. Winter bathing had been a tradition since 1825, but about 1915 the winter bathers formed their own exclusive fellowship in the "Sea Robber Guild". A special feature of winter bathing was, and still is, the prevalence of elderly and very old bathers. As is the custom in male fellowships of this type, many old tales and tall stories are related, and old bathers in particular have supplied much material for these, but we should not take all these stories at face value. We should rather be aware that the commitment itself, particularly in the exploits of the old and elderly – their way of describing these with humour mixed with admiration – tells an interesting parallel story. A beginner tells the story of the day his friend Hansen took him to winter bathing for the first time around the year 1915.

> "Hansen talked me into it, and I must say I've never regretted it; for when winter came with snow and ice, and the bathing assistant had to break a hole in the ice, this was when we felt the greatest pleasure after the bath. Stripping off in front of a warm fire, diving into the sea, swim a dozen metres out, and then back and out of the water as a new and better person. Yes, literally a new and better person. For you could come down and be bad-tempered and sulky, but after a cold plunge it was as though all the bad temper had been washed away and you came out of the water *like a carefree boy.* And in particular those days when the ice was melting but was still on the water like icy gruel, and you climbed out of the water with a covering of ice on your body".[45] (authors italics)

The former landowner, Niels Matzen, who was Denmark's oldest swimmer began as a winter bather at the age of 80. 14 days before his death at the age of 93, he took his last swim breaking the ice at the Rysensteen baths. On his 90th birthday, he swam a race and won a bottle of aquavit. Incidentally Niels Matzen was 30 years older than his father-in-law. On the very seldom occasions that he was obliged to miss his daily plunge because of work or travel, you could hear him comment on the situation when he came back again to the baths.

> "It's the very devil with all the rheumatism that accumulates when you miss your daily plunge".[46]

The draper Erik Lassen could celebrate his 75 years jubilee as an all-year bather at Rysensteen. He had been a bather there since he was 5 years old.

It was said that his bathing ritual lasted more than three hours during which he carefully brushed every article of clothing several times – both inside and out. Even his walking stick was washed and carefully dried. He was bedridden for the last year of his life before he died at the age of 90. It was said that he complained daily that,

> "If only I could get down to "Rysensteen" and have my daily plunge, I would soon get better".[47]

Winter bathing constitutes a fellowship of the elderly, where the biological insistence of the elderly body is, of course, present, but where other bodies and embodiments are parallel and paradoxically revealed, partly in the language – a special bantering jargon – and partly in sensually ritualised body behaviour where the integrative capacity of language is constantly challenged and exceeded.

For the Old Boys as well as for the Sea Robbers, "boyish spirit" was exposed, but was not viewed, as one might perhaps expect, as extrinsic to a boyish physicality, on the contrary, the latter was experienced as a complimentary part of the "boyish spirit" – a kind of external image or projection of the inner boy in men. Therefore these men were often experienced as frivolous and irresponsible, when they tumbled about in sport, gymnastics and ball games. Childhood, adulthood and old age seem to coalesce in the physical culture of these men during the first decades of the new century. This attribute does not disappear, but is retained throughout the century as, for instance, in this occasional song from 1941 by the Old Boys of Aarhus demonstrates.

When we don our sporting gear
We are no longer full-grown men.
As grown-ups we are duty bound
Wherever we may go and when.
As in our youth we still must try
To help, and not to fail our friends.
But on the sporting field we change
To boys again with praise and scold.
We fight, have fun, dispute, compete
But soon become as friends again.[48]

There is apparently more to understanding these men than simply establishing the capability of sport to form character and discipline the body. The rigid control and armouring of the body must be viewed simultaneously – at least when discussing elderly sporting competitors – with a release of body control and an allowance of space for the little boy present in the elderly man, side by side with all the other bodies and embodiments of a lifetime that are lived through and retained in the memory. Barbara Myerhoff refers to this phenomenon as "Body memory". Body memory indicates that tactile and kinesthetic events and sensations experienced from childhood are stored in the body and can be recalled by the activation of the moving body, as we see it here, even at a late age.[49] This might indicate the difference between the younger adult citizen who is in the process of creating a career and therefore must project his body control as a visible part of his self-identity, and on the other hand the older man, who has already reached the top of his career and has therefore little need to manifest the ability for strict physical discipline and control, but can, to a large degree respond in a relaxed and uninhibited manner.

The historian Hans Bonde pleads that men in sporting circles at the turn of the century would, at all costs, try to avoid being identified with homosexual or feminine forms of behaviour.[50] Therefore they could not exhibit gentle or feminine sides of themselves. However the otherwise tabooed childishness was allowed to be exhibited in closed circles.[51] In other words gentle values appeared, not as feminine or homosexual, but as childlike. It is exactly this contrast between age that they lived with and age that they lived by, that is of interest here.[52] In spite of their evident interest in the celebration of special birthdays, these sportsmen did not strictly adhere to the particular rules for behaviour – in the Victorian sense – required by their chronological age, but broke these rules when they celebrated the moods of boyishness and youth.

Age was at that time, as it partly still is, an absolute determiner of physical sporting performance. This assumption was reflected in contemporary medical literature, which was strongly influenced by theories of degeneration and decay. These theories emphasized the inevitable drastic decrease in physical performance with increasing age. This knowledge was transformed into medical advice to sportsmen and athletes as described in the following. In many ways it adequately reproduced the particular discourse about aging that the elderly sportsman was facing.

> "When people pass the age of forty – or perhaps even before – they often become indolent and do not take the trouble to move, any more than their businesses force them to. But it does not pay not to maintain our bodies. We have of course a body, we are not just souls – it often happens nowadays that when people have passed the age of fifty they enter a gymnastics class and continue there for many years. (............) The gymnastics that they take part in is, of course, not as intensive as that of young men in their twenties, but it does not have to be so gentle that it resembles remedial exercise – I had for many years a class for elderly men where most of the participants were over fifty, one was even more than sixty. In the course of the winter many were able to run for $4^{1/2}$ minutes at a time. Of course we proceeded gradual-

ly, starting at ½ or 1 minute, but to run for 4½ minutes is quite good for elderly people.[53]

In spite of contemporary medical health discourse, which held a view of aging which reflected physical aging and age-related exhaustion, and which appeared most visibly in relation to industrial labour and agriculture, a belief in possibilities for the elderly began to make itself felt among sportsmen. Prejudices about physical performance and old age were confronting the practical innovative experiences of these elderly athletes who continued actively to pursue their sporting interests throughout their lives. In accordance with the optimistic attitudes at the beginning of the new century, they struggled to set new standards for exercise habits and training in old age. "Old Boys" was what they called themselves. They represented more than mere echoes of former achievements. It was not only a case of a useless struggle to repeat the manly triumphs of their youth, but apparently it was most of all the more sophisticated and subtle ways in which they dealt with the experience of age and identity, that really characterised their male fellowship.

Lived bodies

This article has so far dealt with the relationship between body and age within the field of body culture forms, such as sport and gymnastics. Anyone who has experience of sport and physical training will agree that the body – and perhaps in particular the aging body – here is staged in a special way which is remarkably different from the usual presentation of the body in everyday life. This applies particularly to physical activity, dress and social conventions. Kathleen Woodward has pointed out, that the body appears as the dominant signifier of age in western culture, and she adds that, "in western culture, aging is represented primarily in terms of the visual, in terms of the surface of the body".[54]

Apparently with veteran performers there can be several types of bodies involved, over and above the normal representation of the aging body as a biological, physical and empirically aged body. Viewed phenomenologically, the elderly's experience of an aging body would under certain circumstances, according to what has previously been shown, seem to revert to and relate to other bodies – that of the youth or the child, for example. The subject of this article has first and foremost been to underline the presence of these other bodies at the interface between nature and culture, and between construction and "lived experience". Thomas J. Csordas suggests that the body should be regarded from two complementary angles.

> "We require a term that is complementary as subject is to object, and for that purpose suggest "being-in-the-world", a term from the phe-

nomenological tradition that captures precisely the sense of existential immediacy to which we have already alluded. This is an immediacy in a double sense: not as a synchronic moment of the ethnographic present but as temporally/historically informed sensory presence and engagement; and not unmediated in the sense of a precultural universalism but in the sense of the preobjective reservoir of meaning outlined above. The distinction between representation and being-in-the-world is methodologically critical, for it is the difference between understanding culture in terms of objectified abstraction and existential immediacy. Representation is fundamentally nominal, and hence we can speak of "a representation". Being-in-the-world is fundamentally conditional, and hence we must speak of "existence" and "lived experience."[55]

A corresponding insistence on a physical being prior to, but in an interplay with the body as a construction, is emphasized by the cultural historian Niels Kayser Nielsen.

The Physical "Lebenswelt", as regarded by Merleau-Ponty and Heidegger in their perception of the factuality and thus the primacy of the sensual "being" in relation to any other discursivity; before we are anything at all we are a body. That is to say, the body has its own world, long before any other perception of the surrounding world exists – and also long before we are at all aware of an "I", let alone a "Me".[56]

These ambiguities of the body mark a break with the predominant tendency, even in socialisation theory, of regarding the body as a biological, anatomical or physiological entity. There is a phenomenological body also, or perhaps several. If we assume the existence of these several bodies, embodiments or physicalities, this may give way to different perceptions of the elderly body, for instance as a biologically aged body with significant signs on the surface of the body: wrinkles, grey hair, bunions, muscular atrophy etc., or with respect to a particular interpretation of the intellectual and psycho-motoric status as a "second childhood", and finally, a third possibility would appear to be the "lived body's" situationally-dependent reactualization of other bodies, for example the child's body.

Old age regarded as a "second childhood" contains at root a paradoxical notion of a second not-yet aged body within an empirically aged body. This widespread representation of the old body also creates a discriminatory infantilization of old people in its wake. Infantilization is embedded in many perceptions of old age and aging, first and foremost in medico-therapeutic discourse.[57] As a consequence of this, using an expression from Jenny Hockey og Allison James, elderly people are transformed and "metaphorically converted into children".[58]

Negative stereotyping of old age and the aging body which appears through infantilization and "second childhood" overshadows, to a certain degree, the presence of other "lived/imaginary/situated" bodies in old age. As an example, old men's delight in the rediscovery of the boy in themselves is often overlooked. This experience often seems to appear in connection with bodily and physical movement and an (almost) sensual activation in sport and general gymnastics, and in the social fellowship of shared physical exertion. It is here – in the interaction between the physical construction (old body) and the experienced physicality (boy's body) – that the aging body of sport can point the way to other possibilities of interpretation of the relationship between old age and childhood than those described above.

---

1. Inscription on "Buller's" (master joiner Olaf Olsen) sundial, presented to him by his Old Boys comrades on his 65th birthday.
2. O. S. Winding 1909, pp. 5-7.
3. A basic and characteristic feature of age divisions in sport is the structural difference between the numerous narrow groupings for the participation of children and adolescents in sport, as compared to the fewer, and much broader, age divisions of adults and elderly people. The following shows the age divisions for children and adolescents in the current tournaments of the Danish Football Association: *Children and Youth:* Microtots under 8 years old, Tinytots under 10 år, Pre-teens under 12 years old, Boys under 14 years old, Juniors under 16 years old, Adolescents under 18 years old. *Adults*: Seniors (males must be at least 16 years old, females must be at least 15 years old), Old-boys (at least 33 years old), Old-girls (at least 29 years old), Veterans (at least 40 years old) (no group here for women), Super-veterans (at least 45 years old), Masters (at least 50 years old), Supermasters (at least 55 years old). It is made plain here that, in the age groups up to 18 years old, there are (at least) six age categories whereas the 18 to 100 years old groups comprise the same number, six. Within recent years, however, an increase in the number of age divisions has taken place, and we will probably see several more age-related divisions in adult and elderly sport.
4. See H. Eichberg 1978, W. Hopf 1981.
5. Age differentiation cannot, however be regarded as a totalising and universal principle, because – paradoxically in relation to the interpretation of the Olympic Games of this century as a modern phenomenon – age has been abolished as regards competing in these games. Anyone who qualifies may compete, regardless of age, which distinguishes the Olympic Games from other international championships where, as a general rule, there is a distinction between senior and junior championships. However, it appears that also here in the Olympic Games there is a change taking place as regards age differentiation, which applies to elderly sports competitors, for whom initiatives have been taken to hold "Senior Olympic Games" and Master's Games, just as there are Youth Olympic Games. This does not change the fact that anyone regardless of age may take part in the traditional and and official Olympic Games.
6. Rowing, Orienteering and Swimming are examples of sports disciplines with a more differentiated age classification system.

7. See for instance National Geographic, 192, no 5 1997: The major theme of this particular volume is Aging. It is striking that the majority of the illustrations are of elderly people doing exercise or sport. The icon of the body in old age is more and more becoming the fit, active, exercised body.
8. See A. Diemer 1913, pp. 13-14. Unfortunately Diemer does not give more precise information about the date and year of the mentioned competitions.
9. These elder sportsmen were first and foremost supposed to beformer competitors in athletics which became popular at the end of the 19th century. They were thus pioneers of this sport in Denmark, which can also perhaps explain the mixture of pathos and enthusiasm which symbolizes the presentation of the association in its first years. In other words, it was these athletes who were to have the experience of becoming old competitors, where old in this context must be seen in relation to what ever it was like to be old at the turn of the century, when the average age for men was about 50 years, and for women 53 years. What happened here can be described as a kind of "generationalization" of athletes, which had not been possible before, because sport did not emerge in a broader sense before the end of the 19th century in Denmark.
10. How old these athletes were, can be seen from the statistics of Old Boys from the 40-year and 50-year jubilees in 1953 and 1963 respectively. When the Old Boys association was founded in 1913, 45 out of 80 founding members were under 30 years, 23 were between 36-40 years, 7 between 41-45 years, 2 between 46-50 years, 2 between 51-55 years and finally one member 56-60years. (In 1953 there were 37 between 46 and 50; 72 between 50 and 60; 46 between 61 and 70; 21 between 71 and 75 and finally 6 over 76 years) In 1963 there were 8 members between 76-80 years, 6 between 81-85, og 1 member over 86 years). Over the years the aging profile of the association increased, as the figures presented in Old Boys – Et jubilæumsskrift 1953 (the Jubilee Review of the Old Boys association of Copenhagen, 1953), p. 31, show.
11. From about 1890 track sports became very popular among sportsmen in Denmark.
12. As time went by, regional and national athletics meetings were established and formalized for elderly athletes.
13. The construction of middle class men and manliness through sport in the period 1880-1920 has been treated extensively by the historian Hans Bonde in his book "Mandighed og sport", 1991.
14. This particular Old Boys cyclist's association in Copenhagen was mentioned, too, in Trangbæk, Hansen, Ibsen, Jørgensen and Nielsen, 1995, Vol. 1 p. 72. The dispute between the two Old Boys associations is described in Et Jubilæumsskrift for Old Boys, København 1938 (The Jubilee Review of the Old Boys association of Copenhagen), 1938 p. 10.
15. ibid. p. 10.
16. ibid p. 15 and J. Wøllekær, 1997, pp. 67-84.
17. A. Lundkvist Andersen 1945, vol. 1, p. 438.
18. Old Boys – Et jubilæumsskrift. København 1953 (the Jubilee Review of the Old Boys association of Copenhagen, 1953), p. 16.
19. Et Jubilæumsskrift for Old Boys, København 1938 (the Jubilee Review of the Old Boys association of Copenhagen, 1938), p. 6.
20. Ibid p. 8.
21. Tourist Sport was at that particular time a range of different activities first of all walking tours, hiking, but also rowing and cycling.
22. Ibid. p. 6-7.
23. The charismatic, self-taught, health-prophet Capt. Jespersen as well as several Danish physicians were from the 1930's – 1950's promoting the moral and aesthetic codex: "Stay young" to prescribe the necessity of systematic physical activity in old age. See J.P. Jespersen 1934, and Carl Ottosen 1940. The fit old body became in the 1980's and 1990's

almost an icon of the will and ability to survive by conquering time and the aging process. See J. Povlsen 1996.
24. Old Boys – Et jubilæumsskrift. København 1953. (the Jubilee Review of the Old Boys Association of Copenhagen, 1953), p. 7.
25. See A. Diemer 1913, p. 34.
26. Handball as a sport has quite a noteworthy history in this connection, although the description of the Old Boys Association's role in the invention and implementation of this particular sport in Denmark has been rather exaggerated, according to the Danish Handball Federation's 100 years jubilee publication. DHF København 1997.
27. Et Jubilæumsskrift for Old Boys, København 1938 (the Jubilee Review of the Old Boys association of Copenhagen, 1938), p. 29.
28. Ibid. p. 11-12.
29. See J. Hansen 1988.
30. The Danish historian Jørn Hansen has investigated the social background of the initiators of the Danish Sport Federation (founded in 1896). He concludes that the pioneers of the Danish Sports Movement around the turn of the century were men characterised by progressive ideas, interest in growth and expansion, and a firm belief in the benefits of civilisation. See E. Trangbæk, J. Hansen, B. Ibsen, P. Jørgensen and N.K. Nielsen 1995, Vol. 1 pp. 24-26.
31. See Berlingske Tidende 25th of August 1926 and Jydsk Idræts Blad 18th of November 1926.
32. J. Frykman and O. Løfgren 1993.
33. See Old Boys – Et jubilæumsskrift. København 1953. (the Jubilee Review of the Old Boys association of Copenhagen, 1953), p. 31.
34. "Buller" is the nickname of masterjoiner Olaf Olsen, who was one of the pioneers of the Old Boys association in Copenhagen. He stayed a highly valued member of the Old Boys association until his death in 1952. Again and again he was the object of festive recognition.
35. Old Boys – Et jubilæumsskrift. København 1953. (the Jubilee Review of the Old Boys association of Copenhagen, 1953), p. 15
36. Ibid. p. 36
37. This motto is affirmed in Denmark's oldest football club: KB: Københavns Boldklub which was founded in 1876. For the role of football in the transition from boyhood to manhood see the cultural historian Niels Kayser Nielsen 1992 , p. 341. Nielsen takes here as his point of departure English sports historical research which, in the 1980's, laid particular stress on male socialisation in football, and an analysis of football at the close of the 19th century and emphasizes: "The local football clubs for boys and youths which arose from back street football and acted as a bridge between childhood and the adult world where: "the enthusiasm of boys for games was transformed into the brash style of the male world. Boys learned to drink and tell jokes, just as they learned the language of physical aggression"." (quoted from Richard Holt: Working class Football and the City, in: British Journal of Sports History, vol. 3 nr. 1 (1986) p. 7. (N.K. Nielsen's quotation)). As can be seen from the preceding, this was a repeated phenomenon of boys becoming men through sport – that is working class boys. Similar ritualised transitions for middle class boys existed in other sports such as fencing, tennis, skating, and gymnastics – all sports with stricter codified rules of behaviour than those which existed in early football. The historian Hans Bonde emphasizes this in his analysis of sport as a test of manhood, and as an initiation ritual on the same lines as the rituals of the boy scout movement. Hans Bonde: 1991, p. 22.
38. See A. A. Koldste 1996 p. 7.
39. See C. Shilling 1993 p. 163ff and C. Wouters 1986 pp. 405-427.

40. See H. Bonde: 1991 p. 21ff.
41. See A. James: Bodies of Knowledge: Growing up and Growing Old in this book.
42. See N. Elias 1978; E. Goffmann: 1969; C. Shilling 1993.
43. The socialization and phenomenological aspects of this fellowship of elderly men has been especially cultivated by the concept historian Søren Nagbøl. See Søren Nagbøl 1990 pp. 24-32.
44. See Ryssensteens historie. København 1933.
45. A. R. Nielsen 1935 p. 1213.
46. Ibid p. 1215.
47. Ibid p. 1214.
48. Idrætsforeningen Old Boys af Aarhus 1921-1996 Jubilee Review, p. 14. The original version of the song in Danish presents itself like this:
   Trækker vi i idrætstøjet
   er vi ikke mere mænd.
   Vi har ganske vist et ansvar,
   hvor så siden vi går hen.
   Som vor ungdom har vi pligter,
   (der er ingen, der dem svigter):
   Men på idrætspladsen er vi
   drenge, som får klap og skænd.
   Vi kan more os og kævles,
   men bli'r venner snart igen.
49. See B. Myerhoff 1984. pp.305-330. On p. 326 Barbara Myerhof writes: In my own fieldwork among the elderly, I was particularly struck by the frequency with which certain actions recalled the past. Songs, ritual storytelling, dancing and gestures were recurrent occasions when time was transcended. One of the elderly women with whom I was working explained this experience most precisely, referring to the significance of a prayer accompanied by certain ritual gestures. When I make movements, circling the Sabbath candles, calling their holiness to me, covering my eyes, then I feel my mother's hands on my smooth cheeks." Often on such occasions the elderly looked transformed. Their posture, energy, movements, facial expressions lightened, quickened, expressed freedom, and took on what can only be called an air of youthfulness. Then their songs, dances, and the like were not about anything else; though symbolic forms, they were not secondary experiences or interpretations, but original experiences, immediate and satisfying in themselves, sui generis.
50. See H. Bonde 1991, p. 56.
51. Tabooed in the sense that a distinction between child/infantility and adulthood, as we have seen earlier, was given decisive importance.
52. John Gillis expands this point concerning "the time we live by, and the time we live with" in his article: A World of Their Own Making. Families and the Modern Culture of Aging in this book.
53. See A.C. Meier 1906, pp. 40-41.
54. See K. Woodward 1991, p. 10 and p. 169.
55. See T. J. Csordas 1994, p. 10.
56. See N. K. Nielsen 1997, p. 26.
57. See H. Hazan 1980.
58. Jenny Hockey og Allison James 1995. James/Hockey also draw attention to the fact that the perception of a "second childhood" has a long tradition behind it and refer to its occurrence already in the works of Aristotle.

Bibliography

Bonde, H. *Mandighed og sport*, Odense Universitetsforlag. Odense, 1991.

Csordas, T. J. (ed.) *Embodiment and experience. The existential ground of culture and self.* Cambridge. Cambridge University Press. 1994.

Danish Handball Federation's 100 years jubilee publication. DHF København 1997.

Diemer, A. *Sport i den ældre Alder,* København 1913.

Eichberg, H. *Leistung, Spannung und Geschwindigkeit. Sport und Tanz im gesellschaftlichen Wandel des 18./19. Jahrhunderts.* Stuttgart, 1978.

Elias, N. The *Civilizing Process.* vol.1: The History of Manners, Basil Blackwell, Oxford 1978;

Et Jubilæumsskrift for Old Boys 1913 – 1938. København 1938.

Frykman, J. and Løfgren, O. *Den kultiverade människan.* Lund. Gleerup. 1993.

Gillis, J. *A World of Their Own Making. A History of Myth and Ritual in Family Life.* Oxford University Press, 1997.

Goffmann, E. *The Presentation of Self in Everyday Life.* Penguin, Harmondsworth, 1969.

Hansen, J. "Fra Crystal Palace til Athen". *Hurtigere, Højere, Stærkere.* Hansen, J. (ed.) Aabybro. Idrætshistorisk Årbog, 4. årg. 1988.

Hazan, H. *The Limbo People.* Routledge, London 1980.

Hermann, Aa. and Andersen, E. *Den Danske Idræts Bog.* Dansk Haandbogs Forlag, Kbh. 1935

Hockey, J. and James, A. "Back to Our Futures. Imaging second Childhood". *Images of Aging. Cultural Representations of Later Life.* (eds.) Featherstone, M. and Wernick, A. London. Routledge, 1995

Hopf, W. *Soziale Zeit und Körperkultur.* Afra Verlag, Münster, 1981.

Idrætsforeningen Old Boys. 50 års jubilæum 1913 – 1963. København 1963.

Jespersen, J.P. *Stavsystemet.* Jul. Gjellerups Forlag, Kbh. 1934.

Koldste, A. A. (ed.) *Old Boys. Idrætsforeningen Old Boys, Aarhus.* 1921-1996. Jubilæumsskrift.

Lundkvist Andersen, A. (ed.) *Dansk Sportsleksikon,* Kbh. 1945, bd. 1.

Meier, A.C. *Idrætsbogen.* Chr. Erichsens Forlag, København 1906.

Myerhoff, B. "Rites and Signs of Ripening: The Intertwining of Ritual, Time and Growing Older". *Age & Anthropological Theory.* D. Kertzer & J. Keith (eds.). London. Cornell University Press. 1984.

Nagbøl, S. "At bade er regionalt, nationalt og overnationalt. Helgoland på Amager".

Kropskultur og Idræt – regionalt, nationalt og internationalt. Jørn Hansen (ed.) Idrætshistorisk årbog. 6. årg. Odense. Odense Universitetsforlag 1990.

National Geographic, 192, no. 5, 1997.

Nielsen, A. R. Vikinger og Sørøvere, *Den Danske Idræts Bog.* Hermann, Aa. and Andersen, E. (eds.) København. Dansk Haandbogs Forlag. 1935.

Nielsen, N. K. *Fra Robin Hood til Fodbold. En kulturanalytisk studie i arbejderklassens kropskultur i England i 1800 tallet.* Odense University Studies in History and Social Sciences vol 154. Odense Universitetsforlag. Odense 1992.

Nielsen, N. K. *Krop og kulturanalyse. Den levede og den konstruerede krop.* Odense Universitetsforlag, Odense 1997.

Old Boys – Et jubilæumsskrift 1913 – 1953. København 1953.

Ottosen, C. *Hold dig ung – og stærk paa Sundhedens Kongevej i fin Form på alle Alderstrin.* De Samvirkende Sundhedsforeninger. Alf Nielsens Forlag, Kbh. 1940.

Povlsen, J. "Den gerontologiserede krop". *Idrætshistorie. Krop og Kultur.* Idrætshistorisk Årbog. Hansen, J. (ed.), Odense. Odense Universitetsforlag. 1996.

Rysensteens historie. København 1933.

Shilling, C. *The Body and Social Theory.* SAGE Publications, Ltd., London 1993.

Trangbæk, E., Hansen J., Ibsen, B., Jørgensen, P. and Nielsen, N. K. *Dansk Idrætsliv. Den moderne idræts gennembrud 1860-1940.* Vol. 1. København. Gyldendal, 1995.

Winding, O. S. "Fodbold", in A. C. Meyer *Idrætsbogen,* vol. 2, København 1909.

Woodward, K. *Aging and Its Discontents. Freud and Other Fictions.* Indiana University Press. Indianapolis. 1991.

Wouters, C. "Formalization and informalization: changing tension balances in civilizing processes". *Theory, Culture and Society,* 4 1986.

Wøllekær, J. "Mellem sport, adspredelse og selskabelighed". *Idrættens steder.* Jørn Hansen (ed.) Idrætshistorisk årbog. 13. årg. Odense. Odense Universitetsforlag. 1997.

Power to the Elders:

The Politics of Aging Amongst the Kikuyu Women of Kenya

Patricia Stamp

To any Kikuyu woman, it is axiomatic that elderhood is a negotiated, socially mediated state of being. For most who continue to live in the rural, clan based villages of the Kenyan central highlands, advancing years are welcomed as a time of increased autonomy and authority. An ideology of female elderhood constitutes the rich discursive ground upon which women stake their claim to, and qualifications for, political power. But this elderhood cannot be conceptualized as an essential state of being. Rather, it is a relational process, where youth prefigures the power of age, and where the seeds of successful elderhood are in turn meticulously planted in the young. Neither can Kikuyu women's elderhood be conceptualized as an individual condition. Moving through the life course in a series of age-graded ranks, women build on the intersubjective and co-operative practices laid down in girlhood, activating their collective power as they enter elderhood together.

The empirical ground of this investigation into the politics of aging amongst Kikuyu women is my research on women elders in the village of Mitero, Kiambu District, in 1974, 1981, 1985, and 1989. This furnished the basis for several articles on women's self-help groups and their relation to the locality and the state in Kenya.[1] The analysis is also informed by a set of vivid life histories from Mutira village in neighbouring Murang'a District collected by Jean Davison.[2] The Kikuyu have been important to study, both because of their status as a typical patrilineal kin-corporate society of the widespread Bantu linguistic group, displaying important general features of gender relations in precolonial and postcolonial Africa, and because of the historically central role they have played since the colonial era, as Kenya's most numerous, and until recently, dominant ethnic group.[3]

The argument in this chapter presupposes an "ethnographic present", a heuristic analytic device used to explore as best one can an African past lost to the inventions of colonial discourses and practices, and to uncover those aspects of the present that are continuous with that lost past – the "long ago or far away," to use Sacks's evocative phrase.[4] It is important to caution that while many Kikuyu continue to live in clan and lineage-organized villages, practising subsistence horticulture at least in part, all Kikuyu (and other Africans) are as modern as any other society on earth, in the sense that global capitalism, the contemporary nation state, and dominant patriarchal gender discourses provide their overarching reality. Moreover, a large number of urbanized or marginalized rural Kikuyu men and women no longer participate in the remnant Kikuyu polity.[5] The methodological path to an understanding of the politics of African women's aging is thus a rocky, indistinct one, along which one must pioneer backward in time, amongst imperfect ethnographies and the shards of old people's recounted memories. It is the vista that opens up along this path that reveals how powerfully culture and history shape the very construction of age, across human time and space.

Biology is not destiny for an aging Kikuyu woman, except in that menopause frees her time and energies from the preoccupations and constraints of childbearing, and creates a neutral sexual status that affords her a wider social stage than that granted to the sexually constrained childbearing mother. But motherhood always remains at the heart of things, even past the childbearing years. It is a permanent empowering condition, both discursively and materially: the maternal life course is the social scaffolding for a complex set of practices and perquisites that evolve as women age. And if motherhood is the pivot of a woman's life course, girlhood is its wellspring. Girls derive autonomy and esteem from their beauty, female camaraderie and controlled sexual freedom, and above all from their potential as future mothers; elderly women appropriate the freedom of girlhood as a nostalgic metaphor for the power and autonomy that comes with age.

The midwife 'Wanoi' of Mutira (a village in Murang'a District similar to the Kiambu District village of Mitero) encapsulates this symmetry succinctly in extolling her newfound post-menopausal freedom:

> "[The Kikuyu say that] 'a woman never challenged does not give birth.' We also say, 'Going wide is seeing and learning much.' The person who just stays in one place is a fool… Of all the changes [in my life], the one that changed me the most was when I gave birth. That's because I knew then that I had become a woman entitled to some duties and respect. But when I stopped menstruating I was happy, because now I am like a young girl again because I am not always having to wait and wash clothes and cook for everybody… If I spend

the night anywhere, nobody can ask me about it, and I do not have any small child who is crying – that makes me happy."[6]

It is not only in the village, but also on the contemporary national stage, that a discourse of motherly elderhood – closely kin to what I have elsewhere called 'combative motherhood', can be invoked.[7] When in 1991 a group of schoolgirls were killed or raped by schoolboys in the infamous 'St. Kizito massacre', the feminist leaders of Kenya constituted themselves as an organization, "Mothers in Action," and went on from their activism regarding the school tragedy to write a feminist agenda into the platform of Kenya's democratic opposition party.[8] In a less tragic but quite fascinating saga (which was followed avidly not only in Kenya but all over Africa), Wambui Otieno, the famous Kikuyu widow who fought through the Kenyan courts for the custody of her Luo husband's body, argued the case for her widow's rights from her moral position as a mother, wife, Christian, and founder of the Kenyan nation, in the course of which she became an almost mythical figure in the popular imagination. "I fought for independence and this judiciary," she asserted in the High Court trial.[9]

The subtlety of the Kikuyu lifecourse and women's complex positions along it highlight the point that for the Kikuyu, youth and old age are neither equal nor opposite, but rather create a complementary relationship: the young serve the old and in turn receive service when they become elders; elders, for their part, pay homage to the ancestors embodied in their young (a father calls his son "grandfather") or seek the origins of their present condition in their youthful past. It is this relational process that shapes the discursive and material power of women in their old age.

Conceptualzing aging and power in East Africa

The Kikuyu of Kenya are one of the African peoples characterized by an age grade structure. East African women's age grades have been very poorly studied; evidence can be found, however, that many societies in the region do indeed have women's age grades, and that these organize women's social, cultural and political life, and provide a collective counterweight to male authority and domination. Amongst the Kikuyu, when a woman enters the 'elders' age grade, *Nyakinyua*, her power and authority instantly increase. Coincident with menopause, elderhood for women furnishes them with discursive and material resources to exercise considerable power in their communities. While age grades are weakening in the current era, the discourse of elderhood remains a strong factor in women's ability to shape local politics and define the terms of "development."

In European and North American societies, the social construction of aging has not until recently become transparent to social science analysis.

Even today we must work quite hard to bring the historical and cultural dimensions of "old age" into focus. A major reason for this is that biology itself as a category has been culturally constructed, as a vessel that contains and explains the human life course. In other parts of the world, different possibilities present themselves because cultural templates of the life course prevent the construction of a purely biological model for aging. The presence of age grade systems in a number of East African societies, for example, suggests an obvious model for framing the concept of aging in these societies. One cannot **naturalize** aging in the presence of such determinant social structures in East African societies. Both men and women pass as members of a cohort through socially defined stages of the life course, with several sub-stages in each of childhood, adolescence, adulthood, and old age. Both are designated at the time of initiation in adolescence as members of an "age set," whose name relates to some current event or conforms to a cyclical formula. (For instance, a northern group of Kikuyu men circumcised in 1926, the year that the airplane was first seen in Kenyan skies, were named Ndege – literally "bird" – the Swahili neologism for airplane).

This model for aging, where biology only loosely guides the formulation of social age, not only configures a notion of aging very different from our predominant Western one, but positions the process of aging as a dominant factor in the dynamics of political, social and economic power. In pre-colonial polities, men held the most direct power in the patrilineal kin corporate societies of precolonial East Africa, in their collective capacity as lineage brothers and elder age set members. But gender relations were complex and counterbalancing, and provided considerable opportunities for women to exercise power and autonomy. These opportunities were grounded in women's dual capacity as wives of the lineage and as members of their elder age set. In some cases, as well, they exercised power as sisters of their natal lineage.[10]

Interestingly enough, the study of East African age grade systems has been an opportunity lost when it comes to exploring the social construction of aging. And the possibility that age grade systems, even vestigial ones, are a key to understanding the politics of the locality in contemporary East Africa has been even less imagined. Almost all the work on age grades was done by anthropologists of the early to mid-twentieth century; and this work, grounded as it was in the problematic of Structural-Functionalism, tended to explain age grades not in terms of the life course but as a structural device counterbalancing the familial descent systems of lineage and clan, thus providing a homeostatic mechanism for the good governance of the "tribe."

The study of women and age grades is an opportunity doubly lost. Age grade analyses, presuming monovalent male power structures, ignored almost completely the phenomenon of women's age grade systems. The

The author with her research assistent Rebecca Chege on left – dancing on tree-planting day with the Mitero-womens groups. (Credit: Charles K. Iruri).

evidence regarding women elders is nowhere systematically or intentionally presented in the mid-twentieth century anthropological treatises that investigated age-grade societies. Women's interaction with each other, or their participation in decision-making with men, is ignored or trivialized in these studies. Where an anthropologist took the trouble to record empirical data regarding women's agency and life course, as did Leakey and Lambert, discussed below, the contradictions between the descriptive evidence and the analytical conclusions are often almost laughable. As for contemporary analyses of African politics, the study of such an "anthropological" topic as age systems is beyond the methodological pale.

One of the few age grade analyses to deal with women, a 1980 study of the Latuka of the Sudan, specifies the women's age set system and explains differences between men's and women's age grade organization in terms of the social imperatives of the maternal life course.[11] Yet the article, in citing the mid-20th century East African anthropology, replicates its silences in the analysis of Latuka women. Thus, the study succumbs to the androcentrism that characterizes most of the East African anthropology. No-one thought to ask: do women elders traffic in power, and if so, how? By a sleight of hand that relegates all social and economic activity of women to the domestic sphere – women, after all, are responsible "only" for women's affairs – the transparent parallels between men's and women's age grade systems (if they have even been noticed) disappear. That men's authority structures are almost entirely to do with "men's affairs," i.e. that men and women have exclusive, if overlapping, domains of power, was simply invisible in an era when the term "man" unproblematically subsumed both men specifically and all humans in general.

Yet the evidence we can find out of the corners of our eyes suggest a way to begin conceptualizing the relationship between power and age in East African societies, an approach that will as well provide a valuable comparative tool for thinking about Western constructions of aging. We may be able to abstract the conditions under which age either confers or diminishes power, and those in which gender becomes a key variable.

The need for such peripheral vision in the difficult backward journey we must make to discover the relation between age, gender and power is exemplified by H.E. Lambert's much-referenced 1956 treatise, *Kikuyu Social and Political Institutions*. The study is intriguing because the author does indeed talk about organization amongst women, but he does so in such a convoluted way that he succeeds in distorting and eclipsing the women's age grade structure and political practices, while leaving rich clues as to their complexity and specificity. Lambert states unapologetically that "[Kikuyu] men say they do not know for certain whether gatherings of women are merely called for specific purposes or whether they are ad hoc committees of permanent and organized *chiama* [councils with political, social and judicial functions]." Men's *chiama*, on the other hand, are minutely analyzed as a core political institution of the Kikuyu. Lambert goes on to discuss the age-based leadership of a sub-group of the Kikuyu, the Meru. Through an androcentric sophistry he characterizes the *agambi* (leaders or "speakers") of the Meru young girls' set as "prefects" responsible for their age mates' etiquette. This schoolroom connotation is then carried over to married women and elders, with women once again remaining mysterious in the eyes of Lambert's male informants. "The young married women, the [male] elder[s] think, have also their *agambi*, who are sometimes called *nkatha*, [which] means a good housewife..." While *nkatha* might be "representatives among the women," this and other leadership terms "have acquired more or less technical meanings in special contexts."[12]

> "... The men apply them to the women whom they suppose to be the female counterparts of their own *agambi*. Whether the women use these words to denote their leaders the men do not profess to know. There is alleged to be a body called *kagiri* (literally 'small enclosure') *ka ntichio* ('committee of crones'), which is described as a "real kiama."... It has the power to inflict fines on women for various faults, though what those faults may be the men ... do not seem to know."[13]

If only Lambert had thought to gain himself some informants from amongst those "prefects," "good housewives" and "crones," we would have a wonderful picture of women's age sets and power structures amongst the different branches of the Kikuyu. Instead, we must read between the lines, to identify each of these caricatures as an overt leadership role, appropriate to the structure and stage within which women found themselves during their life course. Fortunately, a few feminist scholars have begun to tackle the issue of gender, age and power in East Africa, combining their contemporary ethnographic research with interpretive readings of the androcentric anthropology. These studies rescue women from the "domestic" realm: producing up to 90% of the food or managing all the dairy production and veterinary care of the family herd cease to be labelled mere "household tasks." Elder women's management of the affairs of younger women and girls comes to be viewed for the public role in the polity that it is. It is a matter of breaking the giant tautology that has ruled most 20th century anthropology: any work or actions by women – even if it is growing all the food – must be "domestic" because women occupy the private domestic sphere. Once one takes the elementary feminist step of assuming all women's practices to be political, or at least not necessarily private, their role in the governance of African polities jumps sharply into focus, rather like the holographic images that wink at you if you turn them in the light.[14]

It is a frequent mistake to assume that domestic or relational terms like "housewife" denote literal rather than metaphorical qualities. Motherhood, time and wifehood are indeed the assets that furnished an older woman's social world with the human subjects of her newfound political power: grown children, and the younger women – and men – of the local polity. And the younger women were organized into self-governing age sets, just like the men. Payments by younger women to older ones, far from being mysterious fines for "various faults" as Lambert puts it, were a system of fees (and sometime penalties) that provided cohesion to the power structure, marked passage through the age grades, and cemented the symbolic and material power of elder women.[15] The control of younger wives in the village by their female elders, far from being a punitive or largely exploitative relationship, represented a legitimate authority counterbalancing patrilineal control of women, whether by their husbands or their male in-laws. This relationship between older and younger women also put considerable human labour at the disposition of women elders as a group. And all young women could look forward to the time when they would be on the receiving end of the relationship.

Girls become elders

It is not just youthful beauty and freedom that shaped the behaviour of girls. They were already inscribed with their destiny as powerful elders; and in many ways their freedom of action mirrored that of women elders. Old women speak succinctly about the centrality of motherhood in their lives, but eloquently about girlhood, and in the activities so lovingly reminisced can be seen the outlines of a mature subjectivity grounded in self-confidence in one's autonomy, deep reliance on the collectivity of one's age mates, and a healthy scepticism about the shibboleths of patriarchal ideology. The sense of being the cornerstone of the community's material life comes through strongest of all. The mid-wife 'Wanoi': "What am I proudest of having achieved? I know I have achieved a lot of things – like making that granary there. It is me who thought how to make it. My husband never asked."[16]

And the coin of the relation between girls, women and elders was food and service: the materials and labour of women's productive lives. Girls of thirteen or fourteen, still living with their mothers, would form their own *ngwatio* (collective cultivation) groups, thereby shifting their allegiance and energy from their mothers' homestead to their new age set. Their initiation through a cliteridectomy ceremony during the harvest of pigeon peas would inaugurate their age grade status as *muumo*, a stage preparatory to adulthood. They would join newly circumcised boys in a communal life with carefully regulated sexual activity, in a two-month period known as

Irua. The widow 'Wangeci' is eloquent on the importance of this stage of a girl's life.

> "*Irua* taught me how to move from childhood to womanhood... There was the time for women to go for *Irua* and so we did. It had much meaning, as it was a way of doing what the ancestors had done. It was a way of staying part of them... During this time we would go to dances. We would spend the day dancing and we even could decide to spend the night at the [house] of a mwanake kiumbi [a handsome, well-liked young man]. Before we went there we would tie our clothes with a rope. We would get one edge of the skirt at the front and tie it between our legs and round each thigh with the rope – that way you were protecting yourself. We would spend the whole night at this young man's house being turned over by him on the bed. He would only touch our breasts and nowhere else. At times, we would be so many on the bed that the man would ask his friend to come and help."[17]

Girls would also commence fulfilment of a series of ritual obligations to their female seniors. Age sets with names corresponding the boys' sets were the context for their work and play. Old women of Mitero reminisce happily about their *muumo* years. Says one, "When we were older girls, we used to make *mote* [a kind of gruel] in the newly married wives' houses. Also, we used to collect pigeon peas from any woman's *shamba* [agricultural plot], cook and eat, and go home laughing and cracking jokes because we had eaten well... Girls rarely ate at their mothers' houses unless they wished to. It was a custom to cook their own food and eat communally. They also used to cook food in the season for dances."[18]

The *mote* fee permitted girls to join the dances and to receive instruction in a variety of matters: "the proper use of ornaments and clothing, privacy, personal cleanliness, and the rules governing the practice of limited lovemaking which will henceforth be allowed between them and their warrior friends."[19] Further, eating well together meant independence as well as bonding for girls. As one Mitero woman suggests: "Girls always cooked and ate food and made sure they had enough. They fed themselves to become strong, so that they would have the strength to dance."[20]

This fondly remembered period of safe group sex, dancing, good eating, and "hanging out" with each other had a profoundly serious purpose for girls' transition to womanhood, according to the Mitero elders. Successful participation in the collectivity of the age set was a predictor of a girl's future success as a productive and politically active woman – whether in her capacity as wife, mother, or ruling elder. Says one elder, "If a girl did not move about with other girls, automatically her mother would start worrying that she is not with her age group and thus will not know about worldly affairs."[21] As for the dances themselves, they were the material and symbolic focal point of the transition from girlhood to womanhood. Louis B. Leakey, the chronicler of late 19th to early 20th century Kikuyu life, provides (in spite of the stunning androcentrism of this three-volume work) a lambent vignette of this pivotal moment in girls' lives, in his recounting from oral history of the *Kuria Muhothi* ("to eat what has been collected"):

> "As soon as all the *muumo* girls had obtained the right to take part in the dances, they were anxious to achieve full equal status with the senior girls in order that they might enjoy the other privileges, in particular, the right to link little fingers with the senior girls, the right to use the special hand-clapping type of greeting used between girls, and the right to have *nguiko* (restricted intercourse) with the warriors. In order to acquire these rights, the *muumo* girls were required by their seniors to pay a fee called *muhothi* (a collection), which was consumed at a ceremonial feast called *kuria muhothi*. For this feast every junior girl had to persuade her family to let her have yams, sugar-cane, and ripe bananas. The juniors brought their fees together to a place in the bush selected by the seniors, and in the late afternoon the feast began, with the juniors acting as servants to the seniors and peeling the yams, preparing the sugar-cane, etc… A short time after the feast provided by the juniors, the seniors in their turn provided one of these feasts for girls only, to which they invited the juniors. With this act the juniors were acknowledged as equals."[22]

The rights and responsibilities, including restricted sex, taught to juniors by seniors following this feast were a vital part of the transition to the stage of girlhood preparatory to formal adulthood and marriage. The sense of competence, their control over their sexuality, work and social lives, and responsibility to their age mates and girls younger than themselves – and even their participation in the selection of a husband – shines through Leakey's brief account of girls' practices. (It is with a sense of bemusement that one reads, just a few pages earlier, about "the right to control all unmarried, initiated girls" by the eldest warrior age group).[23]

Women thus approached adulthood and marriage with a precise understanding of their place in the structured life course, and a sense of agency grounded in the collectivity of their age set, which strictly governed the transition from girlhood to marriage. Thus empowered, they are difficult to picture as the downtrodden objects of patriarchal exploitation depicted in many of the studies on African women. The reminiscence of the very elderly 'Hannah Nguru', (who was married during the generation of [the age set] Ndege, and hence was about 74), testifies to this empowered, collective agency:

> "A girl used to dance *gichukia* with other groups of girls and boys. When there was no *gichukia* we used to go to the *shamba* and assist with the *shamba* work, such as harvesting millet. Some girls got married after *gichukia*. A boy would go the girl's father if he loved her, to ask whether he could marry her. Then the girl was called and asked whether she wanted to marry that man. She could agree or refuse. Parents used to advise their sons to marry from a particular home where a girls was hard-working or from a good clan. No girl could ever go alone for any type of work, such as drawing water from the river or collecting firewood. They always walked in a group to every function. Especially if a girl went for *thigo* [*nguiko*] in a boy's *ithunwo* [temporary hut] alone, then other girls will say she has her own affairs that she wants to perform. These sort of affairs for girls together were very good. We used to be very happy during our time for it. Today, such affairs for girls are according to their own God, because we do not understand what they are doing."[24]

'Wangeci' and the other Mutira narrators stress the importance of using one's intelligence: being a mature, responsible adult is graphically described in terms of having "more brains". It is worth highlighting these narrators' reflections on intellect and self-esteem because all too often African women are portrayed in scholarly and popular literature as silent victims of sexist behaviour, persons always acted upon rather than acting. Unfortunately, the research that demonstrates women's active agency in African societies is piecemeal and scattered.

The years of young wifehood and motherhood before the children were grown seemed to pass in a blur for Kikuyu women. The Mutira and Mitero women's reports of their time as *Kang'ei* (the age grade of mothers of uninitiated children, i.e. from roughly 18 to 35) are filled with the details of their work in the fields and their duties to their husbands and to women elders. In that Kikuyu society is patrilineal and patrilocal, many wives move away from their natal village. Particularly when they are were newly married they seem to have been under the thumb of their often arbitrary husbands. 'Esther Njeri' vividly encapsulates a common experience of young wives and their feelings about it:

> "Women used to be ordered to perform their duties by their husbands. If a husband saw a mistake at home, such as the goats not fed well, or gruel not made, any time of the day or night she could be woken to do the work. Men of those days were foolish because they did not mind whether the wife had to perform her duties in the middle of the night; for example she could be told to go to the *shamba* and get food for the goats, and he did not care if the hyenas ate her."[25]

171

But with time, the new group of age mates, comprising the lineage wives of a village, including co-wives, consolidated into an effective collectivity. The inculcation into the group began right at marriage, and wives brought to their communal work with other women, including their co-wives, the collective subjectivity, skills in group interaction, and commitment to women's solidarity that was fostered amongst the *muumo* girls. Says Mitero elder 'Jane Njoki':

> "When I was a girl, we used to harvest millet in a group. We used to cook food and build small shades along the road and put food in them for travellers. The food was sweet potatoes, arrow root and roasted bananas. When a girl was getting married, groups of women each carried a bunch of bananas to her home. When I married I joined with a group of women who could come together when there was a house to be thatched. This was the same group that carried stones from the river to build the health clinic in 1948."[26]

So important was this collective activity of young wives that failure to participate, as with too-individualistic girls, brought censure. 'Monica Mundia' states that she joined her women's group "because if I am in difficulty they will help me. The group is like my relatives. Women who are not in the groups are nicknamed by group members – because they can be thieves who steal from other women's homes if they are not doing group work and they are not at home."[27]

It was the cohort of lineage wives – mothers to the next generation of the lineage's men – that constituted the set that would eventually become dominant in the local political economy, once the cohort reached the *Nyakinyua* stage. 'Jane Njoki', who carried stones as a young *Kang'ei* wife in 1948, was by 1974 the leader of one of the most active and forward-looking self-help groups in the village.[28] In the meanwhile, however, the younger members of the *Kang'ei* age grade were at the beck and call of the *Nyakinyua* elders, with their husbands closely monitoring – and sometimes censoring – their age set activities. 'Hannah Nguru' is again informative about this sometimes coercive relationship. Speaking as a *Nyakinyua* in 1974, she said:

> "We used to bring cases against young married women's behaviour. If we saw a fault they were fined. What we used to look at was how the younger women treated their husbands; how they walked and talked in the presence of older women, whether a young wife abused her father-in-law's wives. The *Nyakinyua* women would tell the other *Kang'ei* women not to help her with her work [perform *ngwatio* for her], and they would obey until such a time as she had made *mote* for them and so that her punishment would be over."[29]

For all that *Kang'ei* women's behaviourial lapses appear to have preoccupied *Nyakinyua* elders' thoughts, the chief content of relations between *Nyakinuya* and *Kang'ei*, however, was in the form of service to the elders: the cooking of food, or group cultivation on their *shambas*. In many parts of Africa, such service is necessary for promotion through the ranks, and indeed, it can be seen as a valuable economic and social system whereby youthful labour is usefully deployed according to the collective decisions of elder women (and hence in the interests of women as a whole) at the same time that solidarity of women across the life cycle is discursively and materially reinforced. That the relationship between *Kang'ei* and *Nyakinyua* women was characteristically agonistic did not detract from the benefit in rendering Kikuyu society as a whole more egalitarian, and retaining in the hands of women significant material and ideological resources of the polity. Whether resentfully described as onerous tasks by *Kang'ei* women, or celebrated as the perquisites of authority by *Nyakinyua* women, the details of service were parsed out in ritual foodstuffs for ritual occasions, and formally organized work parties on designated sides of the agricultural plots.

> "*Kang'ei* used to make six gourds of oil from *mbariki* seeds, then each woman would bring food, which the *Nyakinyua* women would eat separately. The oil was divided among the two groups: *Kang'ei* would get three, and *Nyakinyua* would get three. This meeting would be for the purpose of turning the *Kang'ei* women into *Nyakinyua*. If *Kang'ei* women attended *Nyakinyua* events prior to this ceremony, they were fined or published, in the form of cooking for the *Nyakinyua* women."[30]

'Esther Njeri' notes that paraffin and cooking fat have replaced *mbariki* oil in the graduating ceremony. "They continue to do this ceremony today because the older people of the clan who died spoke a kirumi ["curse" or spell] to ensure that the custom would go on. This ceremony is like the religion of Kikuyu people."[31] *Nyakinyua* women had some reciprocal responsibilities in these inter-age grade activities as well, but woe betide the *Kang'ei* woman who complained if they didn't fulfil them:

> "When *Kang'ei* women went to work the *Nyakinyua* roasted bananas for the babies [of the *Kang'ei*]. If they happened to eat them and not give them to the babies, and the *Kang'ei* got annoyed, the *Nyakinyua* women would punish the *Kang'ei* for being annoyed. As punishment they would have to cook food for the *Nyakinyua* women. The *Kang'ei* women should respect the senior women, then they should join them and enjoy."[32]

Kang'ei women's behaviour may have been ruled by the elders, but the organization of their working lives, and much of their social lives, into a woman-centred realm of action provided a powerful counterweight to the patriarchal tendencies of this patrilineal society.[33] The older women talked of *ndundu*, ongoing organizations with economic, social and judicial functions. In Mitero, the *ndundu* was known as *nyumba* (literally, "house"), and its membership comprised the women married into the village lineage, Mutego. *Ngwatio*, co-operative cultivation of each woman's field in turn, and *matega*, a custom where the group would furnish women in childbed with firewood, food and water, were the vital material practices on which women's solidarity rested. And it is these practices which today have been transformed and expanded, in the context of "modern" self-help groups, into co-operative village enterprise, and revolving credit schemes. Both of these put more economic power in the hands of women than they could gain as individuals.[34]

But it was motherhood, above all, that determined a woman's status. "The more children a woman has, the more prosperous she is considered. Mothers who have raised many children are highly regarding by both sexes," remarks Jean Davison.[35] The powerful connection between motherhood and status accounts for so many of the Mitero informants denouncing birth control as "poison," cutting off the life of a future President Kenyatta, "or you, Rebecca" [my research associate]."[36] The Mutira women whose life histories Davison chronicled accorded her the respect of referring to her by the name of her first-born child. Being *Nyina-wa-Stephen* (Mother-of-Stephen) "allowed me to gain an acceptable position in Mutira Location... It was my position as a mother that gave me access to certain information that I otherwise might have been denied."[37] The title "mother" was a generalized term, in fact, for all older women deserving respect. Says 'Wangeci,' "When my children were growing up, I taught them to respect their elders. I told them, 'Any woman married to somebody of your father's *riika* [age set], respect her and call her 'mother.'"[38]

"WOMEN WHO HAVE EXPERIENCED LIFE"

It was when children were grown that women really came into their own. There were two dimensions to the status of a woman at this point of the life course. First, being the mother of grown sons was the acme of social status and political power for women. Says 'Wanjiku,' one of the Mutira narrators:

> "As an old woman, I try and counsel my sons now. Gatae – now that he is a man of the people [assistant chief] – I remind him that he cannot come home late at night with a family here waiting for him. He must learn to carry the country [sublocation] with *rurigi* [strings] rather than *mukwa* [a carrying rope]. We have a saying . . . 'Why carry it with a rope when you can use a string.' When I hear that any of my

sons have quarrelled with their wives, I call that son and tell him it is not good to quarrel because it will teach the children bad behaviour."[39]

This status was more than titular, as Leakey described it in turn-of-the-century society:

"Among some peoples the life of an old woman is one of suffering and hardship, but a Kikuyu woman who had sons was never in this position. The love and respect which a Kikuyu man showed to his mother was quite touching, and exceeded that shown to his father... Few men would openly go against their mother's wishes... Nor would any man whose mother was alive make any decision of importance about his property or his family affairs without first consulting her."[40]

Second, as "women who have experienced life,"[41] the *Nyakinyua* elders held power both within and beyond the village. Several feminist studies chronicle the scope of 19th century Kikuyu women's activities. Although the Kikuyu were primarily a horticultural society, they engaged in trade with surrounding societies, both for consumption and for the acquisition of "prestige" goods. While men controlled the ivory trade, generating wealth for additional wives and hence expanded homesteads, older women travelled to neighbouring pastoral areas bartering food they produced, as well as honey, pottery, and other goods for livestock. These practices, too, enhanced the standing of their marital lineages, especially in regard to their sons' success as lineage leaders. Contrary to assumptions about men having exclusive control of livestock, women had considerable control over the livestock that they brought back from their trading expeditions, as well as over the sheep and goats given to their care at marriage.[42]

There is no doubt that *Nyakinyua* elders saw their authority over younger women as a pleasurable responsibility. Regarding their right to fine *Kang'ei* women for bad behaviour, 'Hannah Nguru' said that the activity was "a sort of enjoyment for *Nyakinyua* women;" all the *Nyakinyua* informants revealed their enthusiasm to carry out the managerial tasks of their age grade. We learn much about female subjectivity and its relation to African social relations and life course regimes from the reflections of 'Wangeci,' a widow in the full flower of her elderhood:

"Which of my roles in life is most important to me? Now, the most important is cultivating my farm and doing the work of the homestead, because those are needed before all else. Then I would say being a member of the Mother's Union and Uritu wa Gatwe ["Power of Gatwe" – a self-help group], because the women's groups help me a lot, as I've said. Being a mother or grandmother is next most important. Then the one of being a wife to my husband, because the role of being a daughter was a long time ago... My strongest character is that I like people and I'm hospitable to all – even when calling you to come and eat my food, it is with a clean and happy heart that I do it. I can't think of anything I'd like to change – I feel satisfied with myself. Being a woman means being able to keep things to myself,to go ahead and do them but not talk about them."[43]

"THESE ARE MODERN TIMES": BREAKING THE TIE BETWEEN AGE AND POWER

In East Africa from colonial times on, age-based authority for both men and women has been undermined by the authority conferred through education, on the one hand, and the formal, specialized political and bureaucratic positions of power on the other. Nevertheless, age remains a powerful factor in the equation of political power. The first president of independent Kenya, Jomo Kenyatta, chose the highly symbolic honorific of "Mzee" ("old man"), while his popular young wife was known as Mama Ngina ("Mother" being a designation often taken by presidents' wives in Africa to denote their aspiration to symbolic motherhood of the nation).

However, the perquisites of age have become a moveable feast in the age of formal Western education, and bureaucratic non-consensual forms of local governance. In Mitero, the old chief Samuel Githimbo, who was the ranking Mutego lineage elder in the village, was supplanted in 1985 by a thirty year old technical college-trained stranger to the area, in spite of campaigning by Mitero for its traditional elder. Younger men who become powerful take on the social trappings of elderhood: by claiming their perquisites, exercising the responsibilities, and dispensing the largesse, they can, in effect, become a young "elder". I knew of one young Kalenjin man in his 20s who, on his return to a very poor village with a new wife and some capital for a new business, established his elderhood very immediately and directly. He built himself a new family compound of the finest rondavels in the village; he made a major donation to the village primary school, enabling the community to commence building a new schoolhouse; and he took charge ten years early of his designated portion of his father's cattle herd. In doing so, he exhausted his business capital, but his status as an elder ten to fifteen years before the designated time ensured his place in the political power structure of the village.

The age-based authority of women has suffered in particular since colonial times. From a position of educational equality women fell behind men, in that formal schooling was and is seen as less vital for women, and their educational levels are consequently much lower. Colonial local government was promulgated as a strictly male preserve, a pattern that persists today. Moreover, stringently Victorian values regarding gender relations were inculcated, via colonial policy, missionary proselytizing and a newly sexist political hegemony. These reinforced and brought to the fore the formerly constrained patriarchal tendencies of Kenyan patrilineal societies. I explore this theme at length in my study of the Otieno burial saga, where I argue for the existence of a "collaborative hegemony" of the political state in alliance with the sub-national kin-organized polities of clans and lineages, both structures having a political and economic interest in the co-optation of gender relations and the control of women. The collaborative strategy conspires to constrain women and younger men, inventing "custom" and manipulating the traditions of motherhood and wifely responsibility, for the purposes of neocolonial capitalist state power on the one hand, and the aggrandizement of locally powerful men on the other.[44]

Mitero and Mutira women express their feeling of loss concretely. Interestingly, they focus less on their increased subordination to their husbands than on the breakdown of the age-based relations between elder women, younger women, and girls. The midwife 'Wanoi' of Mutira said, "Long ago, when a woman had a son as old as [my own], she could become an elder and was made a member of the *kiama* if the woman wanted to. But these days there is no recognition when a woman's child gets circumcised... The old customs are not followed now.[45] 'Cecilia Wangui,' a 50 year-old Mitero woman, complained about the collapse nowadays of a proper distance between elders and juniors. She says the age grade system had been weakened, "because now women's discussion has become free, so that any woman can say anything in the presence of any other woman, no matter whether she is a *Nyakinyua* or a *Kang'ei*. In those days if the *Kang'ei* talked abusively or cracked jokes in the presence of *Nyakinyua*, they were fined – in the form of cooking special food such as millet and black peas. I think this was good because younger women respected older women. These days there are no ways to show that kind of respect among women. If it weren't for these self-help groups we have instead, people could forget one another."[46]

The widow 'Wangeci' of Mutira bemoans the demeaning of girlhood: "There is nothing that can take the place of *Irua* today. Big girls who are grown and mature are playing with girls of their daughters' age. There is no separation of age groups. You can see a girl swinging her hips in front of her father and mother nowadays."[47] 'Monica Mundia,' the chairwoman of a Mitero women's self-help group, asserts that young women "won't agree to help their mother-in-law. They say they have one husband and not two [referring to their mother-in-law]. Today young women say we are foolish, and they do not want to be taught by us. Perhaps when they grow older they will get clever."[48] 'Grace Nyambura', member of a Mitero self-help group named for the *Kang'ei* age grade, sees the attenuation of younger women's service to elders as a consequence of the need for women's groups to earn cash for their rotating credit fund: "We cultivate for other people, and when we are paid we vote who among us is going to receive that money first."[49]

The dissipation of the age grade system is at the heart of the problem, according to 'Wangeci'.

> "Even if we tried to change back to the old ways, everything would go up in the air – it would have no meaning. In my time, one's *riika*-mates were important, but today *mariika* [plural] have no importance to younger women. For us, they still have meaning... Now, a younger woman will talk and joke with a man – even a younger one. In our case, those who were younger than us, if we met with them, we had our own way of greeting them that showed the separation between our ages. Now, it is different."[50]

Conclusion

It is clear that the very constraints and obligations of wife- and motherhood within the Kikuyu gender system – to bear children for their husband's lineage, to produce food and offer hospitality, to manage many aspects of the material life of the locality, and to act as the linchpin in a wide network of affinal kin relations – provided women in the past with the opportunity to exercise political power and the authority to make decisions. The potential for this power and authority, nurtured in girlhood, and largely latent in the childbearing years, came to fruition in elderhood. The age-grade system was a chief means by which women took up this opportunity. It provided the base for their strategies to generate resources and the forum for their collective decision making with regard to matters within their sphere of authority. As Carolyn Clark so succinctly puts it, "Despite an ideology of male dominance pervasive in many kin relations and in areas characterized as the 'prestige economy,' Kikuyu women emerge as the actors with control over resources vital in a system in which relations of production enter into political strategies and are built into the social relations of power."[51]

Today, while the nature of state hegemony has distorted and attenuated the precolonial practices and structures that linked age and authority for women, and has ruptured the web of relations between women and girls, some of the material elements and much of the discursive power of elderhood remains. Not only amongst the Kikuyu, but everywhere in Africa, elderly mothers exercise their power to curse and bless, to manage the affairs of younger women and men, and to practise, in this era fraught with the disintegrating forces of Structural Adjustment and the millennial capitalist order, that special genius for small-scale governance that was the foundation of African civilization, and is its best hope for the future.

1. My research spanning nineteen years with Rebecca Njeri Chege on Mitero village in the Kenyan highlands revealed the centrality of women's collaborative endeavours for the life of rural communities. The practice of cooperation and the discourse of communality surviving from precolonial times animates the women's contemporary self-help groups. Nothing to do with aid projects, the Mitero self-help groups flourish as a means for women to cope creatively with the sweeping post-independence economic and social change and with the exigencies of a neocolonial political economy. *Ngwatio* and another term, *matega*, referring to women's mutual help during childbirth, have taken on new meanings expressing collective economic and social strategies to cope with their double domination, as peasants in an exploitative petty commodity production system, and as women, a subordinated category within the peasantry.
   The chief studies derived from the field research are Stamp 1975-76;1984;1986 as well as "*Matega*: Manipulating Women's Co-operative Traditions for Material and Social Gain in Kenya", Canadian Association of African Studies Conference, University of Alberta, Edmonton, May 1987 and at the Third International Interdisciplinary Congress on Women, Trinity College, Dublin, July 1987.
2. Jean Davison and the Women of Mutira, Voices From Mutira: Lives of Rural Gikuyu Women, Boulder and London: Lynne Rienner Publishers, 1989 (hereafter cited as Mutira). Davison surveyed 101 women, and collected and organized eight narratives from the women surveyed. The study thus engendered is a model of collaborative research between a Western scholar and African women. I am grateful to Davison for conceptualizing the study and providing rich primary data in the published text.
3. Other well-known Bantu ethnic groups around Eastern, Central, and Southern Africa are, for example, the Zulu and Xhosa of South Africa; the Shona of Zimbabwe; the Bakongo of the Congo (formerly Zaire); the Baganda of Uganda; and the Swahili of coastal East Africa (whose language is the lingua franca for the region). The Kikuyu are the group who promulgated the Mau Mau uprising against the British colonialists in the 1950s, while Kenya's first president and earliest apologist for Kikuyu culture, the Kikuyu Jomo Kenyatta, shaped the identity of Kenya from the 1930s to the 1970s. The concept of kin-corporate society, i.e. a precolonial form of political economy grounded in kin relations organized by clan and lineage, is taken from Karen Sacks's (1979) excellent study. The study continues to be the definitive survey text on political economy and gender relations in pre-colonial Africa, as well as for a model methodology to get at "long ago or far away" (cf. Sacks p.3), through the critical use of anthropological and historical texts. The classic texts bracketing the historical and ethnographic study of the Kikuyu are Louis B. Leakey 1977 [1933] (see note 21 below); Jomo Kenyatta 1938 and Godfrey Muriuki 1974.
4. Sacks 1979, p 3.
5. This is to observe O. Onoge's (1977) injunction against "the functional amnesia" of ethnography. For a rigorous and humane account of the historical processes of marginalization amongst the Kikuyu, with an excellent focus on the experience of women, see T. Kanogo 1987. In this study I infer social and political relations of the pre-colonial past from my interviews in the 1970s and 1980s, from historical, anthropological and life-history secondary sources; and from my 30 year study of contemporary Kenyan politics and society. I make it clear in the text when I am referring to the colonial and pre-colonial past or to the transformed post-colonial present, and describing the nature of contemporary local politics.
6. The midwife 'Wanoi', life history in Mutira 1989, pp.167, 168. Wanoi and all other women's names are pseudonyms.
7. Stamp 1991, pp. 808-45; 1995. I first appropriated the term "combative motherhood" from Maxine Molyneux's excellent analysis of feminist discourse in a revolutionary context (1985). See Stamp 1995, p. 76-77.

8. "The political warriors [on the national stage], educated, worldly and economically privileged, draw on the same subject positions as their peasant countrywomen, often using them in a very sophisticated way, and working on a more overtly ideological terrain. Presenting themselves as mothers, wives, providers, responsible social agents, and loyal citizens, they engage with the patriarchal laws and repressive politics of the state." (Stamp 1995, p. 79).
9. Patricia Stamp 1991, p. 819. Wambui lost custody of the body, on the grounds of a sucessful judicial appeal to "customary law," and he was buried in triumph in his ancestral home; but she retained the joint marital property, which had been a target of Otieno's kin who promulgated the case. For both Wambui's ethnic group, the Kikuyu, and her husband S.M. Otieno's, the Luo, precolonial gender relations were not as unidimensionally patriarchal as Otieno's clan's arguments and the court judgements implied, as the discussion in the following sections reveals (see also n. 10).
10. See Sacks 1979 and F. Mackenzie 1990, for a theoretically subtle and empirically rich account of the political economy of gender amongst a sub-group of the Kikuyu, the Murang'a. Gender relations posed a contradictory complexity, however. While the dominance of a patrilineal ideology is suggested by postmarital residence patterns, property rights and the status of children, women occupied an important structural position in the lineage system of both societies. Even today, as mothers and wives and to a lesser extent as daughters, their productive and reproductive roles are crucial for the continuity of the lineage, a core concept in the social structure of all patrilineal East African ethnic groups. Achola Pala Okeyo (1980) presents an excellent historical/-anthropological analysis of Luo gender relations. Stamp (1995) investigates women's agency in contemporary Kenya.

    Wambui Otieno herself claimed her status as "Waiyaki's daughter", a series of her ancestors having played prominent roles in the anticolonial struggle. While women's multiple roles unequivocally testify to the structural importance of women, they also represent contradictions and conflicts in power relations between men and women as political and economic actors within the context of the lineage system. It has been the contradiction between patrilineal ideology and women's structural importance that opened the door to more patriarchal, sexist interpretations of gender relations in the present, as exemplified by the clan's construction of them in the Otieno case. The court judgments are a striking example of the way in which the historic position of women is shorn of its complexities and contradictions in the construction of customary law, to the detriment of women's standing and rights.
11. D. Kertzer and O.B.B. Madison 1981, p.109-10. For all that this study provides a valuable focus on age sets and the life course, it falls prey to the conclusions of the androcentric anthropology of East Africa, uncritically accepting the position on women's organizations put forward by Lambert (see below) and other writers.
12. H.E. Lambert 1956, 97- 98.
13. Ibid.
14. One illuminating study is J. Abwunza 1997. Abwunza conducted a long term ethnographic study of the Maragoli people of Western Kenya, a Bantu-speaking group quite closely related to the Kikuyu. Another is Bonnie Kettel 1992. See also Stamp 1986, p. 31-37. J. van Allen 1972 provides a useful analysis from the other side of the continent of women's collective jurisdiction over both male and female behaviour in the village. This and a host of other studies reveal that there is no public/private dichotomy in most precolonial African polities: marriage is everyone's business, and the politics of gender are seamlessly woven into the political economy of the locality. I critique the public/private dichotomy as one of core the conceptual problems infecting development thinking about women and gender relations in Stamp 1989, p. 113-16.
15. See 'Cecilia Wangui' of Mutira's lament below regarding the disappearance of penalties

for lapses in the deference essential to age grade etiquette, and the negative consequence of this change for women's collective agency.
16. 'Wanoi', Mutira 1989, p. 168.
17. 'Wangeci', Mutira 1989, p. 121, 123.
18. 'Esther Njeri', Mitero interviews, 1974.
19. G. Kershaw 1973. This study, and Kershaw's earlier work with John Middleton 1965, are vital sources for description of life course events amongst the Kikuyu.
20. 'Elizabeth Mwere-ini', Mitero interviews, 1974. Almost all the reminiscent comments cited in this study are from the 1974 interviews, in that the questions in 1981 and 1985 were oriented towards current socio-economic practices and the self-help groups.
21. 'Teresa Wanjiku', Mitero interviews, 1974.
22. L. B. Leakey 1977, Vol. II, p. 738. Leakey's 1400-page, three-volume study, based on his fieldwork in 1937-1938, was published posthumously by his wife Mary Leakey. Louis Leakey had refused to abridge the 650,000 words of his manuscript, and it lay unpublished, prey to insects, until soon before his death. Mary Leakey "corrected and reorganized" the surviving text, and it constitutes today the most comprehensive account of 19th to early 20th century Kikuyu culture, a fascinating archive in spite of its androcentrism. From today's perspective, the Victorian mindset exhibited by Leakey and Lambert, which saw no oddity or bias in focussing exclusively on men and on women viewed through a male prism, is almost incomprehensible. For a feminist scholar, it is a tragedy that Leakey's golden opportunity to capture 19th century Kikuyu women's lives, through oral accounts of women comparable to those of his male informants, was lost. One sifts through the pages of this wonderful text, gleaning the fragments of insight and information that slip through the cracks, and wishes for a time travel ticket to Leakey's camp in Nakuru.
23. Leakey 1977, Vol II, 721. By contrast, the Mutira widow 'Wangeci' describes wonderfully the process by which a young suitor would, over a number of days, hang about a girl's father's compound to elicit the interest of her mother and father, and her own approval, to proceed with an exploration of marriage prospects. (Mutira 1989, pp. 124-25, and see 'Esther Njeri's' account that follows).
24. 'Hannah Nguru,' Mitero interviews, 1974.
25. 'Esther Njeri', Mitero interviews, 1974.
26. 'Jane Njoki', Mitero interviews, 1974.
27. 'Monica Mundia', Mitero interviews, 1974. Hannah was perhaps rather superstitious: she also remarked that "a person with no religion is like a witch."
28. Jane Njeri, Mitero Interviews, 1974.
29. 'Hannah Nguru', Mitero interviews, 1974.
30. 'Mirika Kabura', Mitero interviews, 1974.
31. 'Esther Njeri', Mitero interviews, 1974.
32. 'Patricia Kimani', Mitero interviews, 1974.
33. I have argued elsewhere that patriarchy as a system should not be confused with the patriarchal practices or discourses that may be present in a largely non-patriarchal society; further, patrilineal societies are not necessarily patriarchal. The "bride-wealth sex-gender system," whereby women are pivotal figures in the web of kin, and active agents in their own circulation through society, is the key to the non-patriarchal nature of East African patrilineal societies such as the Kikuyu (Stamp 1986, pp. 33-34).
34. I analyze in depth the transformed organizations of Kikuyu women in Stamp 1986, pp. 37-42. The paper "*Matega*: Manipulating Women's Co-operative Traditions for Material and Social Gain in Kenya," op.cit., describes some of the contradictory aspects of women's co-operative activities in the present, which may be promulgated under a veneer of romanticism about women's togetherness. There are problems with the manipulation of women's cooperative traditions, both by the community, and by

individual women themselves. The 1985 Mitero research showed that the productive capacity of women's groups may be captured by advantaged women, or by male-dominated institutions within the community such as the church or the political party and diverted to ends incompatible with the goals of the groups. Nevertheless, the groups remain the chief means by which rural women empower themselves politically and economically within the community – indeed, the efforts at cooptation in the past two decades are a measure of this fact (see Stamp 1989, p. 84).

35. Mutira 1989, introduction, 27.
36. "Family planning is poisonous. It poisons God's creatures. Though I am old and cannot produce any more, I would not use it. This nation of Kikuyu people was blessed by God to produce and multiply. Suppose you were not born [Rebecca], could you be writing as you are writing what I am telling you today? I think this is the reason why people are not living as well as they used to live. God is annoyed with them for poisoning the people before they are born." 'Anna Wanjiru', Mitero interviews, 1974.
37. Mutira 1989, introduction, p. 27.
38. 'Wangeci', Mutira 1989, p.136.
39. 'Wanjiku', Mutira, p. 55.
40. Leakey 1977, Vol. I, pp. 10-11.
41. 'Sarah Ngendo', Mitero interviews, 1974. Sarah was born in 1920.
42. Carolyn M. Clark 1980, p. 363; Penelope Ciancanelli 1980, esp. p. 29.
43. 'Wangeci', Mutira 1989, pp. 138-39.
44. Stamp 1991, pp. 812-13. Wambui's fall from wifely virtue during the trials became a cautionary tale for women about the boundaries they should not cross in the name of progress and modernity.
45. 'Wanoi', Mutira 1989, p. 167.
46. 'Cecilia Wangui', Mitero interviews, 1974.
47. 'Wangeci', Mutira 1989, p. 121.
48. 'Monica Mundia', Mitero interviews, 1981.
49. 'Grace Nyambura', Mitero interviews, 1981.
50. 'Wangeci', Mutira 1989, p. 122.
51. Clark 1980, p. 368.

Bibliography

Abwunza, Judith. "Back Door Decisions," Part III in *Women's Voices, Women's Power: Dialogues of Resistance from East Africa*. Peterborough, Ontario: Broadview, 1997.

Van Allen, Judith. "'Sitting on a Man': Colonialism and the Lost Political Institutions of Igbo Women". *Canadian Journal of African Studies* 6, no. 2 (1972): 165-82.

Ciancanelli, Penelope. "Exchange, Reproduction and Sex Subordination Among the Kikuyu of East Africa". *Review of Radical Political Economy* 12, no. 2 (1980): 25-36.

Clark, Carolyn M. "Land and Food, Women and Power, in Nineteenth Century Kikuyu." *Africa* 50, no. 4 (1980): 357-69.

Davison, Jean and the Women of Mutira. *Voices From Mutira: Lives of Rural Gikuyu Women*. Boulder, Colorado and London: Lynne Rienner Publishers, 1989.

Kanogo, Tabitha. *Squatters and the Roots of Mau Mau*. London: James Currey, 1987.

Kenyatta, Jomo. *Facing Mount Kenya.* New York: Secker and Warburg, 1938 [reprinted by Vintage Books].

Kershaw, Greta. "The Kikuyu of Central Kenya," in Angela Molnos (ed.), *Cultural Source Materials for Population Planning in East Africa,* Vol III: "Beliefs and Practices." Nairobi: East African Publishing House, 1973.

Kershaw, Greta and John Middleton. *The Central tribes of the North-Eastern Bantu.* London: International African Institute, 1965.

Kertzer, David and Oker B.B. Madison, "Women's Age-Set Systems in Africa: The Latuka of Southern Sudan", in Christine Fry, (ed.). *Dimensions: Aging, Culture and Health.* New York: Praeger, 1981.

Kettel, Bonnie. "Gender Distortions and Development Disasters: Women and Milk in African Herding Systems". *NWSA Journal* 4, no. 1 (Spring 1992): 23-41.

Lambert, H.E. *Kikuyu Social and Political Institutions.* London: Oxford University Press, 1956.

Leakey, Louis B. *The Southern Kikuyu Peoples Before 1903* Vols. I-III London: Academic Press, 1977 [1933].

Mackenzie, Fiona. "Gender and Land Rights in Murang'a District, Kenya". *Journal of Peasant Studies* 17, no. 4, (1990): 609-43.

Molyneux, Maxine. "Mobilization Without Emancipation? Women's Interests, the State, and Revolution in Nicaragua". *Feminist Studies* 11, no. 2 (Summer 1985): 227-54.

Muriuki, Godfrey. *A History of the Kikuyu,* 1500-1900. Nairobi: Oxford University Press, 1974.

Okeyo, Achola Pala."Daughters of the Lakes and Rivers: Colonization and the Land Rights of Luo Women", in Mona Etienne and Eleanor Leacock (eds.). *Women and Colonization: Anthropological Perspectives.* New York: Praeger, 1980, 186-213.

Onoge, O.: "Revolutionary Imperatives in African Sociology," in P. Gutkind and P. Waterman (eds.) *African Social Studies: A Radical Reader.* New York: Monthly Review Press, 1977.

Sacks, Karen. *Sisters and Wives: The Past and Future of Sexual Inequality.* Westport, Connecticut: Greenwood Press, 1979.

Stamp, Patricia. "Perceptions of Change and Economic Strategy Among Kikuyu Women of Mitero, Kenya". *Rural Africana* 29 (Winter 1975-76).

Stamp, Patricia and Rebecca N. Chege "Ngwatio: A Story of Co-operative Research on African Women". *Canadian Woman Studies/les cahiers de la femme* 6, no. 1 (Fall 1984).

Stamp, Patricia. "Kikuyu Women's Self-Help Groups: Toward an Understanding of the Relation Between Sex-Gender System and Mode of Production in Africa", in Claire Robertson and Iris Berger (eds.). *Women and Class in Africa.* New York: Holmes and Meier, 1986.

Stamp, Patricia. *Technology, Gender and Power in Africa.* Ottawa: International Development Research Centre, 1989 (revised edition in progress 1998).

Stamp, Patricia. "Mothers of Invention: Women's Agency in the Kenyan State", in Judith Kegan Gardiner (ed.) *Provoking Agents: Gender and Agency in Theory and Practice,* Chicago, University of Illinois Press, 1995.

Stamp, Patricia. "Burying Otieno: The Politics of Gender and Ethnicity in Kenya". *Signs: Journal of Women in Culture and Society* 16, no. 4 (Summer 1991): 808-45 (Reprinted in *Rethinking the Political: Gender, Resistance, and the State,* eds. B. Laslett, J. Brenner, and Y. Arat, Chicago: University of Chicago Press, 1995.

Wise or Childish?

Ambivalent Images of Grandparents in the Course of the 19th Century

Erhard Chvojka

Shortly after the middle of the 18th century, the prototypes of our modern role patterns of grandmotherhood and grandfatherhood started to unfold. Gradually, old people became defined mainly as reference points for children, particularly for their own grandchildren. According to the works of late enlightenment pedagogues, old people were expected and believed to be able to exercise a very specific grandparental pedagogic effect on children. The roles of grandmother- and grandfatherhood are then closely connected with contemporary bourgeois images of mother- and fatherhood as well as with newly developed understanding of childhood. The roles of grandparenthood must therefore be regarded as inherent elements of the bourgeois conception of family of that time.

I shall now present a survey of selected parts of the empirical approach I used in order to investigate the wide spectrum of diverse role patterns of grandparenthood. The main emphasis of this paper will be laid on paradigms of grandfatherhood, though images of grandmotherhood will also receive their fair share of attention. Methodologically, I am going to pursue the aspects mentioned by examining normative visual representations as well as textual examples of middle-class discourse. As a contrast, I will refer to a selection of autobiographical records in order to work out the permanent interactions between normative paradigms and social practices.

I decided to concentrate on the 19th century because, especially as far as roles of grandparenthood are concerned, this period seems to be most relevant to the strikingly provocative question raised by this book, namely whether Old Age and Infancy may be either regarded as Equals or as Opposites. Nevertheless I will also be looking at the late 18th century as well as the early 20th century. Regarding geographic areas I shall focus on conditions in Central Europe, though I may sometimes look beyond this region too.

Anonymous: Des Grossvaters Unterricht. German Copper engraving from the beginning of the 19th century. Bildarchiv Preussischer Kulturbesitz, Berlin.

As an introduction to the wide range of images of grandparenthood in the 19th century, an anonymous German copper engraving with the title "Grandfathers' Lesson" from around 1800 may provide an example of the stereotype of grandfather as teacher.[1] In this representation, the grandfather is obviously educating a ten- or eleven-year-old granddaughter. While looking at her with a friendly expression, he seems to expect an answer to a question he may have asked concerning the open page lying on his lap. Referring to the normative message, the representation shows then an elderly man in first place representing a moral and educational authority, secondly exercising that power in an innerfamilial and very intimate atmosphere.

This specific conception of grandfatherhood ranks among the basic elements of the remarkably intensive middle-class discourse about old age pervading the second half of the 18th century. As early as 1776, the German pedagogue Friedrich Eberhard von Rochow makes use of an "old grandfather" in order to provide the whole range of contemporary middle class moral values. In 1776, Der Kinderfreund, a magazine designed to be read mainly by bourgeois parents, has a short text under the headline *The Old Man*.

> "On a silent evening, an old farmer was sitting in front of his door. His silver grey hair was shining in the moonlight. Next to him stood his son, to whom he had handed over the farm, and his young daughter-in-law. Their small child was playing on the ground. "My dear children", said the old man, "I feel I am going to die very soon, for I am old and weak – but don't cry about this, and listen to my well-meaning admonitions. Be pious, upright and honest, stay away from envy and miserliness, love God, for whatever you have comes from him. Be charitable towards the Poor, busy in your profession, respectful and obedient towards the authorities. Be peaceful neighbours and married people and raise your children as sensible and upright people through good education and particularly through own good example. Thus you will grow old in honour as I did, and you will once face death without any worries as I can do now". And after he had spoken these words, he died."[2]

It is quite obvious that the author makes use of a wide-spread principle of fiction writing, – messages about moral virtues are much more accepted and appreciated when being proclaimed by old men representing symbolic authorities, particularly when they are described as being on the verge of death.

At the beginning of the 19th century, the image of the old man as teacher became even more specified, as we already saw in the engraving described above. It seems that grandfathers were more and more expected to act explicitly as an extension of the school system. Another example from pedagogic literature, which corresponds nicely to the engraving, was written by the pedagogue Johann Heinrich Campe. In 1806 he published the so-called *Abeze- und Lesebuch* ('ABC and reading-book') being designed for children at primary school age. The whole book is based on a fictitious dialogue between two persons, who are "grandfather and Karl". The grandfather acts as a very friendly and careful teacher. "Karl", the grandson, is described by Campe – not surprisingly – as very obedient and appreciative of this behaviour of his grandfather's.[3]

After looking at some examples from discourse about roles and functions of old men, I shall now turn to the level of representations of personal experiences as reflected in autobiographical records. There is actually some evidence that writings by authors from the middle classes or the nobility correspond somehow with the normative messages of the contemporary works of pedagogues. This is small wonder, if we accept autobiographies as retrospective combinations of widespread cultural stereotypes on the one hand and references to "social reality" on the other. As researchers, we may now try to disentangle those two levels very carefully. As a second possibility, we could also regard the whole representation as a kind of total reflection of the author's cultural disposition – which is permanently shaping not only his or her perception of life, but finally also the social behaviour of the writer. Accepting this assumption, it would even be contraproductive to try to distinguish too rigidly between these two levels, mainly established artificially by rather conventional social scientific approaches.

I shall now present a concrete example, written by Josef Spaun who was born in 1788 to a family of Viennese merchants and civil servants. In his autobiography, he recalls his private school lessons in the 1790's.

> "The teacher Mr. Jobst introduced me and my brother into the secrets of the alphabet. The lessons always took place in the house of grandfather Steyrer, who joined us during the first lesson with goodwill and benevolence. As a reward for our good behaviour and the progress of our studies, we were always served some hot chocolate."[4]

Such autobiographic representation of a grandfather's involvement in affairs of school education is actually typical for middle class autobiographers covering the time around 1800.

Nevertheless, we have to keep in mind that the normative as well as the social basis for such a specific perception were restricted to particular social milieu. When we look at members of the so-called lower classes, we can often see some significant 'collisions' between normative images and stereotypes of typical grandparental behaviour as teachers with the pragmatic conditions of everyday life. Viktor Walter for example, who was born in 1893 in Vienna into a proletarian family, started to attend primary school in 1900. In this context he writes in his autobiography.

> "But there were no private coaching lessons with grandmother or grandfather, because at this time there were still many illiterates among the members of this generation in the lower classes."[5]

It seems to be quite evident that the author is very familiar with the stereotype of teaching grandparents, otherwise he would never have made this particular remark. But due to his very own experience he has to explicitly deny this image.

But in numerous bourgeois autobiographies of the 19th and 20th centuries, the chapters devoted to the remembrance of grandfathers provide a very clear image of them as being in charge of education in conventionally male-dominated fields. Many authors – of both sexes – pretend for instance to owe the most important knowledge in the fields of morals, political ideology and history to their grandfathers. Especially concerning history, grandfathers (and never grandmothers!) are regarded to be particularly suited to teach younger persons, due to their role as "personal witnesses to history".

This specific perception – which, by the way, survives even today – can in fact not be found until the last years of the 18th century, neither in autobiographic sources nor in works of a more normative character. In my opinion, this must be interpreted in accordance with the fact that change and development of the society can actually not be perceived as happening gradually and visibly from generation to generation before the late 18th century. For an illustration of the idea that the aged are 'experts in history' let me now turn again to a visual record.

In a painting of the Viennese artist Johann Nepomuk Mayer,[6] dating from 1842, the interior of a middle class living-room is depicted. There a grandfather is surrounded by four of his grandchildren who are between about four and seven years old. By pointing at a metal bust of the Austrian Emperor Franz I, he seems to be explaining to them something apparently very serious. The grandfather appears friendly, but also quite serious due to the importance of the matter he wants to present. The painting combines then two basic stereotypes of the grandfather role, – their prime function as teaching persons as well as their position as witnesses to the period they are teaching about.

These stereotypes can be pursued easily within middle-class discourses throughout the 19th century. Around 1900 they are finally introduced to contemporary school books, especially for primary schools. In a reading book for third and fourth grade primary female school pupils, published in Frankfurt in 1925, there is a short story with the title "The Grandfather". The first sentence runs as follows: "The grandfather was an old man with a high forehead, on which you could read much more than in any newspaper."[7] It must not surprise us that we again find direct reflections of these widely propagated images when we look at individual forms of perception, formulated and expressed in contemporary autobiographical writing.

Lots of grandfathers appear in the retrospective autobiographical view of their grandchildren as providing knowledge about "big world history". Melitta Elias for example, born in 1911 in Vienna into a middle class family, speaks about an experience she had with her grandfather when she was five years old. At this time, the Austrian Emperor Franz Josef I died, and, very significantly, Melitta Elias went to watch the big funeral ceremony together with her maternal grandfather. At least she does not mention any other family member as being present which, if she had been accompanied by others, would be even more significant.

> "Then there was a really black day. My grandfather took my to the funeral of our Emperor Franz Josef and said to me very seriously: Always remember, my child, now a great period of history has come to its end."[8]

As I have said, there are some really striking references, showing that exactly this image for grandfathers was propagated intensively in contemporary school books. A drawing in another German primary school book, published in 1910, shows an old bearded grandfather with the obligatory pipe in his hand.[9] He is sitting on a park bench next to his grandson and pointing at a monument of the German Emperor Wilhelm I, which was built in remembrance of the French-German War in 1870/71. The grandfather says to his grandson: "I was there too. It is already a long time ago. I think of it very often."

By turning back again to the level of individual expressions, we can detect that many autobiographers actually record the stories of war they have been told by their grandfathers – surprisingly much more often than those told by their fathers! For Franz Obergottsberger, who was born in 1895 in an Upper Austrian village as an illegitimate child of rural servants, the stories his grandfather told again and again about his participation in the Austrian-Prussian war in 1866 rank among the most outstanding elements the author uses for the retrospective creation of the image of his grandfather.[10]

Another Austrian author, Maria Kroufka, born in 1928 in Vienna into a tanner's family, writes in her autobiography about her grandmother. "She could always tell such beautiful fairy-tales. However, after that we always asked grandfather to tell us what it had been like in the First World War."[11] In this particular case we can see that some grandchildren were not only reproducing familiar clichés of grandparenthood within autobiographical writing. They may also have forced their grandparents to behave quite in accordance with the typical grandparental roles being propagated around 1920 in, for example, numerous school books.

We have now been confronted with a couple of examples for the normative construction as well as for the individual perception of the stereotype of grandfathers as wise and experienced authorities. But in the course of

Drawing from: Sandt H., Heinemann K., Fibel für Stadtkinder (Frankfurt/Main 1910) p.56.

history, there are alongside these also some quite contradictory paradigms of old age. A specific type of a rather discriminatory view of ageing is the stereotype of age as a period of second childhood. This normative pattern can be found without any special interruptions from at least the late Middle Ages till the beginning of the 20th century. A famous example of the public reproduction of this long-lived image is the so-called 'Stages of Life'. Reproduced on numerous pictorial broadsheets, this motive was for at least three centuries, from about 1600 to 1900, the most widespread and popular iconographic image of aging throughout the Western World. The verbal commentary on old age which was included was invariably demeaning. While the 70-year-old man is regarded as 'senile', the 80-year-old man is commented on as 'wisdom gone', and the 90-year-old men usually appears as 'the children's ridicule'.[12] In the course of the 19th century, the image of the "Stages of Life" gained an outstanding popularity among different social strata.

There is some evidence that its negative images of very old men also exercised some influence on the role pattern of grandfatherhood. Without any doubt, a significant change in the judgement of mental abilities of old persons occurred during the course of the 19th century. Yet, during the first decades of the 19th century, we still find numerous estimations and depictions of male old age as a life stage of particularly high mental power, corresponding with the stereotype of old men as teaching persons.

In Macklot's *Conversationslexikon* for example, published in 1816, we can read under the entry 'old age' the following description: "In the same way as the power of the body is declining, the mind and the intellect is rising even more and rationality is at the highest level in old age." By looking at Meyer's *Konversationslexikon*, published in 1874 – just 60 years later than Macklot's – we already find the newly created term 'senile decay': "Senile decay or decrepitude can be observed both on mental and physical levels; the first is connected with the diminution of the brain in old age, which causes a serious decline of mental abilities and the process of growing infantile."[13] As a consequence of the "renaissance" of these attitudes towards (male) old age, it is clear that the role of grandfatherhood, too, lost some basic elements of the respect, which it had contained originally – that is before and around 1800.

Mostly scenarios of deficient aspects of age appear particularly in combination with visual and verbal projections of middle class family concepts into rural milieus. Grandparents are now very often depicted as dependent on the members of the younger generations, sometimes even as purely ridiculous creatures of decay. An outstanding pictorial example for this 'normative turn' is provided by S. Lipschitz' lithographic reproduction of an English painting with the title 'Age and Infancy' from around 1850.[14]

In a very romantic scenery, we can see an old grandfather, sitting in a chair in the small court of the house, or maybe in front of the house. Though the old grandfather appears in principle to be a very sympathetic person, – or maybe exactly because of that – he is nevertheless being treated with very

S. Lipschitz: Alter und Kindheit. Lithographie, 1855, Verlag F. Sala & Co, Berlin. Collection Roth, Berlin.

little respect by his grandchildren. Two of his granddaughters are trying to tug away the chair on which the old man is sitting, another one is climbing on his back. Quite consistently, the parents of the children seem unconcerned by the children's amusement at the grandfather's expense. And even the old man himself, who seems to have just been interrupted in reading something to his grandchildren, is depicted as if this rather disrespectful behaviour appears to him in principle acceptable. Despite the romantic, – three generations living harmoniously under one roof according to middle class precepts was itself anachronistic, – we can see a clear reference to the actual deficient position of the elderly within the familial system. Indeed this picture from the middle of the 19th century can be categorized as a certain kind of 'civilized' variant of the motif of the old man becoming 'the children's ridicule'. Yet, around 1800, grandfathers would never have played children's games with their grandchildren. Only a few decades later, in some representations they even appear as 'toys' of the youngest generations! But, on the other hand, we have to keep in mind that around the turn of the century, school books still adopted the image of grandfathers as highly respectable teachers of their grandchildren. So at least on the level of discourse – and this always means somehow in the perception of individuals too – an apparently diverging development of actually very contradictory images of male old age can be observed during the 19th century.

After concentrating so intensively on the wide range of ambivalent images of male old age and grandfatherhood, let me finally draw some attention to the role patterns of grandmotherhood. In this field, again a significant similarity between visualized images of female teachers – which are in reality rather rare in this period – and visual representations of grandmothers can eventually be detected around 1800. This similarity becomes evident, for example, in a painting by Francis Wheatly from around 1790 with the title "The Teacher".

The female teacher depicted is an old, very friendly and sympathetic looking woman, who especially concerning her outfit appears to be almost a prototype of a grandmother, – all dressed in black and gray, wearing a dark bonnet on her head and small round spectacles on her nose. She is sitting in a small class room, surrounded by seven girls and two boys, all of them between about five and eight years old. She seems to teach them to read and write. Having an open book on her lap, she bears a striking resemblance to the visualized stereotypes of grandmothers, reading fairytales from a book to her grandchildren.[15]

In comparison to the image of grandfathers as teachers, grandmothers in the same context appear substantially different. Concerning their educational activities, grandmothers are presented as either telling or reading stories and fairy-tales to their grandchildren, or, more specifically, as teaching granddaughters particular 'female' qualifications, such as knitting, cooking, etc. In some cases, grandmothers are put into the limelight as transferring the basic elements of religion to children. But without any exceptions, grandmothers are never depicted explicitly teaching grandchildren on an intellectual level. Educating children in the field of 'serious matters' of bourgeois refinement seems to be the exclusive preserve of grandfathers. So in terms of comparison with respective images of grandfatherhood, the role patterns of grandmotherhood represent an image, which is almost the obverse. The relatively big number of pictures of male teachers dating from the 18th and 19th centuries never show any comparable similarity to the stereotypical image of the teaching grandfather. While grandfathers are usually presented as very kind, having a sort of 'natural authority' due to their experience and the familial character of the relation to their grandchildren, male teachers are mostly shown either as completely helpless to establish discipline among their pupils, or – maybe in response to this picture – as being extremely authoritarian or even brutal.

However, grandmothers *themselves* never appear as teachers on the level of so called 'high culture', whereas visual representations of real female teachers almost always show them as striking 'grandmotherly' types. So while grandfathers are presented as very pleasant alternatives to the cruelty of regular teachers, female teachers are obviously expected to be correspondingly kind or even indulgent as grandmothers. Alongside the expectation of a fundamentally friendly attitude and behaviour on the part of old women towards children, there is a specific connotation of deficiency regarding them in the context of child education. A kind of slight reference to this image can, for example, be found in a work of the German painter Max Liebermann, dating from 1879 with the title "Kleinkinderschule", in English translation called the "Nursery".[16]

Max Liebermann: Kleinkinderschule, Painting, 1879/80. Gesellschaft Kruppsche Gemäldesammlungen, Essen.

In a rather simply equipped and furnished room we can see all in all fourteen children of both sexes, looked after by an elderly woman. She is sitting somewhat aside in front of a small table and knitting. The children themselves are sitting on benches, talking to each other or playing simple games. However, the nurse does not seem to pay too much attention to the children. When we now try to reveal the normative messages of this painting, we find a wide range of different aspects. It strikes us immediately that the nurse is again an elderly woman, looking somehow 'grandmotherly'. Furthermore, we might also ask if the specific manner of her rather inattentive way of caring for the children may be interpreted as a sort of subliminal critique of the general ability of elderly people to care for children adequately. Indeed the old nurse is caring quite 'badly'. She is neither taking care actively of the physical well-being of the children nor is she behaving in a specifically 'pedagogical' way. She is not talking to the children, reading something to them or playing games with them. Liebermann's painting can thus be interpreted as a kind of understated but clear condemnation of the institution of early kindergartens, in which children were believed to be neglected and deprived of care for their proper pedagogic development.

It does not seem to be just by chance that the painter used an old 'ignorant' woman for expressing these critical nuances in his work. Again since the middle of the 19th century, the clear picture emerges that elderly women, especially those coming from lower social classes, were not regarded as being really capable of caring properly for children. This particular prejudice is not only expressed in textual media, but also in numerous pictorial representations. Grandmothers from lower classes mainly are now very often depicted as 'warning examples'. Mostly due to their age, they appear completely overburdened by the combination of gainful employment on one hand and the raising of grandchildren on the other.

Carl Bumauer: Der Zuckerdieb, Lithographie, 1863, in: Lebenswelten – Alltagsbilder. Katalog zur Ausstellung im Schlossmuseum Linz (Linz 1993) p.50.

In the following, I am going to present two particular examples for this discriminative stereotype. In 1863 Carl Bumauer created a drawing with the title "A Boy Stealing Sugar",[17] in which he presents an image of grandmotherly insufficiency concerning the upbringing of children. In a small room, an old woman who was just doing her mending, has fallen asleep in her chair, while her grandson is stealing some sugar out of the table drawer. The lack of watchfulness of the grandmother does not indeed cause any serious damage. However, the scenery clearly encourages the viewer to imagine much more nightmarish consequences of such a behaviour in an old person who was left in charge of a child.

Another more explicit scenario of probable negative consequences can be seen in Carl Eckel's painting "Die Federnschleisserin" dated 1856 ('the Feather Picker').[18] The excessive strain of domestic work in addition to the necessity of looking after some children, probably grandchildren of the old woman, causes quite a chaotic moment in the small room. In response, the grandmother seems to become very nervous and angry, thus losing control of the whole situation. The end of the story is again left to the imagination of the viewer. Both of the pictures mentioned are quite obviously providing a clear message to viewers, particularly to parents: "Never leave your children to grandmothers!"

Carl Eckel: Die Federnschleisserin, Painting, 1856, Neue Galerie am Landesmuseum Joanneum, Graz. IN I/385.

Looking for some unequivocal explanations for this normative message, I would suggest a very close connection with the contemporary campaign of condemnation of female professional employment, especially articulated by numerous middle-class men. Actually, a significant number of proletarian women employed in early industrialisation had to rely on their mothers support in looking after their children. In this context, the implicit message "never leave your children to (again working!) grandmothers" seems to be directed particularly to proletarian mothers, who should obviously be "encouraged" to adapt themselves to the middle-class family model.

So the male critique from the bourgeois elites is in fact double-edged. On the one hand it is aimed directly at less well-off older women who are still in need of work. On the other hand, less directly, it addresses young mothers from the lower classes, who should be convinced of the 'dangers' of grandmotherly child-caring and so should take upon themselves the responsibility for child education instead of working. The campaign against grandparental child education, launched hand in hand with 19th century industrialization, easily falls back on traditional stereotypes about the inability of old people to be in charge of children. The propaganda offensive relating to this can be followed in different types of media, as e.g. family magazines or family advisers.

Let me highlight some examples of this campaign from the textual media. The American Reverend John Robinson states in an article on pedagogics as early as in 1851 that children, who are raised by their grandparents, 'seldom do well, but are usually corrupted by their too great indulgence.'[19] The French lawyer Demolombe writes in 1870 concerning grandparents that in general they are too old and less competent at child raising. Especially concerning grandmothers, he argues: "It would be extremely dangerous to engage persons as tutrices, whose weakness of gender is connected with that of old age."[20] During the last decades of the 19th century, the pedagogic debate about the adequate familial role of grandparents escalated. In 1910 the English physician Harold Kerr in the scientific medicine journal *Public Health* even called grandmothers "infanticide experts"[21], due to their supposedly old-fashioned knowledge of child-caring.

An Austrian example of an explicitly negative attitude towards old people in the field of child education derives once again from a work of pedagogy. In 1883, the Viennese physician and pedagogue Julius Boss wrote the book *Die Erziehungskunst in der Familie für Eltern, Erzieherinnen und Erzieher*.[22] It is already quite significant that Boss does not mention grandparents in connection with child education at all. Instead he gives only a few remarks about the psychological damage usually caused by grandparents, when they "take their small grandchildren out of the cradle constantly during their visits or spoil them by giving them too many often useless presents".

Boss also provides another example of what he considers to be a possible negative influence of grandparental behaviour towards small children. By condemning the fact that small children are very often confronted with illustrated books of old legends and fairytales full of frightening creatures, he concludes: "the effect is quite the same as if the child were under the regime of terror of old wet-nurses."[23] This very strict judgement of a late 19th century physician and pedagogue leads us to another aspect of discrimination of the elderly, which can be reduced to a specific attitude of enlightenment discourse.

All through the Modern Ages we can trace a constant line for the tradition of the stereotype that old people in general and particularly elderly women should necessarily be kept away from children because of their supposed irrational behaviour. There is a powerful belief that the latter frightens children and damages their psychological development. In the framework of this argumentation, especially old women are very often regarded to be related to witches and witchcraft. In Karl Wander's German Lexicon of Proverbs, for instance, published in first edition in 1867, the heading "old woman" contains the following proverb: "You are never too old to learn, said to the old woman, so she finally started to learn to practise witchcraft."[24]

Indeed most fairy-tales provide a very negative image of old people. Within folk tales, old people, again especially old women, are almost always very closely connected with poison, witchcraft, ugliness, the devil, betrayal, magic. Fairy-tales as for example Little Red Riding Hood, in which the old grandmother is described in a very neutral way, are an exception to this general rule. So on one hand, old people appear as thrilling creatures in fairy-tales. On the other hand, they are accused of damaging the psychological state of health of children by telling them exactly those fairy-tales. So, during the 19th century, the elderly became more and more caught in a specific dilemma: They were seen as creatures as well as creators of horror.

By looking at selected autobiographical records, we are again able to detect the specific impact of this particular image of old people on the perceptions of the authors. In his autobiography, Reinhold Klaus, who was born in 1881 into a weaver's family in the north Bohemian town of Warnsdorf writes about his very unhappy memories of his paternal grandmother: "This grandmother is the one I can remember, I still have her looks very clearly in my mind. She was a small, bent woman with white hair which already had the characteristic glimmer of yellow ivory, as it is sometimes the case for very old people. She always walked leaning upon a walking-stick and always wore a big basket on her back, which was typical for old women in this region. With her hooked nose, she reminded me of the witch in the fairy-tale of Hänsel und Gretel. This old woman had the same degree of love for me as I had an antipathy against her …".[25]

The memoires of Reinhold Klaus clearly represent how easily the positive prejudice of the practically "natural" grandmotherly goodness of heart and kindness could turn into a completely different negative stereotype. If grandchildren did not experience their grandmothers according to the very idealistic leading image of middle class grandmotherhood, but as a rather negative personality, one of the alternative connotations near at hand was obviously the image of the "witch".

But even without any negative experiences of grandparents, some children report their confusion or even fright about the physical appearance of grandparents. Margarete Domonkos, born in 1906 in Vienna into a middle-class family, writes in her autobiography about her first encounter with her paternal grandfather in a Viennese park around 1910.

> "Today an old man with a long beard joined the assembly in the park. My mother jumped from the bench and suddenly cried out, Look Grete, grandfather is coming! She ran towards him and welcomed him very fondly. Mother loved her father-in-law very much and everything would have turned out well if he hadn't had this horrible long beard, which reminded me of a particular figure in fairy-tales, the Silesian mountain ghost "Rübezahl". (…) I regret very much that I confused the friendly grandfather due to his beard with "Rübezahl". When I was a small child, I was told lots of fairy-tales and legends, my mind was full of strange creatures, which didn't always have the best effect."[26]

So Margarete Domonkos gives us another excellent example for what we might expect in general from autobiographic sources, – the description of so-called "objective events", overlapped by an individually shaped manifestation of widespread images and stereotypes. In this particular case, the authors retrospective representation of her perception is clearly affected by the bourgeois imagination of the bad influence of fairy-tales on children.

Let me conclude in a few sentences the substantive aspects I have tried to present and to illustrate by examples both from the level of normative discourse and individual experience. From the moment of the unfolding of modern role patterns of grandparenthood shortly after the middle of the 18th century, grandfathers are mainly regarded as moral authorities and respectable teachers. This concept represents a definite break with the traditional images of male old age as deficient, as provided, for instance by the pictorial motive of the Stages of Life in existence since the 16th century. However, during the second half of the 19th century, a distinct shift in the direction of a more negative judgement of grandfatherhood becomes visible.

Grandmothers are generally stylized, according to an apparently positive prejudice, as "sitting in the corner and dispensing nice stories from their rocking chairs", as a French study on the images of women in early family magazines put it. But as grandmotherly child education increasingly appeared to provide a precondition for female employment, especially in early industrialization, so did the more traditional discriminatory images of female old age become once again instruments in a certain kind of propaganda offensive against the upbringing of children by grandmothers.

---

1. Anonymous, "Des Großvaters Unterricht" (around 1800) copper engraving; Berlin, Bildarchiv Preußischer Kulturbesitz.
2. F.E. von Rochow 1776, p.111f.
3. J.H. Campe, vol.1, pp. 39-53.
4. E. Chvojka and J. Losová 1997, p.15.
5. V. Walter Autobiography p.2.
6. Johann Nepomuk Mayer. "Kinder mit Großvater vor der Büste Kaiser Franz I"; (1842) water colour-painting.Vienna, Historisches Museum, Inv. HM 97.566.
7. K. Bojunga, A. Hoffa , and F. Sandmann 1925, p. 9.
8. M. Elias Autobiography, p.7.
9. K. Heinemann and H. Sandt 1910, p. 56.
10. E. Chvojka and J. Losová 1997, p.38ff.
11. Ibid., p.141.
12. R. Schenda 1983, p. 11.
13. H.J. Kondratowitz 1983, p.393, 404.
14. S. Lipschitz "Alter und Kindheit", (Berlin, around 1855) chalk lithography after the painting "Age and Infancy". Collection Roth.
15. John Coles "Die Schulmeisterin" (1794) copper engraving after a painting by Francis Wheatly. Berlin, Staatliche Museen, Kupferstichkabinett.
16. Max Liebermann "Kleinkinderschule", 1879/80, oil on wood. Essen, Gesellschaft Kruppsche Gemäldesammlungen.
17. Carl Bumauer "Der Zuckerdieb" (1863), oil on canvas. Vienna, private collection.
18. Carl Eckel "Die Federnschleißerin" 1856, oil on canvas. Graz, Neue Galerie am Landsmuseum Joanneum IN I/385.
19. J. Demos 1978, p. 253f.
20. F. Demolombe 1870, p. 178.
21. P. N. Stearns 1980, p. 45.
22. J. Boss 1883.
23. Ibid., p. 81
24. K. Wander 1867, p. 78.
25. E. Chvojka 1992 p. 22.
26. E. Chvojka and J. Losová 1997, p. 49f.

Bibliography

Bojunga, Klaudius, Anna Hoffa, and Fritz Sandmann. *Lebensgut. Ein Lesebuch für deutsche Mädchen.* 2.Teil. 3rd ed. Frankfurt a. M., 1925.

Boss, Julius. *Die Erziehungskunst in der Familie für Eltern, Erzieherinnen und Erzieher.* Wien, 1883).

Campe, Johann Heinrich. *Sämmtliche Kinder- und Jugendschriften*. Neue Gesamtausgabe, vol.1. Braunschweig, 1830.

Chvojka, Erhard (ed.). *Großmütter. Enkelkinder erinnern sich.* (=Damit es nicht verloren geht) vol. 21. Wien/Köln/Weimar: Böhlau, 1992.

Chvojka Erhard and Jana Losová, (ed.) *Großväter. Enkelkinder erinnern sich* (=Damit es nicht verloren geht). vol.36. Wien/Köln/Weimar: Böhlau, 1997.

Demolombe, F. *Cours de Code Napoleon*. vol. 7. Paris,1870.

Demos, John. "Old Age in Early New England". *Turning Points. Historical and Sociological Essays on the Family*. John Demos and S. Boocock Spence (eds). Chicago 1978.

Elias, Melitta. *Autobiography*. Unpublished manuscript in the "Dokumentation lebensgeschichtlicher Aufzeichnungen", Dept. of Social and Economic History, University of Vienna.

Heinemann, K. and H. Sandt. *Fibel für Stadtkinder*. Edition "A". Leipzig/Berlin, 1910.

von Kondratowitz, Hans Joachim. "Zum historischen Konstitutionsprozeß von "Altersgrenzen"". *Gerontologie und Sozialgeschichte. Wege zu einer historischen Betrachtung des Alters*. C. Conrad and H.-J. von Kondratowitz (eds.). Berlin: Eigenverlag DZA, 1983.

von Rochow, Friedrich Eberhard (ed.) *Der Kinderfreund* 1776.

Schenda, Rudolf. "Die Lebentreppe. Geschichte einer Popularisierung". In *Die Lebenstreppe. Bilder der menschlichen Lebensalter*. Katalog zur Ausstellung des Landschaftsverbandes Rheinland. Köln/Bonn 1983.

Stearns, Peter N. "Old Women: Some Historical Observations". *Journal of Familiy History* Vol.5, 1 (1980).

Walter, Viktor. *Autobiography*. Unpublished manuscript in the "Dokumentation lebensgeschichtlicher Aufzeichnungen", Dept. of Social and Economic History, University of Vienna.

Wander, Karl. *Deutsches Sprichwörter-Lexikon*, vol.1. Leipzig 1867.

III

Age in The Future

Age in the Future

Some Implications of New Reproductive and Genetic Technologies

Lene Koch

Recently the first higher mammal was cloned from a cell taken from an adult animal.[1] A clone is a genetic copy of another animal. Earlier, cloning had only been possible using the method of embryonic cloning, i.e. dividing an embryo into two or more omnipotent cells which may all develop into genetically identical individuals. By cloning an adult animal, it is now possible to obtain a copy of an animal whose phenotype is already well known, meaning that we know what the genes are like as they are expressed in a full-grown animal.[2] This event, the creation of the sheep Dolly, is a symbolic representation of the way we may have to think about age and procreation in the future. Dolly challenges all preconceived historical and traditional concepts of age, generational relations between parent and offspring, identity and ancestry. Some have seen Dolly as the key to understanding the ageing process itself and seen from the perspective of the geneticists, one of the most interesting things we may eventually know about Dolly may very well be her age. Will the fact that her genes have already once been in use so to speak, make her life span shorter that other newborns, or will it actually be possible to switch on our genes over and over again? And does this knowledge hold the key to our understanding of the genetic mechanisms behind ageing, the so-called programmed cell death? Another more immediate confusion is that Dolly mixes up our ideas of the order of generations. By being a copy of her mother genetically and at the same time gestated in her mothers body and born by her mother, she simultaneously belongs to two generations – to that of her mother and that of her mother's children. This is a baffling fact that carries remembrances of incestuous sexual relations and this may be an important element in the psychological background for the public outcry against cloning.

Many new and strange perspectives are created by Dolly. The fact that she was created by asexual reproduction has made virgin births possible as well as fatherhood to men who, by the use of surrogate mothers may now create their exclusive male progeny. Interestingly, this asexual form of reproduction eliminates the stochastic nature of sexual reproduction and holds similarities to a more industrial and linear manner of production and in this way an industrial logic is imported into the creation of human beings.

Dolly is then a worthy representative of the modern world of technomedicine and forms a suitable backdrop to a discussion of the cultural and social implications of a number of other better-known and more well-established reproductive and genetic technologies that have changed some of the basic tenets of cultural and social studies of human life.[3]

The most important of the new reproductive technologies is no doubt in vitro fertilisation (IVF) and actually Dolly was only possible because of the use of one of the elements of this technology – i.e. egg retrieval and subsequent manipulation of the egg in vitro, though in this case without fertilisation since embryonic Dolly was not the result of fertilisation. IVF includes egg retrieval whereby eggs are removed from the woman's ovary, made accessible to external technical manipulation and fertilised in vitro in the laboratory. Only after this procedure is carried out, may the fertilized egg, the embryo, be implanted in the uterus and a pregnancy awaited.

This method has already had an immense impact on concepts of individual identity, siblingship, father- and motherhood as well as on family relations in general. Donation of sperm, eggs and embryos creates multiple fathers and mothers, a cultural change that is already commonplace. By freezing embryos it has been possible to produce twins of the same generation, – freeze one or more sisters and brothers, thaw them at any time, implant them in a womb and let them be born, sometimes years apart and thus create a substantial mess in generational patterns. The use of surrogate mothers may take place between strangers as well as inside the immediate family as we have seen in Italy where women have given birth to their own grandchildren. Menopausal women may now give birth to their own children, using frozen eggs or donor eggs. Thus the natural age-limit to giving birth is superceded by technical means and may have some effect on the perception of the boundaries between generations, and how childhood and adulthood are being perceived.

These technical developments, donation, freezing, twinning, spacing etc., have now been supplemented with techniques of genetic quality control. The methods here are either selection or improvement. Selection may technically take place at all stages of the reproductive cycle i.e. embryo, foetus, child, adult, though only few are of any practical interest. Prenatal diagnosis makes selection of foetuses possible in contexts where abortion is acceptable, but the most recent development concerns diagnosis of the embryo before a pregnancy is established, so called pre-implantation diagnosis, whereby only high quality embryos are implanted and abortion is made superfluous.[4]

Genetic improvement, or gene therapy, is as yet technically limited but heavily researched and includes both therapy of the genes of the single sick individual (somatic gene therapy) or therapy of the germ line, i.e. genetic improvement of the sperm and egg that form the basis for future generations. Both selection and genetic improvement would equal a modern form of scientifically based "reform" eugenics.[5]

Improvement may, of course, also take place by, substituting defective body parts, such as organs or parts of organs. Xeno-transplantation is an example of other ways in which age and ideas about age may be influenced by modern medical technology. Xeno-transplantation, aiming at using organs from other species such as pigs or baboons for human use, challenges traditional ideas of human identity and, of course, also affects our ideas about the natural life-span that humans are alotted.

Implications

For the time being the options in reproductive technology only concern a minority of the population directly. Only relatively few employ the new methods of reproduction in the formation of their own family. Still it should be mentioned that on a world-wide basis already more than a quarter of a million babies have been born after IVF. More people are already directly familiar with methods of genetic quality control through prenatal diagnosis and other forms of genetic population screening. But regardless of numbers, of how many actually choose to employ these techniques, there seems no doubt that the ideological impact of these technical options will be strong, and will have broader social and cultural consequences for everybody as our concepts of personhood, family, childhood, motherhood, fatherhood, kinship, ancestry and perhaps even humanity are affected.

Reproductive and genetic technologies have become a central concern in many cultural and social studies because they profoundly affect established notions of what is "natural". Since children may now be born with the assistance of several mothers are they less natural that those born in the old-fashioned way? They are all children one should suppose even though some are only brought to life through complicated technical means implying various selectional and correctional interventions. It is difficult to determine where the limit should be drawn. Is birth by caesarian section more natural than assisted reproduction? Are children born by menopausal mothers less natural than children born by younger mothers?[6] A whole range of problems dealing with where the line should be drawn between the natural and the less natural turn out to be impossible, perhaps not even desirable, to solve and at best reveal to us that preconceived ideas of what is considered natural are socially produced, or to put it in other words, results of a long history. We realize that the line between biology and society, between natural and artificial is flexible, always was and always will be. These biotechnological developments then provide an important input to historical studies, since such notions of the line between the natural and the artifical obviously change over time, even though the way they change nowadays are qualitatively different than in previous times. From a historical perspective, procreation has been re-shaped and technological realities re-made into new "natural facts" and the relationship between biology and social structure is once again recreated.[7] In the future people will have to make choices about life and reproduction under new conditions, which have been redefined by the many new technological options given by reproductive and genetic technologies. It is never easy to make predictions, especially in what concerns the future – to paraphrase a Danish humorist – but since the title of this paper does encourage predictions I shall venture to state a few anyway.

As several anthropologists have stated, concepts of family and kinship constitute one of the areas of important change. We may characterize the new reproductive arrangements as influencing both biological processes of having children but also influencing the reproduction of social relations. The British anthropologist, Marilyn Strathern, has pointed to one of the most important cultural consequences of the reproductive and genetic technologies when she claims that kinship relations as we know them in the Euro-American world are now acquiring a new autonomy apart from the social institution of the family. Furthermore, she argues that where reproduction for most Westerners refers to both the biological process of producing new children and perpetuating social relations in the family through creating new family members, these new technologies make visible the difference between procreation – as a genetically-based biological process – and reproduction understood as reproduction of social relations. This separation has important cultural implications for society and for the individual since it entails a change of ideas and concepts about personhood, family and human relations.

Look for instance at the concepts of fatherhood and motherhood. A substantial though not complete identity between genetic and social parenthood has been the foundation of traditional family life in the Euro-American West. There has been room for adoption, for illegitimate children, though elaborate legal arrangements were required to include these anomalies into the legal framework of the traditional family.[8] The new reproductive technologies have created a number of new actors on the procreative stage, and thereby a number of relationships which find no immediate correlate in the family. The sperm donor, the egg donor, the surrogate mother all have important roles in the procreative process required to produce a child, and some have genetic ties with the child, others biological. Though family ties may be as strong as ever, the range of those involved in the procreative process has become widened, and thus kinship in a procreative sense is becoming dispersed.[9]

There is an interesting parallel in the variety of family arrangements that developed in the 1960's and 1970's, including divorcees and shared children, which document the ways that dispersed kinship may exist even without all the technical procedures discussed here. Rather the partial dissolution of the unity between familial relations and procreative functions is preceded by the domestic arrangements of the politicized extended family unit characteristic of the 1960's and 1970's. Whether it is possible to imagine a new family structure including all the new genetic and biological relations established by assisted reproduction is another and more doubtful matter.

It seems that the post-modern child created by assisted procreation is a child with many genetic and biological parents but not necessarily more relatives in the family sense since only very few genetic actors seem to be included in the socially defined family structure. It is interesting to note how bio-ethical and legislative attempts to regulate the uses of the new technologies have disagreed on the direction they should take, whether the social and relational aspect or the individual genetic aspect should be privileged. Some, and this is characteristic of the Danish situation, have been moved to protect the traditional family from the unwanted intrusion of actors such as the sperm or egg donor by requiring strict anonymity of these parties. Other countries, such as Sweden, have based their legislation on the wish to meet the alleged interest of the child. In Sweden donor anonymity has been abolished with reference to the right of the child to become acquainted with her/his genetic parents, the right to know.

The child of the future may furthermore to some extent be the result of economic transactions. Commercialization of egg donation and of surrogacy has already taken place in some countries – the USA – though there seems to be some agreement on the governmental and professional level that such commercialization should be avoided. These are only trends however, as the regulation of all these technologies are still in the melting pot and has by no means found their final shape.

As the reproductive technologies have deconstructed traditional essentialist ideas of the role of women and men in the reproductive process and reconstructed these in new and unimagined ways, a new essentialism or even fatalism is revealing itself in the uses of the latest genetic technologies.[10] While the human genome project which seeks to map all our genes is approaching its final stages, more and more genes are being identified. And more and more genetic characteristics are open to diagnosis at the foetal stage or, as it happens, in the adult. Traditionally genetics had to rely on family pedigrees to obtain knowledge of the individual's genetic risk or chance of inheriting a genetic trait. The position of the individual in the family and the close congruence between family structure and genetic kinship was the precondition for such genetic predictions. And also for the development of human genetics as a scientific activity. Modern molecular genetics has changed all that. In the future – and here I am still engaging in predictive guesswork – it may no longer be necessary to obtain a family history to make predictions about genetic risk. Till now most genetic diagnoses have been made not on the basis of knowledge of the gene itself but through knowledge of so-called markers positioned very closely to the gene. These differ from family to family, and this makes it necessary to obtain DNA from a relative with the relevant characteristic, in order to compare the genetic profile of, for example, an affected parent and child at risk. But as the knowledge of the genome is increasing and as more genetic characteristics are being mapped, sequenced as it were, it may become possible to read the genes directly from a blood sample of an individual person. If this theoretical possibility becomes a realistic technical option for more than just a few genetically conditioned traits, we may begin to think of ancestry and genetic kinship in completely different terms. To be linked or related by blood, the bodily substance which is used as the traditional metaphor for genetic relations, no longer constitutes our physical and biological identity. It is often stated that genes connect people, since they are hereditary and make people dependent upon each other, for example, in families where hereditary diseases occur, but the other side of the coin is also very real. Social and genetic relatedness no longer go together unquestioned. In the new world of genetic essentialism, genes may become a metaphor for individuality rather that relatedness. And some studies point to a lay understanding of the genetic profile as that which makes up the uniqueness of the individual human being. And as knowledge of genetics becomes accessible to a larger part of the population, more and more people will know about the difference between genotype and phenotype, i.e. the difference between what we inherit and that which we interpret as our individual expression. Strathern develops the point further. "People now "know" they are endowed not with traits but with the potential for them. Perhaps that knowledge will turn what once was a symbol for the immutables of human existence (genetic endowment) into a symbol for the open-endedness of possibilities (the realization of potential) that only the individual will manifest".[11] This may mean that one's genetic constitution will be thought of as a potential and environmental factors may be seen as a barrier to full individual expression. And if the genetic element becomes stronger in the constitution of individual personhood in the future, this will stand in a marked contrast to the stress laid on the importance of the social ties between parent and child of future families established by new reproductive technologies. And if this is true, social relationships may mean less in the future for the construction of personal identity than genetic characteristics.

AGE IN THE FUTURE

I want to end by mentioning a few other technologically based phenomena which will most definitely have an impact on how age will be lived and experienced in the future.

One recently highlighted issue is the flexible limit between foetus and child, and abortion and birth. As new technologies have developed, still younger foetuses may be kept alive. Even extremely premature children may survive with the aid of modern incubators, at the present time from the age of 23 weeks of gestation. At the same time legal abortions are being performed as late as the 27th week of gestation since Danish legislation sets no upper limit to abortus provocatus agreed in consultation with the health authorities. This has led to a protest from Danish midwives that legal abortion may be performed on foetuses which theoretically might survive if born prematurely.

At the present time it is being debated whether the legally valid line between what counts as an abortion and what counts as a child should be revised. Danish authorities have proposed to move the limit from 28 weeks to 24 weeks, others want to move the limit further down. Whether a limit of 20, 24 or 28 weeks will be agreed upon, the controversy illustrates the impossibility of referring to natural criteria in setting such limits.

Organ transplantation, medically assisted methods of suicide and euthanasia, are other important areas of technical change affecting the age issue. Both have gained considerable media coverage and both will be practiced in the tense field between individual autonomy and the restrictions created by living in either a family or other intimate social structures.

As the possibility for performing organ donation was developed in the 1970's and 1980's – mainly through immunological research into tissue compatibility – a worldwide ideological campaign to change old established concepts of what constituted the line between life and death was launched. The cessation of heart-beat had gradually become unacceptable as a criterion for death as the quality of useful organs would quickly deteriorate and cerebral death took its place to keep organs alive while waiting for a suitable recipient. I shall not go into the issue of the death criterion, but only stress that the technological options here never really succeeded in reshaping public perceptions of death, or the proper behaviour in a terminal situation. Most people never sign a will themselves but silently prefer to let things take their natural course at the death bed, which means letting the surviving family decide. The controversy has not been closed as new technologies and new regulatory initiatives enter the stage.[12]

Conclusion

All these developments have changed human identity, the way we think of ourselves and the way we relate to others. Our human nature has indeed become a social and technical construction. We have become cyborgs, cybernetic organisms, or mutants between two forms of being, that of the living biological organism and that of the machine.[13] As a consequence we look at our body parts, and perhaps also to some extent to our bodies, as property, as things, commodities even. Organs such as hearts and livers may be used and reused by others after death, reproductive organs may be deconstructed and reconstructed for instrumental reasons such as having children, or offering surrogacy, and cells may be genetically manipulated for particular purposes.

This definitely moves the human body out of the natural domain and into that of the artefact, not overnight, but gradually and with great certainty. What are our options? Either we can engage in "an anti-science metaphysics", demonizing technology or we can take notice of the fact that we are cybernetic organisms, that our existence is inseparable from that of modern technology. As a consequense we could take responsibility for the factual social relations of science and technology. This would mean embracing the difficult "task of reconstructing the boundaries of daily life, in partial connection with others, in communication with all of our [bodily] parts".[14]

---

1. I. Wilmut et al 1997.
2. It should be mentioned that the feat of the British team which cloned Dolly seems to have been modified by the insight, that only a part of Dolly's DNA was actually a copy of her mother's, i.e. the chromosomal DNA. What was not copied was Dolly's mother's cytoplasmic DNA, which lies outside the nucleus of the cell. This means that there is a minor though not insignificant difference between the DNA of Dolly and that of her mother.
3. See S. Franklin 1993 and 1995, P. Spallone 1989, M. Strathern 1992, D. Haraway 1991.
4. See L. Koch 1997.
5. See H.J. Muller 1936 and G.R. Searle 1976.
6. H. Zwart 1998.
7. S. Franklin 1995.
8. L. Koch 1988.
9. M. Strathern 1992.
10. L. Koch 1988.
11. M. Strathern 1992, p. 358.
12. T. Brante og M. Hallberg, 1989.
13. D. Haraway 1991.
14. ibid p. 181.

Bibliography

Brante, T. and Hallberg. "Kontroversen om dödsbegreppet". *VEST* 10-11:1989.

Franklin, S. *Technologies of Procreation: kinship in the age of assisted conception* (Manchester University Press, with Jeanette Edwards, et al). Manchester 1993.

Franklin, S. 'Postmodern Procreation', in F. Ginsburg and R. Rapp (eds) *Conceiving the New World Order.* Berkeley, Calif.: University of California Press, 1995.

Haraway, D.J. *Simians, Cyborgs, and Women.* London: Free Association 1991.

Koch, L. "Mater est... eller: Hvem er moderen?", in: T. Andersen et al.(eds): *Den tredie skønhed.* Aarhus: Aarhus Universitetsforlag, 1988.

Koch, L. "A new Danish law on assisted reproduction". in: *Biomedical Ethics, Newsletter of the European Network for Biomedical Ethics* 3:1997.

Muller, H.J. *Out of the Night. A Biologist's View of the Future.* London: V. Gollancz 1936.

Searle, G.R. *Eugenics and politics in Britain* 1900-1914. Leyden: Noordhoff, 1976.

Spallone, P. *Beyond Conception.* Basingstoke: MacMillan Education, 1989.

Strathern, M. *Reproducing the future. Essays on anthropology, kinship and the new reproductive technologies.* New York: Routledge, 1992.

Wilmut, I., A.E. Schnieke, J. McWhir, A.J. Kind, and K.H.S. Campbell. "Viable offspring derived from fetal and adult mammalian cells". *Nature* 385: 810-13, 1997.

Zwart, Hub:"Can nature serve as a criterium of the reasonable use of reproductive technologies?" The case of menopausal IVF. in Elisabeth Hildt and Dieter Mieth (eds.) *In vitro fertilisation in the 1990's. Towards a medical, social and ethical evaluation.* Ashgate: Aldershot, 1998.